CHILDREN'S MENTAL HEALTH AND EMOTIONAL WELL-BEING IN PRIMARY SCHOOLS

Sara Miller McCune founded SAGE Publishing in 1965 to support the dissemination of usable knowledge and educate a global community. SAGE publishes more than 1000 journals and over 800 new books each year, spanning a wide range of subject areas. Our growing selection of library products includes archives, data, case studies and video. SAGE remains majority owned by our founder and after her lifetime will become owned by a charitable trust that secures the company's continued independence.

Los Angeles | London | New Delhi | Singapore | Washington DC | Melbourne

CHILDREN'S MENTAL HEALTH AND EMOTIONAL WELL-BEING IN PRIMARY SCHOOLS

A WHOLE SCHOOL APPROACH

COLIN HOWARD, MADDIE BURTON AND DENISSE LEVERMORE

2ND EDITION

Learning Matters
An imprint of SAGE Publications Ltd
1 Oliver's Yard
55 City Road
London EC1Y 1SP

SAGE Publications Inc.
2455 Teller Road
Thousand Oaks, California 91320

SAGE Publications India Pvt Ltd
B 1/I 1 Mohan Cooperative Industrial Area
Mathura Road
New Delhi 110 044

SAGE Publications Asia-Pacific Pte Ltd
3 Church Street
#10-04 Samsung Hub
Singapore 049483

Editor: Amy Thornton
Senior project editor: Chris Marke
Project management: Swales and Willis Ltd,
Exeter, Devon
Marketing manager: Dilhara Attygalle
Cover design: Wendy Scott
Typeset by: C&M Digitals (P) Ltd, Chennai, India
Printed in the UK

Library of Congress Control Number: 2019946419

British Library Cataloguing in Publication Data

A catalogue record for this book is available from
the British Library

ISBN 978-1-5264-6822-2
ISBN 978-1-5264-6821-5 (pbk)

At SAGE we take sustainability seriously. Most of our products are printed in the UK using responsibly sourced
papers and boards. When we print overseas we ensure sustainable papers are used as measured by the
PREPS grading system. We undertake an annual audit to monitor our sustainability.

CONTENTS

ABOUT THE AUTHORS

Colin Howard is a Senior Primary Lecturer in Initial Teacher Education at the University of Worcester. He has been involved in primary education for over 24 years, of which 14 years have been spent as a successful head teacher in both small village and large primary school settings. He has a strong research interest which includes primary science, aspects of professional practice and teachers' professional identity. He is a SIAMS inspector of the Diocese of Hereford.

Maddie Burton is a Registered Mental Health Nurse and for several years worked in both inpatient and community CAMHS. She has an MA in Psychodynamic Approaches to Working with Adolescents from The Tavistock and University of East London. She is currently Senior Lecturer in Child and Adolescent Mental Health at the University of Worcester. She continues to maintain close links with CAMHS practice and works with schools from a CAMH perspective. She holds membership of the Association for Child and Adolescent Mental Health and the Association for Infant Mental Health. Maddie's research interests include suicide and self-harm in children and young people, and infant, maternal and parental mental health. Maddie is also a Fellow of the Higher Education Academy.

Denisse Levermore is a Senior Lecturer in Child and Adolescent Mental Health at the University of Worcester. Her qualifications include: Registered General Nurse, Registered Children's Nurse, Diploma in Social Work and MSc Child and Adolescent Mental Health. Denisse has over 15 years' experience of working with vulnerable families and child and adolescent mental health in her previous roles as a Nurse Therapist within CAMHS and as a Family Nurse within Family Nurse Partnership. She maintains her clinical practice within CAMHS currently by way of an honorary contract, undertaking family and individual therapy with children, young people and their families. Her research interests include domestic violence and the impact on children and young people's mental health, infant mental health and the mental health of young parents.

Co-author on the first edition

Rachel Barrell, then Principal Lecturer and Course Leader in Initial Teacher Education at the University of Worcester, was co-author on the first edition of this text, published in June 2017.

ACKNOWLEDGEMENTS

The authors would like to thank all of the students and practitioners who inspired and supported this text. Where necessary, case studies and examples used in the book have been adapted and anonymised.

1

MENTAL HEALTH AND EMOTIONAL WELL-BEING

CHAPTER OBJECTIVES

By the end of this chapter you should be aware of:

- what we mean by *whole school approach* in relation to emotional health and well-being;
- how schools can help;
- common psychological and mental health problems affecting children and young people;
- origins and prevalence;
- impact of early-life and adverse childhood experiences (ACEs) on children and young people's mental health;
- being curious about any change in children and young people's behaviour;
- changes in behaviour may be context-specific or about a potential emerging mental health problem;
- the importance of getting a balance and not always pathologising and medicalising children and young people's behaviour;
- some presenting behaviours can be considered 'normal' when the context is understood, so the 'context' beyond the child may require attention;
- being mindful of children who live in difficult circumstances, including looked-after children, refugees and asylum-seeking children;
- treatments, interventions and therapeutic approaches;
- changing and rephrasing the language we use.

TEACHERS' STANDARDS

This chapter supports the development of the following Teachers' Standards:

TS8: Fulfil wider professional responsibilities

- Take responsibility for improving teaching through appropriate professional development, responding to advice and feedback from colleagues.
- Communicate effectively with parents with regard to pupils' achievements and well-being.

Introduction

This chapter will consider aspects of child and adolescent mental health with a brief overview of some of the most common presenting problems, together with consideration of the role schools and teaching and educational staff can play. Although eating disorders and self-harm tend to occur from age 11 and on through adolescence, a short description has been included in the chapter. Other important considerations in relation to child and adolescent mental health, such as self-esteem, risk and resilience theories and their application, are explored in Chapter 4.

The No Health Without Mental Health strategy (Department of Health, 2011 a) stated that over half of lifetime mental health problems begin to emerge by age 14, and three-quarters by the mid-20s. Where it arises mental ill health really is a concern, at what should be an optimum time of life, requiring appropriate supportive responses and interventions. These children and young people are in our schools, often when mental health problems are emerging. Good mental health is the foundation of healthy development. But having mental health problems early in life can have adverse and long-lasting effects (Murphy and Fonagy, 2012; Young Minds, 2018). Teaching staff and other school staff are the professionals spending the most time with children and young people – more than any other professional group – and are well placed to notice any behaviour changes which may indicate a problem (Weare, 2015). School is a major part of children and young people's lives; they spend over a third of their time in school, meeting and making friends there, and teaching staff play a large part in their development (Royal College of Psychiatrists, 2016, p11). A parent advocate aptly stated:

> My daughter trusts her teacher more than anybody … As they get older that trust becomes even more precious … They are going to talk to their teachers. School is a unique opportunity but … there is [also] an awful lot of pressure on teachers.

> (Menzies et al., 2018, p22)

We have a 'window of opportunity' because of the progressing and continuing developmental aspects, unique to children and young people, for offering early help and support so that lifelong outcomes can be improved.

The Pursuit of Happiness report (CentreForum Commission, 2014, p36) and the House of Commons Health Committee (2014) recommend that teaching and educational staff should receive training in child development, mental health and psychological resilience so that vulnerable children and children at risk can be identified. The CentreForum Commission recognised that teachers are not mental health professionals but they should have skills of recognition and know how to access help and when to refer to Child and Adolescent Mental Health Services (CAMHS). Other recommendations in the report include a requirement for the National Curriculum to include teaching on children and young people's mental health and improving their resilience.

The topic of child and adolescent mental health is now frequently featured in the media and is the subject of political debate. Future in Mind: Promoting, Protecting and Improving Our Children and Young People's Mental Health and Well-being (Department of Health, 2015) set out the findings and recommendations of the Children and Young People's Mental Health and Wellbeing Taskforce. It firmly sets a whole-child and whole-family approach, promoting good mental health at the earliest ages and moving away from only thinking about mental health from a clinical position. It acknowledges the role schools are already playing in supporting pupil mental health and that this needs to be further developed by earlier identification of issues and early support.

In 2017 the government set out its commitment: *Transforming Children and Young People's Mental Health Provision: A Green Paper* (Department of Health, Department for Education, 2017). This was followed in 2018 by: *Government Response to the Consultation on Transforming Children and Young People's Mental Health Provision: A Green Paper and Next Steps* (Department of Health and Social Care, DfE, 2018). It firmly shifts the lens on to schools in terms of early recognition of potential mental health problems with a commitment to designated senior leads for mental health in schools, mental health support teams and a 4-week waiting time for access to specialist CAMHS. £1.4 billion has been set aside to support the School Designated Lead and Mental Health Team, although only reaching one in four schools by 2022–2023. This is a timely reminder that CAMHS represents under 1 per cent of the total NHS budget and that the Green Paper commitment only provides for one in three children and young people able to access specialist support, thus leaving two out of three reliant on others or with no support (RSA, 2018).

Teaching children and young people how to improve their resilience should be a whole school approach with the promotion of emotional health and well-being embedded into the culture and core business of school settings. Promoting and supporting the emotional well-being of the whole school community is noted as very important given that educational staff have high rates of work-related stress. (CentreForum Commission, 2014, pp32–33; Weare, 2015). The MindEd e-portal was introduced in 2014 as an online electronic resource for professionals interested in child and adolescent mental health and provides clear guidance on children and young people's mental health, well-being and development. *Mental Health and Behaviour in Schools* (Department for Education, 2018) proposes that a whole school approach should pervade all aspects of school life, including the culture, ethos and environment, teaching and partnerships with families and the wider community.

In 2017 the Prime Minister Theresa May announced a commitment to improve mental health and well-being, including mental health first-aid training for all secondary school staff with an additional emphasis on improving mental health in the workplace for staff (British Association of Counselling and Psychiatry, 2017). Again in 2019 Theresa May unveiled a plan for all new teachers to be trained in identifying early signs of mental illness but questions remain over resourcing such a plan (Ward, 2019).

Prevalence

Public Health England (2015) identified that in an average class of 30 15-year-old pupils:

- three may have a mental disorder;
- ten are likely to have witnessed their parents separate;
- one may have experienced the death of a parent;

- seven are likely to have been bullied;

- six may be self-harming.

These figures in 2015 were based on the previous prevalence study (Department of Health, 2004), so the most recent 2017 statistics are likely to indicate an increase in those areas. In November 2018 the *Mental Health of Children and Young People in England, 2017* report was published (NHS Digital, 2018), announcing that one in eight (12.8 per cent) children and young people aged between five and 19, surveyed in England in 2017, had a mental disorder. This is an increase from one in ten (10 per cent) in the previous published research in 2004. Emotional disorders for 5–15-year-olds showed the most significant increase over time whereas all other types of disorder have remained stable.

Under-fives were not included in the previous 2004 study (Department of Health, 2004). For the first time 2–19-year-olds were included in the 2017 study (NHS Digital, 2018). Findings showed that one in 18 2–4-year-olds were identified with at least one disorder, with boys more likely than girls to have a disorder. Research has suggested that 50–60 per cent of children showing high levels of disruptive behaviour at ages 3–4 years will continue to have these problems at school age (Murphy and Fonagy, 2012). For primary-age children the figure rises to one in ten. At a House of Commons round-table event a parent advocate stated: *My magic wand would be looking after your mind as a subject in school from reception up so that they can start to recognise when they don't feel themselves* (Menzies et al., 2018, p24).

Understanding mental health in children and young people

Many mental health problems have their origins in childhood (Dogra et al., 2009; Young Minds, 2018). An accepted view is that mental health and ill health arise from a context of variables, including biological factors such as genetics and brain development, psychological variables that include coping mechanisms and how these then interact in relation to either adverse or positive environmental circumstances or experiences. Another way to consider this is that early experiences also impact on brain development and it is by the impact of these experiences on inherent temperament and character that psychological development, therefore, becomes influenced. MindEd has a useful exercise, 'Putting Information Together', using the '4 Ps' model which can be helpful in understanding the influence of context (Nikapota, 2016). The '4 Ps' model is a model for understanding *why* someone has developed a mental health problem and what may be preventing that person from recovering. It looks at the factors which:

- *predisposed* someone to the mental health problem;

- *precipitated* the mental health problem;

- *protected* the individual from the mental health problem (or may help that person recover from it); or

- *perpetuated* the mental health problem.

You can consider these in relation to the case studies later in the chapter.

An individual's inherent genes can be triggered by experiences in childhood. The Adverse Childhood Experiences (ACEs) study was carried out in the USA in the late 1990s (Felitti et al., 1998). It consisted of 17,000 participants and looked at how adverse experiences in childhood impact health and behaviour across the life course. The study found that a larger number of ACEs greatly increases poor health, whether physical, social or emotional. The study found a strong link between trauma and chronic disease in adulthood as well as social and emotional problems, as shown in the trailer for the film *Resilience: the Biology of Stress and the Science of Hope* (see Further reading). Nadine Burke Harris explains in a TED talk how childhood trauma affects health across a lifetime (see Further reading).

There are clear definitions and measurements of what an ACE is. Examples include maltreatment, violence and coercion, inhumane treatment, prejudice, household or family adversity, adjustment, adult responsibilities, bereavement and survivorship. Despite experiencing ACEs not all children will have a poor outcome but children experiencing four or more ACEs are four times more likely to have low levels of mental well-being (Young Minds, 2018, pp28–29). A recent study of over 9,000 participants aged 8–21 years linked traumatic events such as growing up in poverty, accidents and sexual assault with increased mental ill health and effect on brain development (Gur et al., 2019)

There is now an increased dialogue on trauma and the effect of trauma on development with life-long consequences. This includes a move to areas, including schools, being 'trauma-informed'. Trauma Informed UK Schools is a useful resource (https://www.traumainformedschools.co.uk/).

Many children and young people have lived, and often remain living, in difficult circumstances and will have experienced a few or a range of ACEs, all of which are extrinsic to them. Looked-after and refugee and asylum-seeking children will have experienced extreme distress, and for refugee children this is often compounded by less than positive experiences once settled or while awaiting status decisions. Sadly, they often continue to experience bullying and discrimination yet often have the capacity to draw on protective resources, which will be discussed in Chapter 4. Our task is to understand in order to respond appropriately and with compassion and empathy. There is also a developing dialogue on the intergenerational transmission of trauma *thinking across generations* (Gray et al., 2017).

Responses from the classroom

It is also important to consider and be mindful that most presenting mental health conditions are medicalised and are an interpretation of behaviours considered to be beyond what would be accepted as normal behaviour. We remain quite attached to a medical model of understanding and interpreting behaviours, especially in adult mental health but less so in child and adolescent mental health. Behaviours can also be thought about from a psychological perspective. Often children and young people are 'acting out'. Acting out is a defence mechanism which defends the individual from anxiety and is an emotional and externally visible response to overwhelming and unmanageable feelings (Burton et al., 2014). It is important to try and understand the behaviour within the young person's context. For children who have experienced ACEs, events in the classroom such as the behaviour of other pupils or perceived criticism can act as a trigger, leading the young person into safety-seeking behaviours such as escaping, running away from the perceived threat or becoming challenging and 'fighting' the perceived threat, parallel to the fight, flight or freeze automatic responses when threatened.

In relation to perceived poor behaviour, approaches based on punishment which focus on the negative tend to be common. For example, practice such as using zone boards or writing the child's name on the classroom board for the day or withholding playtime in younger children does not get to the bottom of the problem. It is not helpful to come from a position that sees poor behaviour as intentional or under the child's control – bear in mind that usually it is not. School exclusions are more common for children with a mental health disorder, particularly those with a behavioural or hyperactivity disorder. One boy in ten with a disorder has been excluded and one in 20 on three or more occasions (NHS Digital, 2018).

Try and see the whole child and what the child may have experienced (ACEs) behind the behaviour and, instead of focusing on negatives, focus on positive characteristics (as discussed in Chapter 4; Weare, 2015, p11). Incidentally, play is a right under Article 31 of the United Nations Convention on the Rights of the Child (1989), so there is no justifiable case for withholding or rewarding play.

Usually behaviours can be understood within their context and may be temporary and a reaction to adversity and are extrinsic not intrinsic to the child. For example, a child may become anxious and not want to leave a parent and go to school. But if there are changed family circumstances such as bereavement, domestic abuse or parental mental or physical illness this could explain the changed behaviour. A clinical judgement is still required if a child is highly anxious or likely to be depressed, as it would be important to follow this process in order to access appropriate treatment.

Using the term 'mental disorder' or problem indicates that the problem resides within the child, and is not always helpful, but problems or disorders can develop as a reaction to external circumstances, as shown by the chapter case studies (Murphy and Fonagy, 2012). One of the most important things to remember is that, when a change of behaviour is observed, be curious and explore what may be happening in the child or young person's context. We often make the mistake of expecting children and young people to 'behave' within what is considered 'normal' in the class and school settings but that can sometimes be an impossible task for young people struggling to deal with any problems they may have or have encountered. If they feel misunderstood, criticised and ultimately unsafe it is likely to make things much worse for them, as it would for any of us in their shoes. Having a supportive relationship with an identified person is key. It can be helpful to change the language we tend to automatically use. Instead of 'challenging behaviour' consider 'distressed behaviour'. Instead of 'What's the matter with you?' ask 'What has happened to you?'

Typical mental health problems: children and young people

Children and young people can experience the same mental health problems as adults. The difference between adults and children, which is important to understand, is the requirement to think about these presentations within the context of the developmental phase.

There is a considerable overlap across the range of problems and conditions, with an emotional element consistently present throughout. Some children may have both physical illnesses and mental health problems or disorders as a combination or comorbidity. For example, a young woman with diabetes may place herself at risk through non-compliance with diet and medication, which could be considered an aspect of self-harming behaviour. Overall children with mental health problems are also at increased risk of physical health problems (Department of Health, 2015, p25; NHS Digital, 2018). This was evidenced in the ACEs study (Felitti et al., 1998).

Presentations (what we see) need to be thought of in the context of normal development which is on a continuum of constant change. It is important to remember that risk-taking behaviours and mood changes are considered normal adolescent behaviour. Physical and hormonal changes leave the adolescent brain less able to regulate emotion and impulse (Weare, 2015). Sarah-Jayne Blakemore (2012) has given an informative TED talk on the mysterious workings of the adolescent brain (see Further reading).

Potential symptoms need to be considered not only from a developmental perspective but also within the context of the child or young person and his or her experiences – what is and what has been happening (Burton et al., 2014).

The most common mental health problems for children and young people are emotional disorders, including depression and anxiety, conduct disorders, attention deficit hyperactivity disorder (ADHD), and autistic spectrum conditions (ASC) (Murphy and Fonagy, 2012). Trauma disorders such as post-traumatic stress disorder as a result of traumatic experiences or persistent periods of neglect and abuse are now increasingly recognised (Department for Education, 2018). Other significant mental health conditions include eating disorders such as anorexia nervosa, attachment disorder, self-harm, suicidal behaviours, mood changes, behaviour changes, relationship and attachment difficulties, substance misuse, changed eating patterns, isolation and social withdrawal and somatic problems. Somatising features and problems (physical symptoms with psychological origins) include, for example, headaches, enuresis and encopresis (faecal soiling), tummy aches and sleep disturbances, and often present in younger children and can be common with varying degrees of severity, frequency and persistence. Only appropriately trained professionals should diagnose a mental health problem, but schools are in a unique position on a daily basis to observe children who may be experiencing, or are at risk of experiencing, a mental health problem (Department for Education, 2018).

Emotional disorders

Depression and anxiety

Depression is now recognised as a major public health problem in the UK and worldwide. It accounts for 15 per cent of all disability in high-income countries. In England one in six adults and one in 20 children and young people at any one time are affected by depression and related conditions, such as anxiety. In all, 0.9 per cent of children and young people are seriously depressed (Department of Health, 2015). The *Mental Health of Children and Young People in England, 2017* report (NHS Digital, 2018) found that one in 12 (8.1 per cent) 5–19-year-olds had an emotional disorder, with rates higher in girls (10.0 per cent) than boys (6.2 per cent). Anxiety disorders (7.2 per cent) were more common than depressive disorders (2.1 per cent).

According to the *International Classification of Diseases* (ICD 10) (World Health Organization, 2016) (ICD 11 will come into effect in January 2022) and the *Diagnostic Statistical Manual* (DSM–5) (American Psychiatric Association, 2013), depression is characterised by an episodic disorder of varying degrees of severity characterised by depressed mood and loss of enjoyment persisting for several weeks. There must also be a presence of other symptoms, including depressive thinking, pessimism about the future and suicidal ideas and biological symptoms such as early waking, weight loss and reduced appetite (NICE, 2013 a).

The criteria are similar for children and adults but with important differences (Keenan and Evans, 2009). With children and young people developmental perspectives and context are highly relevant, as already discussed. For example, eating and sleeping disturbances often present as potential symptoms, but these would be common in childhood anyway. Tearfulness and crying have a very different meaning and incidence in childhood compared with adulthood. It is not uncommon to feel depressed at times. It is also important to 'normalise' sadness as a passing human condition. If sadness becomes persistent over time this is different and a cause for concern (Burton et al., 2014; Royal College of Psychiatrists, 2017 a).

Anxiety, it must be remembered, is normal. Anxiety becomes pathological when the fear is out of proportion to the context of the life situation and, in childhood, when it is out of keeping with the expected behaviour for the developmental stage of the child (Lask, 2003). It is also one of the most common mental health problems; it is estimated that 300,000 young people or 3.3 per cent in Britain have an anxiety disorder (Department of Health, 2015; Royal College of Psychiatrists, 2017 a). For example, separation anxiety is considered normal for infants (leaving a primary carer) but less so for a teenager.

In a relatively short time span, in comparison to the full length of human life, children move from a state of limited emotional understanding to becoming complex individuals. The number and complexity of emotional experiences together with modulation of human expression increase with age. It is therefore not surprising that some children and young people are easily overwhelmed and experience emotional disorders, which if they persist are debilitating and require intervention and help.

There are many variations of anxiety and children can experience anxiety in some of the following ways: worries, phobias, separation anxiety, panic disorder, post-traumatic stress disorder and obsessive-compulsive disorder. Thinking about the above variations in how anxiety is expressed it is useful to consider a developmental perspective: there are different fears for different years. In infancy if secure attachment is accomplished, fear of separation from caregiver diminishes. Separation anxiety usually begins in the pre-school years any time after the attachment period but typically in late childhood, early adolescence. Other fears, such as of the dark and then as the imagination develops, ghosts and monsters can appear. Animal phobias such as a fear of spiders or dogs usually begin in childhood. Performance anxiety can emerge in late childhood and social anxiety in adolescence.

Fears and anxieties are normal developmental challenges facing the maturing individual. During adolescence autonomy and independence are major developmental challenges, when young people are endeavouring to balance compliance with rules and expressing independent autonomy. It is normal to experience conflict to some level, but the challenge posed by emerging autonomy can trigger or exacerbate interpersonal problems that require negotiation with the accompanying anxiety (Burton et al., 2014; Young Minds, 2016; Royal College of Psychiatrists, 2017 b).

Conduct disorders

The *Mental Health of Children and Young People in England, 2017* report (NHS Digital, 2018) found that one in 20 (4.6 per cent) 5–19-year-olds had a behavioural disorder, with rates higher in boys (5.8 per cent) than girls (3.4 per cent).

> *Conduct disorders nearly always have a significant impact on functioning and quality of life. The 1999 ONS [Office for National Statistics] survey demonstrated that conduct disorders have a steep social class gradient, with a three to fourfold increase in prevalence in social classes D and E compared with social class A. The 2004 survey found that almost 40% of looked-after children, those who had been abused and those on child protection or safeguarding registers had a conduct disorder.*
>
> (NICE, 2013 b, p4)

These figures are comparable across the breadth of mental ill health with those who have experienced ACEs. Conduct disorder refers to aggressive, destructive and disruptive behaviours in childhood that are serious and likely to impair a child's development. In DSM–5 (American Psychiatric Association, 2013) there is a distinction between oppositional defiant disorder (characterised by recurrent negativistic defiant, disobedient and hostile behaviours) and conduct disorder, which includes the presence of repetitive persistent violations of societal norms and other people's basic rights. In ICD-10 (World Health Organization, 2016) oppositional and conduct problems are both included under the heading of conduct disorder.

Many behaviours included in the diagnosis are common in normal child development, but when they are persistent and frequent they bring increased risks in later life, including antisocial behaviour, a range of psychiatric disorders, educational and work failure and relationship difficulties (Moffitt et al., 2002). There is frequently comorbidity with other illness, including substance misuse, anxiety and ADHD. Individual risk factors include low school achievement and impulsiveness; family risk factors include parental contact with the criminal justice system and child abuse; social risk factors include low family income and little education (NICE, 2013 b). Parenting practices in families of conduct-disordered children are reported as often hostile, critical, with harsh discipline, a lack of consistent rules, low monitoring of behaviours and parental disagreements.

Where there is a combination of inherited vulnerability plus negative parenting, especially early negative effect and intrusive control, these factors contribute to the development and persistence of conduct problems. These are often highly vulnerable young people and can be at risk to themselves and others (Burton et al., 2014).

Hyperactivity disorders

Hyperactivity disorders include disorders characterised by inattention, impulsivity and hyperactivity. The number of children with a hyperactivity disorder, as defined by ICD-10 (World Health Organization, 2016), is likely lower than the number of children with ADHD (as defined by DSM–5: American Psychiatric Association, 2013), as hyperactivity disorders have a more restrictive set of criteria. In England about one in 60 (1.6 per cent) 5–19-year-olds had a hyperactivity disorder, with rates higher in boys (2.6 per cent) than girls (0.6 per cent) (NHS Digital, 2018).

A total of 1.5 per cent of children and young people have severe ADHD (Department of Health, 2015). Characteristics of ADHD include a triad or constellation of impairments in the following areas:

1. poor concentration;

2. hyperactivity;

3. impulsiveness.

It is important to recognise that displaying the above behaviours does not necessarily mean ADHD is the explanation. These behaviours may indicate psychological causes. Think about how you might behave if you were in a stressful situation, experiencing stress and anxiety: all the above areas are likely to show changes. A key factor is the persistence and frequency in all domains (Burton et al., 2014).

A problem for children and young people is that their ADHD impairments can impact significantly on educational experiences and attainment. Young people with ADHD have a higher rate of behavioural and disruptive disorders and are disproportionately represented in the youth justice service. Children with ADHD struggle to regulate activity and they are not able to evaluate their responses beforehand or subsequently. Exhortations often made of them to 'try harder' or 'learn to concentrate' are impossible to fulfil, unhelpful and tend to reinforce failure.

The range of possible lifetime impairment extends to educational and occupational underachievement, dangerous driving, difficulties in carrying out daily activities such as shopping and organising household tasks, in making and keeping friends, in intimate relationships (for example, excessive disagreement) and with childcare (NICE, 2018).

As with other disorders ADHD is classified in both ICD 10 (World Health Organization, 2016) (hyperkinetic disorder) and in DSM–5 (American Psychiatric Association, 2013). Severe ADHD corresponds approximately to the ICD 10 diagnosis of hyperkinetic disorder. This is defined as when hyperactivity, impulsivity and inattention are all present in multiple settings, and when impairment affects multiple domains in multiple settings. Part of the assessment process includes collecting information from parents and from teaching staff in educational settings. Diagnosis is a matter of clinical judgement, which considers the severity of impairment, pervasiveness, individual factors and familial and social context (NICE, 2018).

There are strong genetic influences and often history taking reveals other family members exhibiting ADHD traits that are undiagnosed; this is significantly so in earlier generations where ADHD was unrecognised. No single gene has yet been identified. Environmental factors include maternal drug and alcohol use in pregnancy. In addition, the ongoing effects of individual and parental substance misuse and poor or hostile parenting also need to be considered. It must be remembered that all of these factors also constitute ACEs and their impact cannot be underestimated.

It can be helpful to reframe the negative symptoms of ADHD in terms of positive aspects. It is not always helpful to focus on reducing 'unwanted' behaviours; alternatively it is better to harness the positives (as discussed in Chapter 4). There is potential for these young people as they usually have energy and enthusiasm by the bucket load. They have a 'feet first' activist approach which during childhood and adolescence can get them into trouble but also has advantages. But it can be difficult to 'fit in' to 'systems', especially the demands of education, which can be stacked against a child or young person with ADHD (Burton et al., 2014).

Autistic spectrum conditions

The *Mental Health of Children and Young People in England, 2017* report (NHS Digital, 2018) found a prevalence of 1.2 per cent for ASC. Autism in Britain was first labelled as childhood psychosis at the beginning of the twentieth century. In 1944 it was named 'Kanner's syndrome', and then in the latter part of the twentieth century 'autism' (Wing, 1996). Asperger's syndrome was identified in 1944, although it took until 1979 for Asperger's work to be translated from German to English. It wasn't until 1991 that the term 'Asperger's syndrome' was recognised in Britain. The difference between autism and Asperger's syndrome is that 'Aspies' are of average or higher intelligence and develop language skills in the normal developmental way; the reverse is true for autistic people (Bradshaw, 2013, p55).

ASC or autistic spectrum disorders form a very broad variation in presentation. 'Spectrum' indicates that, while sharing the same condition, there is a wide range of difficulties experienced in different ways. Thinking of the spectrum as a scale from 0 to 100, a social and communicative person would appear at 0. Someone with a few autistic traits such as a need for routine would appear further along the spectrum. The stronger the autistic traits the further along the spectrum, so a person with no speech and limited responses to others would be at 100 (Muggleton, 2012, p31). There may be accompanying learning disabilities. ASC is a lifelong condition and, unlike all the other conditions discussed in this chapter, has a biological origin and is a disorder of development. Autistic people often experience sensitivity to sounds, touch, tastes, smells, light or colours (The National Autistic Society, 2013).

Autism is characterised by a triad of features related to functioning in all situations:

1. impairment of social communication;

2. impairment of social understanding;

3. impairment in social imagination and play.

There are also accompanying and ritualistic stereotyped interests and behaviours. These are usually evident from infancy, although they may not be recognised at that point. Play is often a preoccupation with repetitive activities.

Again, as with children and young people with ADHD, it is helpful to consider positives for Asperger's children. Having a diagnosis does not in itself change anything but it can help parents and teachers to understand a child's needs and put in place supportive measures. Strengths can be in individual sports, for example. Another trait is honesty; never ask 'Does my bum look big in this?' If you are not prepared for an honest response, do not ask if the truth is going to hurt! Similarly, language needs to be straightforward. If you ask an Aspie to 'Hold your horses', i.e. slow down, you will have a puzzled response, with the person wondering, where exactly are the horses? (Burton et al., 2014).

Eating disorders

The *Mental Health of Children and Young People in England, 2017* report (NHS Digital, 2018) identified an overall prevalence of 0.4 per cent with an eating disorder. Eating disorders can develop in childhood or adolescence, in keeping with other mental health disorders becoming most frequent, with an age of onset of between 15 and 35 years (BEAT, 2015). Anorexia nervosa has a mortality rate which is twice the level of any other illness and has the highest death rate of any mental illness (Treasure and Alexander, 2013). Anorexia has always been considered a predominantly female disorder, borne out by the statistics; nevertheless boys and young men do develop anorexia which professionals also need to be mindful of (Wright et al., 2018). It is generally considered that, as with other psychological disorders and mental illnesses, eating disorders arise from a combination of biological/medical, psychological and social or environmental factors, as discussed above. The articulation and inter-relation of these overlapping theories, together with risk and resilience factors, as a combination, lead to understanding and interpreting the causes of eating disorders, rather than a single application of a model (Burton, 2014).

However, the case for being driven predominantly by the medical genetic origin is quite strong. More recent research suggests a strong genetic link and predisposition and demonstrates that anorexia nervosa is not a lifestyle choice but rather an inherent gene which is most probably present and becomes vulnerable when exposed to other factors (Lask et al., 2012).

Other factors include psychological attributes, with perfectionism implicated as both a risk and a maintaining factor (Fairburn and Harrison, 2003; Wade and Tiggeman, 2013). Typically, young people with anorexia often have perfectionist traits and can be academically high achievers. But they often have low self-esteem and find it difficult to express or externalise negative emotions (Dhakras, 2005). Media and societal attitudes towards thinness are often cited as 'reasons' but they are not reasons in isolation; rather they can act as contributing factors or triggers. Other predisposing factors centre on the negotiation of transitional points, for example, the negotiation of adolescence in combination with an adverse life event such as bereavement, parental divorce or sexual abuse, together with an inherent psychological vulnerability (Burton, 2014).

Self-harm and suicidal behaviour

The *Mental Health of Children and Young People in England, 2017* report (NHS Digital, 2018) found that 25.5 per cent of 11–16-year-olds with a disorder self-harmed or attempted suicide, whereas 3 per cent of 11–16-year-olds without a disorder self-harmed or attempted suicide. Self-harm and suicidal behaviour are emotional disorders on a similar continuum as they are both in response to stress. Self-harm tends to be about coping whereas suicidal behaviour can be associated with giving up or seen as a solution to overwhelming and intolerable feelings, although not necessarily about wanting to die. Young people who self-harm are at a higher risk of suicide. Unfortunately, self-harm is frequently stigmatised, with individuals being described as 'attention seeking'. This is unhelpful and it is important to maintain curiosity over why the young person may be expressing his or her feelings in such a way, in order to be able to offer appropriate support. Again, a reframing of language is helpful, considering 'attachment needing' or 'attachment seeking' instead of 'attention seeking'.

All of us have an attachment quality which develops during the first 5 years of life. Many children and young people (and adults) who experience negative problems during this crucial and critical period when the architecture of the brain is forming may have an impaired attachment quality, which then tends to be borne out in all future relationships and affects the capacity for emotional and self-regulation. Schore (2014) describes the effects of neglect on brain development (see Further reading).

ACEs are associated with an increased risk of suicide (Department of Health, 2011 b; Cleare et al., 2018). There have been relatively few studies of children in care and self-harming behaviours. Studies that have been undertaken have shown that they are a high-risk group with high self-harm rates. These are children most likely to exhibit attachment-seeking behaviours due to poor and adverse early experiences (Burton, 2019). It is important to assess all episodes of self-harm individually in a person-centred and systemic way, as failure to do so can lead to individuals feeling misunderstood (NICE, 2004).

Young people are vulnerable to suicidal feelings. The risk is greater when they have mental health problems or behavioural disorder, misuse substances, have family breakdown or mental health problems or suicide in the family (Department of Health, 2011 b). Adolescence is the most turbulent developmental period after infancy with the biggest challenges and changes in all areas of biological, psychological and social change. Predisposing vulnerabilities such as poor or adverse early experiences can be activated during the adolescent phase (Anderson, 2008). Triggers influencing self-harm and suicidal behaviour include ACEs such as: bullying, difficulties with parental and peer relationships, bereavement, earlier abusive experiences, difficulties with sexuality, problems with ethnicity, culture, religion, substance misuse and low self-esteem. Contextual triggers include adverse family circumstances, dysfunctional relationships, domestic violence, poverty, parental criminality, time in local authority care, frequent punishments and family transitions.

Bell (2000) describes that the cause given is the trigger precipitating suicidal behaviour. But it will often be the reason given by the young person, their families, and even doctors and other clinical staff. Reasons given might include an argument with a close friend or family member or failing exams. The notion of a trigger as an explanation often leads to a minimising of the level of seriousness surrounding the suicide attempt which is *never* about the stated reason. Rather, it is a rationalisation of the event rather than an explanation as it may be a frightening prospect for all concerned to consider serious mental disturbance. This is a very important point to bear in mind and is the key to understanding suicidal ideation. For example, not all individuals who have arguments and fail exams make attempts on their lives, therefore those who do so for those reasons given are responding to a trigger (the argument, exam failure) to much deeper intolerable problems.

Suicide and suicidal ideation always take place within the context of relationships which is the important challenge to explore and understand. Studies of suicidal behaviour in young people confirm that relationship difficulties predominate (Hawton et al., 2012). Usage of triggers as an explanation can lead to collusion and denial of the seriousness of the event, not only by family members but clinical staff also, and therefore it is highly risky not to take the attempt seriously. Suicide attempts should be taken seriously and must never be minimised by describing somewhat trivial reasons such as relationship disagreements or exam failure which are in fact the precipitating triggers (Burton, 2014).

The difference with self-harming behaviour, as opposed to an intention to kill oneself, is that with self-harm the person is in touch with his or her body through the physical reality of pain. The skin becomes a medium for communication (Gardner, 2001). Physical pain is often easier to manage than emotional pain and when inflicted can change mood which in turn can be habit forming. There can also be something about experiencing first-aid 'patching up' and 'repairing' either by the individual or helpers, with these repairing acts experienced as therapeutic (Burton, 2019).

KEY REFLECTIONS

- It is estimated that one in eight children have a diagnosable mental health condition.
- Half of lifetime mental health problems (excluding dementia) begin to emerge by age 14 and three-quarters by the mid-20s.
- Children who have experienced ACEs are at greater risk of developing mental health problems.
- Mental ill health arises from a context of variables – genetic biological factors (biomedical) and psychological factors – and how these articulate with lived experiences (psychosocial).
- When considering children and young people potential symptoms need to be considered from a developmental and contextual perspective; for example, 'risk-taking' behaviour could be considered part of adolescent pathology and therefore normal.
- Children and young people can experience the same mental health problems as adults.

Interventions, strategies and therapeutic treatment approaches: how can schools help?

The *Annual Report of the Chief Medical Officer 2012, Our Children Deserve Better: Prevention Pays* included a key message that service design should recognise the role, importance and potential of schools in fostering the development of resilience and opportunities for delivering interventions that can improve mental health (Murphy and Fonagy, 2012, p12). Child and adolescent mental health sits within a medical and psychological diagnostic model. Children and young people, as already identified, tend to receive a diagnosis if an assessment reveals this to be appropriate. This will primarily be a medical interpretation but the approach to both interpretation and treatment is one which considers all factors, including psychological and sociological. An appropriate treatment or intervention is then recommended according to the diagnosis.

Freeth (2007), as cited in (Prever, 2010, p57), argues that this model does not sit well with the 'person-centred' approach, although CAMHS workers do adopt a 'person-centred' approach where the focus is on relationship building alongside the treatment or intervention. Regardless of what sort of approach is used – cognitive behavioural therapy, solution-focused therapy, eye movement desensitisation reprocessing (EMDR; which is receiving more attention for the treatment of post-traumatic stress disorder in CAMHS) (NICE, 2005; Tufnell, 2005) or family therapy and family work – the point is not primarily to pathologise an individual according to a diagnosis, but to adopt a person-centred relationship approach. In terms of children this can be further considered as being 'child centred'/'child focused'.

The person-centred approach is the most widely known of the humanistic approaches developed by Carl Rogers in the 1950s. Rogers' core conditions of empathy, unconditional positive regard and congruence tend to underpin all approaches of therapy and are the mainstay of the therapeutic relationship and effective communication (Rogers, 1957). In child and adolescent mental health, as discussed previously, a person-centred/child-centred approach also considers the child and young person in relation to that individual's context of family. Similarly, for teaching staff it is essential to consider the child or young person's context in order to assist with understanding of what may be happening. Whilst doing so it is very important to remain 'child-focused' and to be in a position that maintains and supports the child or young person from an appropriate developmental position. Whilst the family can sometimes be seen as part of the problem it is important to avoid a blaming stance and also to see the family as a resource for change.

Interventions and therapeutic approaches in CAMHS Tiers 2–4 usually include: play therapy, art therapy, parent–infant psychotherapy, under-5s work, cognitive behavioural therapy, individual work, family work, parenting work and family therapy. There will often be a combination model of a psychological and pharmacological intervention and approaches, as shown in the case studies below.

For conduct disorder multidimensional treatment can include parent work and individual work. Psychosocial therapies are the main approach to conduct disorders, involving close working with parents through parenting programmes and parent–child interaction therapy, with the key feature being positive parenting (Murphy and Fonagy, 2012). It can be combined with risperidone (pharmacological approach) for a short period alongside other approaches as above (NICE, 2013 b). Treatment approaches for ADHD include a pharmacological approach as first-line treatment (in conjunction with parenting and individual programmes) for ADHD using a prescribed psychostimulant (methylphenidate) (NICE, 2018). Medication can help children with concentration so has a valid use in supporting children in school settings. It can buy thinking time so impulsivity is reduced and it does help significantly with concentration. It can help with symptom (triad of impairments) control and does not remain in the system for more than a few hours. Treatment 'holidays' can be taken so, for example, the young person may not take need to take medication at the weekend or in the school holidays.

Management of ADHD includes parent and teacher training in behavioural techniques as well as individual support for the young person. A multifaceted and multiagency approach in the management of ADHD includes teacher training in behavioural techniques. There are however side effects, including loss of appetite and difficulty getting to sleep (Burton et al., 2014).

In schools there is an emerging and promising evidence base for mindfulness, not just for children but also school staff, and it provides an opportunity for implementation, adoption and embedding into the curriculum as part of a whole school approach to emotional health and well-being (CentreForum Commission, 2014; Weare, 2015; Mindfulness in Schools Project, 2019). Other whole school approaches include 'circle time' for younger children. In addition, nurture groups, peer mentoring and buddy systems offer important opportunities to build on children and young people's resilience factors and therefore mitigate risk factors, as discussed in the Chapter 4.

Strategies for improving the mental health of children and young people can operate at multiple levels. A goal for teaching and school staff is to develop relationships and partnerships with local agencies who can provide specialist support through service partnerships. But it is recognised this is against a backdrop of reductions in CAMHS budgets, mainly in the Tier 1 and 2 early intervention services. This has led to higher thresholds for referrals to CAMHS, leaving children, young people and families not able to access services until their problem is severe. It is interesting to consider this would be completely unacceptable for childhood cancer services (CentreForum Commission, 2014, p34). An increase in the tiny 6 per cent child and adolescent mental health budget of the overall mental health budget is long overdue (House of Commons Health Committee, 2014, points 80 and 86).

Some of the most effective school interventions have proved to be Targeted Mental Health in Schools (TaMHS), where early identification and support prevent problems escalating. Weare (2015) noted that often schools wait too long, not wishing to 'label' and often thinking children will 'grow out' of problems. Where possible, working with local agencies and CAMHS brings education and health together to think about children and young people where and as soon as concerns are raised.

KEY REFLECTIONS

- Schools have potential and opportunities to mitigate children's mental health through whole school approaches being embedded into the curriculum.
- Examples of these include mindfulness, nurture groups, buddy and peer mentoring systems.
- It is essential to consider the child's context as this contributes to understanding: 'What has happened?'
- There are multiple treatment approaches, including psychological and pharmacological support.
- Many approaches are primarily about working with parents.
- Try to make links with professionals in CAMHS for joined-up working and wrap-round support.

CASE STUDY: JOE

Joe has a diagnosis of ADHD so he is easily distracted and finds it difficult to concentrate for very long and is sometimes impulsive.

Joe is 7 and in a primary school class with 20 other boys and girls. The classroom is sunny and bright with equipment, bookshelves and storage boxes all around the room. There are posters and pictures on the walls. The teacher has a whiteboard. All the children sit at tables which join each other in a group. So there are four children to each group of tables. They are facing each other and not the teacher, who is standing at the front of the class. There is a teaching assistant helping Joe with his task.

Joe is colouring in letter shapes and then cutting them out to stick on a poster. While he is colouring he keeps looking around the classroom and shouts over to his friend on another table who waves back. Joe starts talking to the boy opposite him. The other children round the table are busy working and cutting out.

Joe is trying to concentrate but finds it difficult to stay on task. The teaching assistant reminds Joe to keep on colouring and then she helps him with the scissors and cutting out a letter R. Joe manages to cut out a letter L, for which he receives praise. At the end of the lesson Joe receives a gold star for working hard. He rushes outside at break and tears round the playground with the other boys.

Case study reflections

- Consider classroom layouts; for children like Joe it can be harder to concentrate when he is facing other children, not the class teacher.
- Joe is having great support from the class teaching assistant.
- Joe is praised and rewarded for staying on task, which will have been difficult for him.
- Playtime is a really important opportunity to let off steam and play before the next class.
- Sometimes children like Joe who find it difficult to concentrate and get into trouble have play curtailed, or minutes deducted. This is not helpful and is counterproductive.
- It can be helpful to reframe potential negative characteristics and focus on positive aspects of ADHD, such as higher energy levels and 'up for anything' traits.

Integrating psychological care into Tier 1 universal settings such as schools can work as a preventive and protective strategy. School-based counselling is an available and accessible form of psychological therapy for young people in the UK. *Future in Mind* (Department of Health, 2015) suggests a whole-child and family approach with a move away from thinking purely clinically about child mental health, and emphasising prevention, early intervention and recovery, and that this needs to be considered and implemented universally across settings.

The Pursuit of Happiness report (CentreForum Commission, 2014, p36) recommends that for children with less severe and emerging mental health problems there should be greater accessibility to psychological therapies in schools and that the service could be provided by a practitioner with a child and adolescent mental health background.

The 2017 Green Paper (Department of Health, Department for Education, 2017) and response (Department for Health and Social Care, Department for Education, 2018), discussed in the introduction to this chapter, proposes educational mental health practitioners (EMHPs) in schools and training for these roles commenced in January 2019. In secondary schools young people should have routine access to a named CAMHS worker; this will be met through the EMHP role, although not all schools will have one.

School nurses can be an essential resource; a significant proportion of their workload consists of supporting children and young people with emotional and psychological difficulties (Bohenkamp et al., 2015). They often, however, lack mental health training. This has been recognised by the Royal College of Nursing as an important issue and they have asked for country-wide standardised mental health training (Brown, 2015). School nurses are in the front line in terms of being a health professional accessible to young people in schools and are well placed to offer support and make links within their school community and staff and with other professionals and CAMHS.

Counselling and psychotherapy for children and young people are very different from the traditional adult approaches and need to be developmentally appropriate, individualised, flexible and creative. They need to engage young people who are often reluctant to talk or find it difficult to recognise or understand their feelings. The young person's context or system also requires attention as they are inter-related, and one cannot function in isolation from the other. Children and young people are usually one part of a wider family and are often relatively powerless to change their situation unless their family are supportive of the changes. Typically, a young person may be receiving age-appropriate support individually but ideally, and if possible, this would also be alongside parent and family work (Burton et al., 2014).

CASE STUDY: SARAH-JANE (WITH THANKS TO DR CLARE SMITH)

Sarah-Jane (S-J) is 5. She started in reception class in September and is one of the older children, having had her fifth birthday in late September. It is now mid-February and S-J's teacher, Miss Jennings, is becoming increasingly worried as, although S-J's school attendance has been very poor since she began school, it is getting worse. S-J's attendance has averaged about 50 per cent since the start of term. Her mother is very good at letting school know when S-J is off by phoning in the morning when she's going to miss school and always sends a note when S-J goes back to school. The reasons she gives for keeping S-J off sound genuine, but just seem to be very frequent (cold, cough, earache, sore throat etc.).

Miss Jennings is especially concerned that S-J, who has always been very quiet, has become almost silent. S-J seems very withdrawn and doesn't play much with other children at school. She is becoming harder and harder to engage, although she seems to be an exceptionally polite girl who appears keen to please. During the last week, S-J has cried frequently at school, often over little things.

S-J lives with her mother, father and younger sister, who is 3. Mum used to be a librarian but did not return to work after having S-J. Dad works installing telephone networks and commutes by train into a nearby city, walking to the station each day – a total commute of about one-and-a-half hours each way door to door. Sometimes he works away from home for a week at a time. The family moved to this town so as to be within walking distance of Mum's work and a bit nearer Dad's workplace to shorten his commute, a year or so before S-J was born. Both sets of grandparents live in the town where S-J's parents used to live, about 45 minutes' drive away. All the grandparents work full time, so the family has very little grandparental support. S-J's mum has a driving licence but doesn't like to drive.

S-J is always immaculately dressed for school. Her mum walks her to and from school every day, with her little sister in the push chair. S-J's teacher has noted that Mum is very quiet and tends not to chat with the other mothers in the playground.

Case study reflections

- There were several external factors affecting S-J.
- Miss Jennings realised that S-J was becoming more and more anxious because she was getting behind at school (her projects weren't as good as the other children's because she wasn't there enough to get on with them) and this worried S-J.

- Miss Jennings recognised that Mum was keeping S-J off because she (Mum) was anxious about sending S-J to school, and so not sending her when she had even the slightest snuffle or hint of being even a tiny bit unwell.
- She realised that Mum's anxiety about S-J was partly because she had no local support networks and hadn't made friends amongst the other mothers, so was socially isolated.
- Miss Jennings discussed the situation with the other reception class teacher and made a plan to support the situation, such as identifying a member of staff to support S-J to integrate successfully with her peers at playtime.
- They asked for Mum's help with hearing the children read in the other reception class (not S-J's). They suggested she come into school whenever the 3-year-old sibling was at nursery. They guessed that if Mum had a commitment to come into school then S-J would have to come into school, too, so she wouldn't miss as much school and would become more confident.
- The plan worked. Both S-J and her mother became more confident and their self-esteem grew. Both became less anxious. Mum helped more and more at school and started to talk a little with the other mothers in the playground.

CASE STUDY: JANEK (WITH THANKS TO DR CLARE SMITH)

Janek is 8. He is in year 4 at a mainstream primary school. He lives with his mother, Ania, and his younger brother, Marius, who is 5. The family is Polish but have lived in the UK for about 7 years. They travel back to Poland every summer to see Ania's parents. Janek's and Marius's parents separated when the boys were 5 and 2 and they see their father, Osa, on alternate weekends when they spend Sunday afternoon and have tea with him and his new partner, Lindsay (who is white British); they live in another town. Both boys seem to get on well with Dad and Lindsay and do lots of fun things with them, but get home very tired on Sunday night. They also behave quite aggressively both at home and at school on the Monday and Tuesday after the weekend when they've seen Dad.

Mum works part-time in a local greengrocer's and is able to drop the children off at school on her way to work and finishes work in time to collect them from the after-school club at 4.30 each day. She gets a discount on the fruit and vegetables in the store, so the children have a very healthy diet. Mum appears to be warm and caring. She has no problems with Janek's behaviour at home unless she tries to get him to do homework, which he resists strongly.

Janek has a large, red birthmark covering one cheek (a port-wine stain). The other children at school are used to it and don't comment on it or tease Janek about it.

Janek's teacher, Miss Freer, complains that Janek is very disruptive at school. He shouts out and disrupts the class, drawing attention to himself and making the other children laugh. This is especially problematic during literacy lessons or when the children have to settle down to their writing. Miss Freer feels that Janek does everything he can to avoid tasks that require prolonged writing.

(Continued)

(Continued)

When the class are doing PE or sport, Janek is able to focus well. He can be quite responsible in these settings and likes to help the teacher by carrying equipment. He thrives on the praise he receives for his efforts.

In the playground, Janek gets on well with his peers. He usually plays football at playtime with a large group of friends. He's a good, popular player who doesn't hog the ball and is able to set up others to score goals.

Janek got on well at Beavers but can be a bit disruptive at Cubs (which he has only just started), though he is fine when they are doing activities outside.

Case study reflections

- Points to note: avoidance of writing tasks; tired and aggressive after seeing Dad; a bit disruptive at Cubs.
- Summary: Janek is an 8-year-old Polish boy who displays disruptive avoidant behaviour when he has to undertake effortful writing tasks. When not faced with such tasks he can behave with maturity. He can also be a little disruptive at Cubs, which might be related to his avoidance of writing or might be due to issues around his facial birthmark. He is good at sport and gets on well with his peers. He appears to be well supported by his parents, though he only sees his father fortnightly for a few hours. Janek and his brother also behave quite aggressively for about 2 days after seeing their father, which may be related to tiredness after a busy day or the change in routine/structure (safeguarding issues were ruled out in this case).
- Plan: discuss with staff involved (such as teacher, special educational needs coordinator (SENCo)) to seek their opinions and feedback on your thoughts.
- Consider with them whether further assessment of Janek's writing difficulty would be helpful at this stage (sensory/motor/coordination problem = occupational therapist; cognitive problem, e.g. possible dyslexia = SENCo or educational psychologist).
- Discuss your thoughts with Janek, Mum (and Dad if possible) so as to develop a collaborative plan with them.
- Think about asking them:
  - Would Janek be happy to have extra help with writing tasks.
  - Are they prepared to see someone to find out more (assessment)?
  - Would Dad be happy to have the boys on a Saturday instead of a Sunday?
  - How would Janek or Mum feel about talking to the Cub Scout leader about possible issues with Janek's birthmark or with tasks involving writing when he's at Cubs?

Whatever issues children and young people exhibit, it is vital that all interested parties work together to support an individual's future mental health and well-being. This will be facilitated by a whole school approach to mental health and well-being which involves its leaders, the voice of the child, the school's learning environment, the expertise of the setting's professionals and a strong partnership with individuals, parents, carers and outside agencies. Such an approach must be a proactive response to provide timely support to any mental health or well-being issues as they arise. This may in turn lead to the promotion of a continual drive to promote resilience within children and young people in schools.

Teachers

FURTHER READING

Anna Freud Centre for Children and Families. *Talking Mental Health*. Available at: https://www.youtube.com/watch?v=nCrjevx3-Js (accessed June 2019).

Blakemore, S.-J. (2012) *The Mysterious Workings of the Adolescent Brain*. Available at: https://www.bing.com/videos/search?q=TED+talkk+the+adolescent+brain&docid=607999632361456058&mid=7ABC4D52DCCFC26E642C7ABC4D52DCCFC26E642C&view=detail&FORM=VIRE (accessed 25 July 2019).

Burke-Harris, N. *How Childhood Trauma Affects Health Across a Lifetime.* Available at: https://www.ted.com/talks/nadine_burke_harris_how_childhood_trauma_affects_health_across_a_lifetime (accessed 25 July 2019).

Geopel, J., Childerhouse, H. and Sharpe, S. (2015) *A Critical Approach to Equality and Special Needs and Disability: Inclusive Primary Teaching.* Northwich: Critical Publishing.

Geopel, J., Childerhouse, H. and Sharpe, S. (2015) *Primary Inclusion and the National Priorities: Key Extracts from Primary Inclusive Teaching.* Northwich: Critical Publishing.

Public Health England (2013) *How Healthy Behaviour Supports Children's Wellbeing.* Available at: https://www.gov.uk/government/uploads/system/uploads/attachment_data/file/232978/Smart_Restart_280813_web.pdf (accessed June 2019).

Resilience: The Biology of Stress and the Science of Hope. Trailer available at: https://www.youtube.com/watch?v=We2BqmjHN0k (accessed 25 July 2019).

Schore, A. (2014) *Attachment Trauma and Effects of Neglect and Abuse on Brain Development.* Available at: https://www.psychalive.org/video-dr-allan-schore-attachment-trauma-effects-neglect-abuse-brain-development/ (accessed 25 July 019).

Van Der Kolk, B. (2015) *The Body Keeps the Score: Mind, Brain and Body in the Transformation of Trauma.* London: Penguin Books.

Young Minds (2018) *Addressing Adversity.* Downloadable as an e-book and with access to posters re ACEs. Available at: https://youngminds.org.uk/resources/policy-reports/addressing-adversity-book/ (accessed June 2019).

REFERENCES

American Psychiatric Association (2013) *Diagnostic Statistical Manual (DSM–5).* Available at: http://psychiatry.org/psychiatrists/practice/dsm (accessed June 2019).

Anderson, R. (2008) A psychoanalytic approach to suicide in adolescents, in *Relating to Self-Harm and Suicide Psychoanalytic Perspectives on Practice, Theory and Prevention.* East Sussex: Routledge, p61.

BEAT (2015) *Eating Disorder Statistics.* Available at: https://www.b-eat.co.uk/about-beat/media-centre/information-and-statistics-about-eating-disorders (accessed June 2019).

Bell, D. (2000) Who is killing what or whom? Some notes on the internal phenomenology of suicide. *Psychoanalytic Psychotherapy*, 15(1): 21–37.

Bohenkamp, J.H., Stephan, S.H. and Bobo, N. (2015) Supporting student mental health: the role of the school nurse in co-ordinated school mental health care. *Psychology in the Schools*, 52(7). Available at: http://onlinelibrary.wiley.com/doi/10.1002/pits.21851/pdf (accessed June 2019).

Bradshaw, S. (2013) *Asperger's Syndrome – That Explains Everything: Strategies for Education, Life and Just About Everything Else.* London: Jessica Kingsley.

British Association of Counselling and Psychotherapy (2017) *BACP Welcomes PM Speech on Mental Health and Shared Society.* Available at: https://www.bacp.co.uk/news/news-from-bacp/2017/9-january-2017-bacp-welcomes-pm-speech-on-mental-health-and-shared-society/ (accessed June 2019).

Brown, J. (2015) School nurses need better mental health training. *Children and Young People Now*. Available at: http://www.cypnow.co.uk/cyp/news/1153192/school-nurses-%E2%80%98need-better-mental-health-training%E2%80%99 (accessed June 2019).

Burton, M. (2014) Understanding eating disorders in young people. *Practice Nurse*, 25(12): 606–610.

Burton, M. (2019) Self harm in young people and children. *Practice Nursing*, 30(5): May 2.

Burton, M., Pavord, E. and Williams, B. (2014) *An Introduction to Child and Adolescent Mental Health*. London: Sage.

CentreForum Commission (2014) *The Pursuit of Happiness: A New Ambition for Our Mental Health*. Available at: https://www.ahsw.org.uk/userfiles/Other_Resources/Reports/the-pursuit-of-happiness-2.pdf (accessed June 2019).

Cleare, S., Wetherall, K., Clark, A., Ryan, C. and Kirtley, O. (2018) Adverse childhood experiences and hospital-treated self-harm. *International Journal of Environmental Research and Public Health*, 15(6): 1235. DOI:10.3390/ijerph15061235.

Department for Education (2018) *Mental Health and Behaviour in Schools*. Available at: https://assets.publishing.service.gov.uk/government/uploads/system/uploads/attachment_data/file/755135/Mental_health_and_behaviour_in_schools__.pdf (accessed June 2019).

Department of Health (2004) *The Mental Health and Psychological Well-being of Children and Young People. CAMHS Standard. National Service Framework for Children, Young People and Maternity Services*. Available at: https://www.gov.uk/government/uploads/system/uploads/attachment_data/file/199959/National_Service_Framework_for_Children_Young_People_and_Maternity_Services_-_The_Mental_Health__and_Psychological_Well-being_of_Children_and_Young_People.pdf (accessed June 2019).

Department of Health (2011 a) *No Health Without Mental Health: A Cross Government Mental Health Outcomes Strategy for People of All Ages*. Available at: https://www.gov.uk/government/uploads/system/uploads/attachment_data/file/213761/dh_124058.pdf (accessed June 2019).

Department of Health (2011 b) *Consultation on Preventing Suicide in England*. Available at: http://webarchive.nationalarchives.gov.uk/20130107105354/http://www.dh.gov.uk/prod_consum_dh/groups/dh_digitalassets/documents/digitalasset/dh_128463.pdf (accessed June 2019).

Department of Health (2015) *Future in Mind: Promoting, Protecting and Improving Our Children and Young People's Mental Health and Wellbeing*. Available at: https://www.gov.uk/government/uploads/system/uploads/attachment_data/file/414024/Childrens_Mental_Health.pdf (accessed June 2019).

Department of Health, Department for Education (2017) *Transforming Children and Young People's Mental Health Provision: A Green Paper*. Available at: https://assets.publishing.service.gov.uk/government/uploads/system/uploads/attachment_data/file/664855/Transforming_children_and_young_people_s_mental_health_provision.pdf (accessed June 2019).

Department of Health and Social Care, Department for Education (2018) *Government Response to the Consultation on Transforming Children and Young People's Mental Health Provision: A Green Paper and Next Steps*. Available at: https://assets.publishing.service.gov.uk/government/uploads/system/uploads/attachment_data/file/728892/government-response-to-consultation-on-transforming-children-and-young-peoples-mental-health.pdf (accessed June 2019).

Dhakras, S. (2005) Anorexia nervosa, in Cooper, M., Hooper, C. and Thompson, M. (eds.) *Child and Adolescent Mental Health Theory and Practice*. London: Hodder-Arnold, pp156–163.

Dogra, N., Parkin, A., Gale, F. and Frake, C. (2009) *A Multidisciplinary Handbook of Child and Adolescent Mental Health for Front-line Professionals*, 2nd ed. London: Jessica Kingsley.

Fairburn, C.G. and Harrison, P. (2003) Eating disorders, as cited in: *The Lancet* (2003) 361: 407–416.

Felitti, V.J., Anda, R.F., Nordenberg, D., Williamson, D.F., Spitz, A.M., Edwards, V., Koss, M.P. and Marks, J.S. (1998) Relationship of childhood abuse and household dysfunction to many of the leading causes of death in adults. The Adverse Childhood Experiences (ACE) study. *American Journal of Preventative Medicine*, 14(4): 245–258: https://www.ncbi.nlm.nih.gov/pubmed/9635069 (accessed June 2019).

Freeth, R. (2007) as cited in: Prever, M. (2010) *Counselling and Supporting Children and Young People: A Person-Centred Approach*. London: Sage, p57.

Gardner, F. (2001) *Self-Harm: A Psychotherapeutic Approach*. East Sussex: Routledge.

Gray, S.A.O., Jones, C.W., Theall, K.P., Glackin, E. and Drury, S.S. (2017) Thinking across generations: unique contributions of maternal early life and prenatal stress to infant physiology. *Journal of the American Academy of Child and Adolescent Psychiatry*, 56(11): 922–929. doi:10.1016/j.jaac.2017.09.001

Gur, R.E., Moore, T.M., Rosen, A.F.G., Barzilay, R., Roalf, D.R., Calkins, M.E., Ruparel, K., Scott, J.C., Almasy, A., Satterthwaite, T.D., Shinohara, R.T. and Gur, R.C. (2019) Burden of environmental adversity associated with psychopathology, maturation, and brain behavior parameters in youths. *JAMA Psychiatry*, DOI: 10.1001/jamapsychiatry.2019.0943. Available at: https://www.sciencedaily.com/releases/2019/05/190531085404.htm (accessed June 2019).

Hawton, K., Saunders, K. and O'Connor, R. (2012) Self-harm and suicide in adolescents. *The Lancet*, 379(9834): 2373–2382.

House of Commons Health Committee (2014) *Children's and Adolescents' Mental Health and CAMHS, Third Report of Session 2014–15*. Available at: http://www.publications.parliament.uk/pa/cm201415/cmselect/cmhealth/342/342.pdf (accessed June 2019).

Keenan, T. and Evans, S. (2009) *An Introduction to Child Development*. London: Sage.

Lask, B. (2003) *Practical Child Psychiatry: The Clinician's Guide*. London: BMJ Publishing Group.

Lask, B., Frampton, I. and Nunn, K. (2012) Anorexia nervosa: a noradrenergic dysregulation hypothesis. *Medical Hypotheses*, 78(5): 580–584.

Menzies, L., Bernardes, E. and Huband-Thompson, B. (2018) *Schools and Youth Mental Health: A Briefing on Current Challenges and Ways Forward*. Available at: https://www.lkmco.org/wp-content/uploads/2018/06/Schools-and-Youth-Mental-Health.-Menzies-et-al.-2018.pdf (accessed July 2019).

Mindfulness in Schools Project (2019) Available at: https://mindfulnessinschools.org/ (accessed June 2019).

Moffitt, T.E., Caspi, A., Harrington, H. and Milne, B.J. (2002) Males on the life course: persistent and adolescence-limited antisocial pathways: follow up at age 26. *Developmental Psychopathology*, 14: 179–207. Available at: http://journals.cambridge.org/action/displayFulltext?type=1&fid=100938&jid=DPP&volumeId=14&issueId=01&aid=100937 (accessed June 2019).

Muggleton, J. (2012) *Raising Martians from Crash Landing to Leaving Home: How to Help a Child with Asperger Syndrome or High-Functioning Autism*. London: Jessica Kingsley.

Murphy, M. and Fonagy, P. (2012) Mental health problems in children and young people, in *Annual Report of the Chief Medical Officer 2012, Our Children Deserve Better: Prevention Pays*, Ch. 10. Available at: https://www.gov.uk/government/uploads/system/uploads/attachment_data/file/252660/33571_2901304_CMO_Chapter_10.pdf (accessed June 2019).

National Institute for Clinical Excellence (NICE) (2004) *Self-harm: The Short-term Physical and Psychological Management and Secondary Prevention of Self-harm in Primary and Secondary Care*. Available at: https://www.nice.org.uk/guidance/cg16 (accessed June 2019).

National Institute for Clinical Excellence (NICE) (2005) *Post-traumatic Stress Disorder (PTSD): The Management of PTSD in Adults and Children in Primary and Secondary Care* (Quick Reference Guide). Available at: http://assisttraumacare.org.uk/wp-content/uploads/NICE-PTSD-Quick-Ref-CG026.pdf (accessed June 2019).

National Institute for Clinical Excellence (NICE) (2013 a) *Depression in Children and Young People, Quality Standard QS48*. Available at: https://www.nice.org.uk/guidance/qs48 (accessed June 2019).

National Institute for Clinical Excellence (NICE) (2013 b) *Antisocial Behaviour and Conduct Disorder in Children and Young People: Recognition and Management*. Available at: https://www.nice.org.uk/guidance/cg158/resources/antisocial-behaviour-and-conduct-disorders-in-children-and-young-people-recognition-and-management-35109638019781 (accessed June 2019).

National Institute for Clinical Excellence (NICE) (2018) *Attention Deficit Hyperactivity Disorder: Diagnosis and Management*. Available at: https://www.nice.org.uk/guidance/NG87 (accessed June 2019).

NHS Digital (2018) *Mental Health of Children and Young People in England, 2017*. Available at: https://digital.nhs.uk/data-and-information/publications/statistical/mental-health-of-children-and-young-people-in-england/2017/2017 (accessed June 2018).

NHS England (2015) *Model Specification for Child and Adolescent Mental Health Services: Targeted and Specialist levels (Tiers 2/3)*. Available at: https://www.england.nhs.uk/wp-content/uploads/2018/04/mod-camhs-tier-2-3-spec.pdf (accessed July 2019).

Nikapota, A. (2016) *Providing Care in the Right Way, Putting Information Together* (MindEd tutorial). Available at: https://www.minded.org.uk/Component/Details/447157 (accessed June 2019).

Prever, M. (2010) *Counselling and Supporting Children and Young People: A Person-Centred Approach*. London: Sage.

Public Health England (2015) *Promoting Children and Young People's Emotional Health and Wellbeing: A Whole School Approach*. Available at: https://assets.publishing.service.gov.uk/government/uploads/system/uploads/attachment_data/file/414908/Final_EHWB_draft_20_03_15.pdf (accessed July 2019)

Rogers, C. (1957) The necessary and sufficient conditions for therapeutic change. *Journal of Consulting Psychology*, 21: 95–103.

Royal College of Psychiatrists (2016) *Values-Based Child and Adolescent Mental Health System Commission: What Really Matters in Children and Young People's Mental Health*. Available at: https://www.rcpsych.

ac.uk/docs/default-source/members/faculties/child-and-adolescent-psychiatry/cap-values-based-camhs-summary-document.pdf?sfvrsn=337bdd8a_2 (accessed June 2019).

Royal College of Psychiatrists (2017 a) *Depression in Young People: Helping Children to Cope; for Parents and Carers*. Available at: https://www.rcpsych.ac.uk/mental-health/parents-and-young-people/information-for-parents-and-carers/depression-in-young-people---helping-children-to-cope-for-parents-and-carers?searchTerms=depression%20children%20and%20young%20people (accessed June 2019).

Royal College of Psychiatrists (2017 b) *Worries and Anxieties – Helping Children to Cope: For Parents and Carers*. Available at: http://www.rcpsych.ac.uk/healthadvice/parentsandyouthinfo/parentscarers/worriesandanxieties.aspx (accessed June 2019).

Royal Society for the Encouragement of Arts, Manufactures and Commerce (RSA) (2018) *A Whole School Approach to Mental Health*. Available at: https://www.youtube.com/watch?v=ORn-5AOvjLg (accessed June 2019).

The National Autistic Society (2013) *What is Autism?* Available at: http://www.autism.org.uk/about-autism/autism-and-asperger-syndrome-an-introduction/what-is-autism.aspx (accessed June 2019).

Treasure, J. and Alexander, J. (2013) *Anorexia Nervosa: A Recovery Guide for Sufferers, Families and Friends*. London: Routledge.

Tufnell, G. (2005) Eye movement desensitization and reprocessing in the treatment of pre-adolescent children with post-traumatic symptoms. *Clinical Child Psychology and Psychiatry*, 10(4): 587–600.

United Nations Convention on the Rights of the Child (1989) *Article 31 Right to Play*. Available at: https://downloads.unicef.org.uk/wp-content/uploads/2010/05/UNCRC_PRESS200910web.pdf?_ga=2.195589615.2130650609.1561407161-1394268396.1528870769 (accessed June 2019).

Wade, T.D. and Tiggeman, M. (2013) The role of perfectionism in body dissatisfaction. *Journal of Eating Disorders*. Available at: https://jeatdisord.biomedcentral.com/articles/10.1186/2050-2974-1-2 (accessed June 2019).

Ward, H. (2019) *Mental Health Training for All New Teachers says PM*. TES 16.06.19. Available at: https://www.tes.com/news/mental-health-training-all-new-teachers-says-pm (accessed June 2019).

Weare, K. (2015) *What Works in Promoting Social and Emotional Well-being and Responding to Mental Health Problems in School?* London: National Children's Bureau.

Wing, L. (1996) *The Autistic Spectrum*. London: Constable.

World Health Organization (2016) *International Classification of Diseases* (ICD 10). Available at: https://icd.who.int/browse10/2016/en#/F90-F98 (accessed June 2019).

Wright, K., Burton, M. and Baker, L. (2018) in *Essentials of Mental Health Nursing: Care of People with Eating Disorders*. London: Sage, Ch. 38.

Young Minds (2016) *About Anxiety*. Available at: http://www.youngminds.org.uk/for_parents/worried_about_your_child/anxiety/dealing_anxiety (accessed June 2019).

Young Minds (2018) *Addressing Adversity*. Available at: https://youngminds.org.uk/resources/policy-reports/addressing-adversity-book/ (accessed June 2019).

2

PROMOTING A WHOLE SCHOOL APPROACH

CHAPTER OBJECTIVES

By the end of this chapter you should be aware of:

- the rationale behind a whole school approach to mental health and well-being;
- why and how the leadership and management of a school should promote such an approach;
- the importance of the school's ethos, culture, curriculum, practice and environment in promoting a unified approach to mental health and well-being;
- the role of children and young people in providing a voice to inform and support change;
- how continuing professional development (CPD) underpins the successful whole school approach;
- how a partnership between parents, carers and outside agencies is vital in supporting whole school mental health and well-being.

TEACHERS' STANDARDS

This chapter supports the development of the following Teachers' Standards:

TS8: Fulfil wider professional responsibilities

- Take responsibility for improving teaching through appropriate professional development, responding to advice and feedback from colleagues.
- Communicate effectively with parents with regard to pupils' achievements and well-being.

Part Two: Personal and professional conduct

- Having regard for the need to safeguard pupils' well-being, in accordance with statutory provisions.
- Teachers must have proper and professional regard for the ethos, policies and practices of the school in which they teach.
- Teachers must have an understanding of, and always act within, the statutory frameworks which set out their professional duties and responsibilities.

Introduction

This chapter will focus on the need for a whole school approach to mental health and well-being. It will examine the role that the leadership and management of a setting can play in promoting a clear, agreed policy to underpin such an approach. It will examine how the establishment of such a policy may serve to inform and therefore to pervade the life of the school. This may be seen in terms of the setting's ethos, culture, learning environment, curriculum and professional practice. The role of children and young people and their voice will be considered with regard to the important part they can play in establishing, informing and underpinning such a whole school approach. Finally the role of teachers' CPD will be considered as a means of enhancing practice. Alongside this, the partnership between parents, carers and outside agencies will be outlined for the vital role it plays in supporting a whole school approach to mental health and well-being.

Why is a whole school approach to mental health and well-being needed?

As children and young people move through their schooling, hormonal and physiological changes will inevitably lead to variations in expression of emotions and feelings. Given such changes it could be argued that such an all-pervading whole school approach to mental health and well-being is vital, as children and young people will be learning how to recognise and manage the ebb and flow of emotions as a result of the maturation process. A whole school approach to mental health and well-being may therefore be seen as a proactive, progressive response to provide a timely response to any mental health or well-being issues as they may arise. This in turn may promote a school's continual drive to promote resilience within the children and young people in their care. Schools can promote resilience to mental health issues by:

> providing pupils with inner resources that they can draw on as a buffer when negative or stressful things happen.

> (Department for Education, 2016, p19)

For some children and young people who face additional challenges at home and within their families, a whole school approach, providing support for them when it is needed, can offer an important role in an individual's life (Weare and Nind, 2011). Schools can provide a 'protective health asset', which can thus provide children and young people with a positive identity and learning opportunities as well as the skills needed to mediate against life's challenges (Brooks, 2012, p6). A whole school approach to mental health and well-being can also serve to help children and young people navigate through, and become more resilient towards, the range of their many social pressures. As well as peer relationships, this may include their use of social media, which may lead to unwanted peer pressure through activities such as cyberbullying. Such activities must be seen as a growing concern for individuals and by the government (Department of Health and Social Care and Department for Education, 2018). In research by the National Children's Bureau (NCB) and Association for School and College Leaders (ASCL) (NCB/ASCL, 2016; Newson, 2016), school leaders reported that over 40 per cent of young people indicated a large problem centred on cyberbullying, with nearly eight out of ten individuals (79 per cent) reporting an increase in self-harm or suicidal thoughts.

Concerns linked not only to cyberbullying but also the harmful effects of social media are being taken very seriously by the government. This will lead to a White Paper originating out of the *Internet Safety Strategy Green Paper* (HM Gov, 2017), which clearly identified the origins and pressures on children and young people's mental health as a result of their access to the internet. This White Paper will not only produce a detailed assessment of the impact that technology has on the mental health of individuals but will also outline new policies to support improvements in what may be seen as a major source of concern linked to children and young people's mental health and well-being.

Given this, it seems vital that schools remain vigilant and respond in a proactive, timely, whole school manner to the myriad of life's challenges that may now affect the mental health and well-being of children and young people.

A whole school approach to mental health and well-being is not meant to provide a substitute for specialised clinical support. However, it should serve to complement the many things that teachers can do to support children and young people with school-based strategies, providing a holistic drive to support the prevention and deterioration of mental health and well-being. Stirling and Emery (2016) note that often a focus on mental health and well-being can be seen as a distraction for schools given the pressure placed on them by budgets, the curriculum and the Standards agenda. However, given the current government guidance (Department for Education, 2019), which signals the vital importance of looking at mental health as part of an effective educational provision and as a means of supporting the 'whole child' within their care, its place in school-based provision cannot be ignored. As Stirling and Emery (2016) note, if done well, not only can attainment be raised and enhanced but it may also lead to a reduction in exclusions and positive relationships which may lead to the attraction and retention of school staff.

Schools can play an important role in the central social positioning of children and young people's development. As Cowie et al. (2004) suggest, individuals' relationships with their peers in schools can be crucial in supporting emotional well-being. Educational settings should promote healthy, positive peer relationships, as well as supporting those isolated or withdrawn due to factors such as bullying. The Department of Health (2015) suggests that, due to their position in children and young people's lives, schools fit well with what may be seen as a universal services-led approach. Their positioning not only promotes, but also leads, prevention-based activities linked to delivering and supporting the mental health and well-being of children and young people (Department of Health, 2015). However, for researchers such as O'Reilly et al. (2018 b, p660):

> there are issues with sustainability of universal approaches, and that success, to some extent, relies on cooperation, training and involvement of the schools and the young people themselves.

Many reports, such as those by Brooks (2012) and Public Health England (2015), clearly indicate that the implementation of a whole school approach to mental health and well-being, if applied consistently, not only has a positive impact in promoting a child or young person's physical health and mental well-being but also can serve to prevent mental health problems from arising or developing further. However, Weare (2015, p6) cautions against what can be seen sometimes as *vague and diluted* approaches. It is important to remember that, despite the valuable role that schools can play in promoting and supporting individuals who themselves have developed mental health and well-being issues linked to factors outside school, such settings themselves may in turn lead unwittingly to unwanted personal well-being issues through poor attainment or through moments of school or secondary transition (Brooks, 2012). As Banerjee et al. (2016, p11) note:

> school-based experiences of being bullied or socially excluded, of damaging instructional and assessment practices and of repeated and chronic school failure can potentially have long-lasting impacts upon later well-being.

Thus, given the significant role that schools can often play in the development of the health and well-being of individuals, they have a duty to support individuals in their own trajectories whatever the personal journey such children and young people are on. Wyn et al. (2000) suggest such work is part of schools' core business.

Such ideals seem to be shared by our inspection regime given that Ofsted have placed such a focus in their Inspection Framework (Ofsted, 2015, 2019) when judging the quality of leadership and management with regard to schools seeking to overcome barriers for learning. By monitoring the provision and actions of the school and by scrutinising a range of records such as those of bullying, racism and homophobia incidents, Ofsted (2015, 2019) will be able to be informed of how well a school provision not only contributes to the physical safety of children and young people but also in regard to their emotional health, safety and well-being. 'Outstanding' schools will ensure that the interaction and interplay between families and such settings create environments where:

> children make consistently high rates of progress in relation to their starting points and are extremely well prepared academically, socially and emotionally for the next stage of their education.

(Ofsted, 2015, p75)

However, Weare (2015) cautions that, despite our best efforts, without identification and support, the mental health and well-being problems of children and young people will not go away. This is a result of the many encountered problems being multiple and often going undetected in schools.

KEY REFLECTIONS

- Why is a whole school approach to mental health and well-being vital to success for a school's children and young people?
- How might such a whole school approach fit in with a school improvement agenda?

A whole school approach to mental health and well-being

The state of children's and young people's mental health and well-being has been highlighted by an ongoing raft of publications and reports over many recent years. For example, Public Health England (2015) indicated that there was a worrying level of children who may be found to be suffering from mental health and well-being issues, whilst Young Minds (2017) suggest that 90 per cent of school leaders have seen a rise in the numbers of individuals who exhibit anxiety or stress over the last 5 years.

Such concerns have now placed the topic of the mental health and well-being of our children and young people in the UK at the very centre of government policy. Through the government's Green Paper (Department of Health and Social Care and Department for Education, 2018) entitled *Transforming Children and Young People's Mental Health*, as well as the Scottish Government's *Mental Health Strategy 2017–2027* (Scottish Government, 2017) and the Welsh Government's *Written Statement: Providing for the Emotional and Mental Health Needs of Young People in Schools* (Welsh Government, 2017), attention has now been firmly focused on the types of policies needed to best support this important agenda.

Alongside such vision is a clear message that schools have a shared, clear and vital role to play in supporting the delivery of interventions that can best help those more vulnerable children and young people. For some children and young people this may mean strategies to promote resilience, for example, mindfulness, which may help to support ongoing issues that individuals face. For others who encounter daily mental health issues in education statutory support may be needed linked to the *Special Educational Needs and Disability* [SEND] *Code of Practice* (Department for Education, 2015) through items such as an Education, Health and Care plan which will allow for an integrated and comprehensive support package to be put in place to support the child or young person.

As with a school's approach to SEND, a graduated approach to promoting mental health and well-being in its children and young people may allow each setting to consider a targeted and progressive approach to delivery support, with universal provision for individuals being made available through programmes such as PHSE, targeted interventions, for example, through the use of nurture groups and then more specialist interventions being delivered by, for example, Child and Adolescent Mental Health Services (CAMHS).

Therefore it is not only our duty to do our very best for all children and young people in our care, but also it seems vital that a whole school approach to mental health and well-being should be placed at the very centre of the life and practices of a school. At times this may seem problematic given the difficulties faced in terms of, for example, a lack of funding, appropriate trained and willing staff, as well as the need for clarity and consistency in what mental health is and means (O'Reilly et al., 2018 b). However it is important that schools and leaders seek to overcome such issues given that schools form an educational context and pervasive environment which are able to *build the rights of agency, security, and personal freedom in young people* (O'Reilly et al., 2018 b, p648). Arguably, though, such a whole school approach may be found to be part of a multipronged attack to support mental health and well-being of individuals (for example, using the curriculum, school-based strategies and through the use of a shared agreed school policy); O'Reilly et al. (2018 a) suggest what is lacking is a limited research base that can best be used by schools to identify and support their practice.

Given such a macro-driven policy for promoting mental health and well-being, a whole school approach to this issue must be underpinned by settings creating a shared ethos for the practical implementation of such ideals and practices. Allied to this, there is a need for effective support mechanisms to be established so that those at risk from mental health and well-being issues in our educational settings may be best supported. This macro-commitment by schools is important if such an approach wishes to be all-pervading in each school, thus allowing for the best of class-based practice as well as fostering a culture of belonging for individuals.

All elements of this approach and practice should be nourished by the voice of the child and young person, through the support and relationships offered and by the school's commitment to all staff's continued professional development to support such a focus. As Weare (2015) concludes, it is important for schools to begin with a central universal focus on positive well-being. Such a collective universal approach promotes the development of a culture where mental health and well-being are seen as the norm that allows for emotions and feelings to be discussed, where asking for help is fine in a non-stigmatising environment and where the attitudes and skill base of individuals can provide support when needed.

Figure 2.1 illustrates the central role that a whole school approach to mental health and well-being should play in school life as well as the contributory factors needed to maximise the effectiveness of such an approach.

Leadership and management

Leadership and management are central to any effective strategy in schools, holding a strategic position in a school's development as well as being pivotal in planning for, and bringing about, whole school change centred on a coherent whole school policy for mental health and well-being. Such a whole school policy provides the basis for a climate which challenges and prevents any stigma attached to mental health and well-being issues. For some schools this work may be underpinned by governmental initiatives to create within each setting *Designated Senior Leads for mental health in schools and colleges* (Department of Health and Social Care and Department for Education, 2018, p6). Though not deemed mandatory, such strategic roles will allow schools, through identified trained staff, to work alongside special educational needs coordinators and the school's safeguarding leads to establish a whole school approach to mental health and well-being. Such an approach is seen to combine preventive activities and the promotion of good mental well-being and resilience amongst teaching professionals, children and young people (Department of Health and Social Care and Department for Education, 2018).

However, whoever the lead is for establishing and promoting the mental health and well-being of children and young people in any one setting, it is important that the school has a clear whole school mental health and well-being policy. This not only outlines a school's position on the topic, but also serves to outline the many practices that a setting may employ to support this whole school

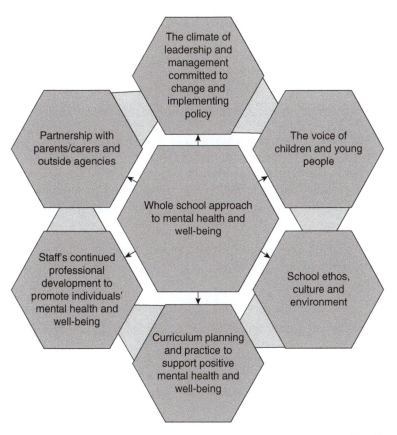

Figure 2.1 A whole school approach to mental health and well-being

focus. It is important that this policy should not sit in isolation from other school policies but the school's agreed actions are *integrated, sustained and monitored* and are:

> *referenced within improvement plans, policies (such as safeguarding; confidentiality; personal, social, health and economic (PSHE) education; social, moral, spiritual and cultural (SMSC) education; behaviour and rewards) and practice.*

(Public Health England, 2015, p7)

Other aspects of a school's work that may support children and young people in this aspect of their lives may also be found in policies such as:

- drug education;
- inclusion;
- anti-bullying;
- attendance.

School leaders also need to acknowledge that, for a whole school approach to mental health and well-being to be effective, the outlining of policy alone is not enough. For any approach to be effective it must encompass the 'whole school' and avoid focusing on disconnected singular approaches. Weare (2015, p5) suggests that in order for schools to have an effective whole school approach to promoting well-being and mental health issues it must be seen in terms of being a coherent *multi-component approach* which uses and encompasses the full potential of the entirety of a school's experience. This may in future include accessing the support of 'mental health support teams' who may help deliver interventions in or close to settings for those who exhibit mild or moderate mental health needs (Department of Health and Social Care and Department for Education, 2018). Or as the Welsh Government (2017) suggests, using CAMHS practitioners as link workers as part of a multidisciplinary model not only to diminish emotional distress and stop mental illness but also to offer early support, relevant referrals and interventions as needed (Welsh Government, 2017).

As Weare (2015, p5) rightly notes, a whole school approach to mental health and well-being should be *everyone's business, with genuine involvement of all staff, pupils, governors, parents and the community and outside agencies.*

However, before any such whole approach can become effective in any setting, as Stirling and Emery (2016) suggest, it has to be based around the establishment of what may be seen as a shared understanding and commitment for such a focus. If such a policy is to be shared and owned by stakeholders then it is vital that all members of staff alongside the wider community of the school are involved in its establishment. This must start with a shared and agreed definition of what social and emotional well-being and mental health mean in the school setting. As Stirling and Emery (2016, p5) note:

> *a shared understanding of the language you use in your school about social and emotional wellbeing and mental health problems helps clear and consistent conversations internally with staff and students with external services, parents and carers.*

So how does a school go about developing such a process? Such an approach is outlined by Stirling and Emery (2016) in their self-assessment and improvement tool for school leaders. In this document Stirling and Emery outline several key questions and activities that you should consider when promoting a dialogue around a shared language (if this is not already the case) and a commitment to change and development. These include:

- What is your consistently understood definition for social and emotional well-being for individuals, children and young people in your setting?
- Where you hold differing views, do they centre on interpretation?
- When you share agreed ideas, what are the key priorities and are any actions needed?
- If items are not accepted or understood, try and ascertain why this is currently the case.
- How might the evidence base inform your practice?
- What universal and targeted approaches work for you and which cause concern?

- What mental health needs do individuals have in your setting and are there issues that you are currently avoiding?

- What individuals or group will lead and implement this change, be accountable for it and prioritise this approach and its actions?

- How are children, young people, parents/carers and external partners given a voice in this process in your setting?

(Stirling and Emery, 2016)

It is important to remember that support for the senior leadership is vital if such work is to be acknowledged and embedded within any setting (Public Health England, 2015). This role may be supported by having a knowledgeable and sympathetic governor who is able to champion mental health and well-being issues. Alternatively, such a role may also be found outside that of senior management just as long as the individual has the support of the leadership, management and governors of the school (Public Health England, 2015).

For any policy to be effective it must remain current and reflect the evolving needs of each setting. Therefore once a school's leadership and management team have created such a policy it must be reviewed regularly, be seen as being 'live' and be capable of responding to the ongoing needs of each setting (Public Health England, 2015).

KEY REFLECTIONS

- How might a mental health and well-being policy support a successful approach to this focus?
- What steps might the leadership and management take to establish such a policy?
- Why must all stakeholders be involved in its establishment?

The school ethos, culture and environment

Once the leadership and management team have led a whole school community through the process of engaging in and establishing the values that underpin a whole school policy for mental health and well-being, the agreed commitment may permeate the life and practice of the school through its culture and ethos. It is important to note however that such agreed school cultural changes must be underpinned by a real commitment and resourcing by school leaders if such a vision is to be owned and realised. As O'Reilly et al. (2018 b, p660) note:

more attention needs to be paid to the culture of schools as part of any intervention, as there is little value in implementing programmes when it is already known that the factors needed for their success are not in place at the time or are not sustainable in the long term.

In a successful inclusive school's ethos, cooperation between all parties will be seen as the norm, with the voice of the individual being heard, with colleagues taking a collegiate approach towards one another (Cole, 2015). The ethos of a school, as Weare (2015) suggests, provides a tone which is all-pervading throughout the setting. It provides a context in which children feel secure, know they are valued as individuals, are safe from emotional and physical harm and are able to discuss their interests and voice their fears in a supportive atmosphere (Ofsted, 2005). A supportive and positive school ethos will, as Weare (2015) rightly acknowledges, allow for a feeling of acceptance, that of being respected, and the creation of strong bonds between individuals and their settings. This may ultimately lead to low levels of conflict, respectful communications, appropriate expression of emotions and an environment which is responsive to individual needs (Weare, 2015).

A supportive, safe and positive ethos for mental health and well-being will no doubt manifest itself through the school's culture of an open-door policy, through staff who are approachable and through its use of nurture groups and quiet areas or rooms in the school. There will be clearly identified individuals for children and young people to approach if worried or concerned. It will forge a school where diversity is celebrated and accepted.

Strategies to support the mental health and well-being of its children and young people at classroom level will seek to develop an individual's sense of self-esteem. This could include having an individual's personal strengths celebrated by use of class-based rewards systems or features such as 'star of the day'. The classroom can also present a supportive and safe environment in which children can discuss and develop areas of low self-confidence or self-esteem through the use of PSHE-based strategies and practices such as circle time or items such as 'worry boxes'. The culture that has been created will mean that relationships between the teacher and the children and young people will be positive. This is important, as:

> the social environment in which staff and pupils spend a high proportion of each weekday may have a profound effect on their physical, emotional and mental health.

> (Public Health, 2014, p7)

It is important to realise that in schools it is not only the school ethos and culture which are of significance but also those of the whole school environment, including the teaching and learning opportunities provided. You may wish to consider whether your school offers the following:

- a school environment which allows for quiet areas as well as areas to promote play to support the range of individual needs;

- a respectful school and classroom environment which allows all pupils to feel safe and valued;

- school grounds and toilet areas which make it harder for young children to be intimidated or bullied out of sight;

- a school building which promotes a positive sense of mood by its quality of decoration and display;

- a staffroom which provides a quiet, comfortable place away from the pressures of the school day for staff.

- Why are a school's ethos and culture so valuable in establishing a climate that supports mental health and well-being?
- How might the wider school environment support individuals' emotional well-being?

Curriculum planning and practice

Surely one of the key roles that the planning and delivery of curricular items in schools can have in promoting resilience with regard to mental health and well-being is that of promoting emotional intelligence within children and young people. As Weare (2015, p10) suggests:

skills are not acquired by osmosis, they involve the school taking a conscious, planned and explicit approach through the taught curriculum.

Such recognition of the importance of the school curriculum and the role it can play in the teaching of children and young people about physical health, mental health and well-being has been signalled by the government's intention to make health education a compulsory element of the curriculum by September 2020 (Department of Health and Social Care and Department for Education, 2018). By such a stance it is hoped that children will receive information to make informed decisions about their own well-being and health and be more able to recognise and seek support as issues arise.

Despite such aspirations (Department of Health and Social Care and Department for Education, 2018), many opportunities can be currently provided by each setting to promote and develop social and emotional skills not only through their use of PSHE and SMSC provision, but also through the wider curriculum in general.

This may include, for example:

- physical education – as well as fostering feelings of positive self-esteem and self-worth, PE can bring about many physical as well as mental health benefits. Research such as that by Glazzard (2018) also shows how projects such as Cambridge Mind Your Head can identify the importance of physical activity in promoting positive mental health;

- music, art and design, where a variety of media are used to explore feelings and emotions;

- literacy, where fiction, non-fiction and a range of writing genres can be explored, promoted and linked to life issues (such as in the novel *The Story of Tracey Beaker* by Jaqueline Wilson);

- religious education, which promotes an exploration of topics such as spirituality.

SMSC is seen by Ofsted (2015, 2019) as an important aspect of an individual's development. It may be seen to pervade the life of the school both in many aspects of the taught curriculum, such as cultural development through religious education, as well as through opportunities such as circle time, which allows children and young people to develop the knowledge, skill and understanding that may underpin their social, moral and spiritual development. As children grow into young people SMSC may be seen to manifest itself in terms of a 'citizenship curriculum'. This forms part of the Key Stage 3 and 4 curriculum which serves to ensure that individuals can form an important and valued part of society whatever their contribution can be.

PSHE may be seen as a means of complementing and enhancing the statutory content of the National Curriculum (Department for Education, 2014, 2019). Most recent changes suggested for PSHE will see its coverage being linked to part of schools' relationships education, relationships and sex education, and health education in England (Department for Education, 2019). Such PSHE content will include mental well-being, internet safety and harm, physical health and fitness, healthy eating, drugs, alcohol and tobacco, health and prevention, and the changing adolescent body (Department for Education, 2019). This will allow PSHE further to support and enhance the school's delivery of the curriculum whilst making clear links to other guidance around drug education, physical activity and healthy lifestyles.

PSHE should be embedded into the educational life of an individual learner through a spiral of learning that will revisit as well as promote positive behaviours by challenging and meeting the needs of children and young people as they grow older. This may be achieved through whole school strategies such as circle time and social and emotional aspects of learning (SEAL), Brain Gym, visiting speakers' reflection time and work around anti-bullying. For some of the most vulnerable in our care consideration must also be given to how best to prevent shared experiences becoming too personal throughout PSHE. Strategies to support such individuals may be found by the use of role play and puppets to provide advice in non-real situations, which may allow for the exploration of dealing with such scenarios (PSHE Association, 2015). As Weare (2015) and the PSHE Association (2015) indicate, for learning to be effective it needs to provide good problem-solving skills. PSHE can:

> *promote the skills, knowledge, understanding and language that will enable pupils to adopt healthy thoughts, behaviours and strategies and to seek appropriate and timely support when they or a friend need it.*
>
> (PSHE Association, 2015)

Through empowering learners to make decisions about their lives in a safe and supportive environment, all individuals can use their experiences to make informed decisions about how best in practice to deal with the situation and issues that are eroding their mental and emotional well-being. Such empowerment may be seen as that of a *growth mind-set* which allows individuals to feel in control of their own abilities and skills in order to facilitate change (PSHE Association, 2015). PSHE may also promote positive relationships between professionals and those in their charge so that each individual feels valued and so that strategies can be deployed to best support the most vulnerable of children and young people.

Though PSHE should pervade the curriculum, despite the best of planning it is important to realise that at times PSHE may also need to respond to situations that are immediate and current for both individuals and for their settings. For example, an issue such as the severe injury or death of a pupil, which can affect children and young people's mental health and well-being, may require discrete teaching.

Additional guidance to support the teaching of PSHE in your setting may be found at **www. pshe-association.org.uk**. Similarly, if you need any guidance, help or advice on supporting the prevention of drug and alcohol-related issues in your setting, further information may be found at **http://mentor-adepis.org**.

KEY REFLECTIONS

- How might the SMSC and PSHE curriculum underpin the teaching and learning related to mental health and well-being?
- How might other aspects of the curriculum support such an agenda?

The voice of children and young people

As Weare (2015) indicates, since mental health and well-being rest on an individual's ability to have a sense of control and self-efficacy it is important that children and young people feel they have a genuine voice, that they are consulted about decisions regarding their own learning and that of school life, and that their rights are respected and listened to. Not only is this vital, but under Article 12 of the United Nations Convention on the Rights of the Child:

> *Children have the right to express their views freely and for their views to be given due weight in matters affecting them.*

> (Robinson, 2014, p18)

Healthy Schools (2007) point out that children and young people's involvement should not be tokenistic; for it to be empowering it should be realistic and meaningful. Robinson (2014) suggests that in schools that take a rights-respecting approach there may be a reduction in incidents of bullying as well as an improved ability for individuals to deal with the conflicts they encounter. However, such an approach involves the need to avoid the temptation of listening to the most vocal and motivated of children and young people (Healthy Schools, 2007; Weare, 2015).

It is important for settings to realise that it is often those who are most marginalised who are struggling to be heard and are in need of being listened to the most. Therefore, schools must do all they can to promote inclusion amongst all individuals and to promote their involvement in change that comes from them and is not part of a predetermined agenda. If children and young people are to feel connected to their setting and to make a meaningful contribution to the decisions that affect their school lives and future well-being then there must be an equal and honest dialogue between individuals and adults. Therefore mechanisms such as school councils should represent the range of individuals in a setting and hence of opinions expressed. Not only does such a body need to be inclusive, but it must be given status and the children and young people should be taught and given the skills necessary to promote the democratic system they are involved in. As Weare (2015) suggests, pupil voice when effective promotes a defensive school connection which can lead to an enhanced feeling towards self, as well as promoting social skills. Individuals in a school that has a rights-respecting approach feel valued, respected, cared for and listened to (Robinson, 2014). All of this should be embedded in relationships with staff where genuine concern is shown toward well-being.

Other school-based strategies that a setting might provide to promote dialogue and involvement include:

- pupil interviews or pupil-based evaluations of school-based activities;

- questions on parent questionnaires;

- assessment for learning approaches such as smiley/sad faces, thumbs up;

- presenting at assemblies;

- reporting back on actions and decisions made by school or eco-councils;

- suggestion/worry boxes;

- opportunities through PSHE/SEAL/circle time activities to share;

- opportunities outside lesson time for adults to share conversation, such as out-of-school activities;

- relationships in nurture groups or with assigned/named adults.

In some settings, pupils' voices can be harnessed in what may be called peer mentoring, peer review or peer support in order to support and improve pupils' well-being. This approach can prove effective if children and young people are given suitable and appropriate support and training. Given such induction they may then be able to work proactively in schools in some form of buddying or peer support approach. This may lead to the promotion of social and emotional skills amongst their peers or the ability to model alternative ways of thinking and behaving (Weare, 2015). The Department for Education (2016) suggests in some settings this can offer an effective, as well as low-cost, support to individuals and can act as a preventive measure against low levels of self-esteem. Weare (2015), however, indicates that the success of such schemes may be found in terms of the ownership and engagement they provide for children or young people.

For children with social, emotional and mental health difficulties (formerly referred to as behavioural, emotional and social difficulties) a useful approach is 'circle of friends' (Farrell, 2006 cited in Cole, 2015). This allows an individual to explore the feelings and issues being created between individuals involved in the scenario during each other's absence. By promoting a sense of empathy with the situation and individuals involved, an agreement can be forged between each party about the best way forward to improve the situation encountered.

Outside the school setting, organisations such as MIND provide comprehensive peer support for a range of issues, and further information may be found by accessing their website: **www.mind.org. uk/get-involved/peer-support**.

```
KEY REFLECTIONS
```

- Why are children and young people's voices so important in promoting their positive mental health and well-being?
- How might a school facilitate and promote the establishment of the voice of an individual?
- How might peers be used to support an inclusive school environment?

Staff and continuing professional development

Teachers who do not have any specialist mental health and well-being training can be left to feel ill equipped and lacking in confidence to identify and deal with the huge range of mental health and well-being issues being presented by children and young people in their everyday teaching lives. As Public Health England (2015) indicates, if school staff are to be equipped to identify mental health issues in their learning population, then they need access to CPD training so as to increase their knowledge of this important aspect of school life. These claims have been backed up by research such as that by O'Reilly et al. (2018 a); this author notes that teachers did not have the skills, time or resources to address issues around mental health. Therefore such training seems vital, as teachers need to be competent in order to recognise and support children and young people with mental health difficulties (O'Reilly et al., 2018 a) given their pivotal role in such children's lives.

Cole (2015) notes that school staff also need training not only to understand the importance that pastoral support can provide but also with regard to accessing specialist support services such as CAMHS.

Let us hope, as O'Reilly et al. (2018 a) suggest, that by upskilling teachers to identify mental health concerns not only will the referral rate to specialist services go up but also teachers will be more able to signpost parents to support outside the school gates. Much of what is desired will rest on sufficient funding and for researchers such as O'Reilly et al. (2018 a) the funding of mental health is currently inadequate.

Despite such claims it is heartening to recognise that at least the government has acknowledged the need for further funding and a need for more consistent training for staff with regard to children and young people's mental health. This has led to a promise by the prime minister that all secondary schools will be offered mental health training (Gov UK, 2017 a) and this will now include every primary school by 2022 (Department of Health and Social Care and Department for Education, 2018). Such a commitment has been coupled with the desire to train identified staff as *Designated Senior Lead for mental health* (Department of Health and Social Care and Department for Education, 2018) to identify and drive forward high-quality mental health provision within schools. Though such moves should be welcomed for the obvious benefits they may bring, it is important to note, as O'Reilly et al. (2018 a) indicate, that any such training does not always lead to an effective transformation of practice when implemented. This may be linked to the challenges and complexities of understanding mental health issues.

As the government has pledged ongoing CPD, it is also necessary for teachers to receive training in order to support the ever-evolving issues which can lead to issues for the mental health and emotional well-being of individuals. For example:

- the Child Exploitation and Online Protection Command, or CEOP, offers training to reduce issues around cyberbullying and child sexual exploitation;

- Prevent (part of the government's counterterrorism strategy) – training linked to the safeguarding of children around issues of radicalisation;

- child protection/safeguarding training.

Therefore, it is important that the leadership and management of any setting promote regular CPD for teachers as a central part of promoting a whole school approach to supporting mental health and well-being, not only for staff, but also the children and young people in its care. For many schools training will take the form of youth mental health first aid (MHFA) (Mental Health First Aid England, 2018). Not only should this type of training form part of any whole school aspiration for all staff, but given Ofsted's (2015, 2019) view on CPD – that it can have a positive impact on teachers' teaching as well as pupils' learning – it should form a vital part of all schools' improvement planning to make them an outstanding institution.

However, despite the best-laid plans to support staff development, barriers may exist to stop the effective delivery of teachers' professional development. Firstly, there is often a meagre funding budget available to train more than a limited number of staff through government funding initiatives and CPD course budgets. Sometimes such funding may have to be channelled to focus on a school improvement agenda, perhaps linked to a recent disappointing Ofsted inspection or to supporting the effective delivery of underachieving core subjects such as literacy and numeracy. Research by the Education Policy Institute has also shown how the long hours worked by English teachers, compared to those of most other countries, have hindered their access to CPD (Frith, 2016). Given the many challenges faced with workforce development linked to children's and young people's mental health, it is important to:

> be clear about who you need in your team and if they have the right skills to the roles you need them for.

> (Frith, 2016, p36)

Such strategic thinking will no doubt be at the foremost of all leaders' minds given the pledged injection of funding by government to support mental health training (Department of Health and Social Care and Department for Education, 2018). As noted earlier, for the majority of schools such training will be seen in terms of MHFA courses for staff and designated leads. For some schools the creation of mental health champions (Gov UK, 2017 b) will be linked to a focus for training within their setting. Therefore it is heartening that recent research acknowledges that youth MHFA training has overall:

> resulted in MHFA Champions' increased confidence in knowledge, skills and awareness of the complexities surrouding mental health needs within current school context.

> (Robert-Holmes et al., 2018, p64)

As indicated earlier, mental health and well-being CPD may take many forms in schools but it should be founded on a clear assessment of a teacher's professional needs as well as on what is needed to support whole school development. This may be achieved through the use of a school's performance management systems so as to encourage, challenge and support teachers' improvement (Ofsted, 2015). However, although CPD may be seen as being a particular course of training to support an individual's needs, at times for the promotion of consistency of an approach in a setting, whole school training may be needed. This may be achieved using items such as teacher development days for the most effective means of delivering whole school CPD.

Not all staff development should be seen to centre on teachers being allowed to go out of school in order to be trained to promote the personal and social development of its pupils. MindEd is a free educational resource on children and young people's mental health, which offers e-learning modules that any adult with an interest in this area can access. There are options to dip in and out of subject areas or to complete whole modules and gain certificates of learning. MindEd also provides children and young people's mental health e-learning aimed at families; if parents express concern or an interest in their child's mental health and well-being, it may be useful to direct them to this resource, which can be accessed at **www.minded.org.uk**.

Ofsted (2006) suggest that for some less experienced and newly appointed staff, assigning them an experienced school mentor can be seen as being beneficial to supporting the needs of their many pupils. Given the government's drive to promote Champions for MHFA and Designated Senior Leads for mental health, such key school personnel will no doubt provide, not only for less experienced but also for more established members of staff, a knowledgeable, valuable resource for individuals to tap into. This may involve adopting a coaching and team-teaching approach for staff as a means of building the capacity of teachers when dealing with the social, emotional and mental health of pupils. For researchers such as O'Reilly et al. (2018 a), such in-class teaching provides staff with practical strategies to support their mental health training.

Though this section has talked about the need for quality training for teachers, leaders must not forget that training in itself can cause issues for even the most trained of professionals (for example, youth MHFA Champions). Research has shown that concerns regarding trained mental health professionals centre around a lack of supervision or debriefing having worked in such roles and with identified individual children and young people (O'Reilly et al., 2018 a; Robert-Holmes et al., 2018). Unless schools seek to address such concerns of teaching professionals being able to offload the emotional result of working with children and young people, they too may find such work has a negative impact upon their own mental health. Such a situation is far from ideal as regards the outlook for the future profession and levels of teacher retention. Some commentators have even suggested with regard to workload that the role of being a teacher is becoming unmanageable and that there has been insufficient focus on teaching professionals mental health, and that this should change if we are to develop the well-being of future generations of children and young people (Stanley, 2018).

If you require further information to support your training on CEOP, MHFA, Prevent or child sexual exploitation, please visit **www.ceop.police.uk**, **www.mhfaengland.org** and **www.prevent forschools.org** or **http://paceuk.info/about-cse/keep-them-safe**.

KEY REFLECTIONS

- Why is professional CPD so important?
- What might prove a barrier to providing CPD?
- How might in-school CPD be supported?

Partnership with parents, carers and outside agencies

When supporting any child or young person with regard to mental health and well-being, it is vital that a partnership is forged between parents, carers and families to secure the best outcomes. As Weare (2015) acknowledges, the effectiveness in this partnership lies in the support and understanding of a child or young person's needs that parents and carers can offer schools. This may be in addition to the role schools can play in developing and supporting their parenting skills and attitudes towards any such issues. By supporting parents and carers through what often are challenging scenarios for their most vulnerable of charges, a school can help improve relationships through mutual cooperation as well as making them more ready to engage with learning and the school setting. As the Department for Education (2016) indicates, such collaborative partnerships between parents and carers can lead to an improved likelihood of reducing a child or young person's difficulties as well as the ability to support his or her emotional development (given the child or young person's appropriate consent).

When considering the issue of partnerships, not only is such a collaboration desirable but it is an expectation of Ofsted (2015, 2019) that schools engage with parents and carers in order to support their child or young person's safety and SMSC development alongside guidance to help support their improvement. The school setting may be able to signpost more vulnerable parents to agencies such as Parent Partnership so that they can be given the appropriate guidance and support to help their child.

Given that children may be in care in our school communities, it is also important that settings have clear strategies to promote successful partnerships with foster carers, members of the extended family and social workers. For looked-after children such clear mechanisms can provide a vital bridge to support what is happening in the home setting and how this may be mitigated against when in the school setting.

Allied to this partnership it is important that settings engage with outside agencies to support a child or young person's mental health and well-being. In some cases such provision is arranged and/or funded by the setting directly depending on the funding arrangements – for example, loss or bereavement counselling. Outside agencies, through their specialised knowledge of how best to identify needs and of the range of support available to individuals, are often best placed to provide support outside that of the school's expertise and graduated response. External partnerships are seen by Ofsted (2015, 2019) as a means of allowing leaders to identify and support children and young people effectively. Such support may take the form of in-school input with specialist support by professionals such as the school nurse or health visitor, educational psychologists or through outside interventions by their general practitioner, CAMHS practitioners or paediatric consultants.

More recently such an idea has seen the piloting by the Welsh Government (2017) of CAHMS practitioners forming a link between themselves and schools. This has resulted in specialist CAMHS support being available when needed by schools. Whatever support is provided, there will need to be close collaboration between such agencies and the school so that appropriate and complementary support may be given to the child or young person when in their educational setting. In some cases it may be that not only will the school have to use outside agencies to support children and young people but such support may also be needed to support family members as a whole through their own mental health and emotional problems. Taking such actions may prove the best route in order to best support the individual at the centre of a school's concerns.

As children and young people get older it will be a school's duty to signpost to agencies that can discuss and support them with personal and emotional issues. To find out more information regarding the range of support and services available to you to support the mental health and well-being of your children and young people, visit the Youth Wellbeing Directory at **www.youthwellbeing.co.uk**.

KEY REFLECTIONS

- Why are partnerships with parents and carers vital?
- How might a school use outside agencies to support their mental health and well-being agenda?
- Why is it so important for schools to have a whole school approach to mental health and well-being?
- What strategic role can leadership and management play in such an approach?
- What role can the school ethos, culture and environment play in supporting individual mental health and well-being?
- How can the school curriculum and school practice complement and support the work of the school?
- How can the voice of children and young people support and enhance the whole school approach?
- Why is CPD necessary to support professionals, children and young people?
- How can working with parents, carers and outside agencies support a school's approach to mental health and well-being?

CHAPTER SUMMARY

- Mental health and well-being are most effectively dealt with through a whole school approach.
- The school's leadership and management can play a pivotal role in providing a vision and means to support the mental health and well-being needs of its stakeholders.
- Providing the right ethos, culture and environment can best support individuals both in the school and classroom.

(Continued)

(Continued)

- The curriculum and practice of a school can significantly contribute to a climate in which children and young adults with mental health and well-being issues can flourish.
- The voice of individuals can serve to inform and enhance an understanding of how best to support children and young people in their setting.
- The CPD of school staff will help them all have a clear role to play in identifying and supporting children with behavioural issues linked to their mental health and well-being.
- The partnerships between parents, carers and outside agencies are fundamental in facilitating a holistic approach to providing support for children and young adults.

FURTHER READING

Boingboing provides opportunities to learn more about promoting resilience: www.boingboing.org.uk.

MIND (2016) *Making Sense of Peer Support*. Available at: http://mind.org.uk/information-support/drugs-and-treatments/peer-support/peer-support-for-specific-groups/#.WByT5IXXIdU (accessed 4 November 2016).

Young Minds (2016) *About Self-esteem*. Available at: www.youngminds.org.uk/for_parents/whats_worrying_you_about_your_child/self-esteem/about_self-esteem (accessed 1 January 2016).

REFERENCES

Banerjee, R., McLaughlin, C., Cotney, J., Roberts, L. and Peereboom, C. (2016) *Promoting Emotional Health, Well-being and Resilience in Primary Schools*. Available at: http://ppiw.org.uk/files/2016/02/PPIW-Report-Promoting-Emotional-Health-Well-being-and-Resilience-in-Primary-Schools-Final.pdf (accessed 25 September 2016).

Brooks, F. (2012) Life stages: School years, in Annual Report of the Chief Medical Officer (2012) *Our Children Deserve Better: Prevention Pays*. Available at: www.gov.uk/government/uploads/system/uploads/attachment_data/file/252657/33571_2901304_CMO_Chapter_7.pdf (accessed 23 July 2016).

Cole, T. (2015) *Mental Health Difficulties and Children at Risk of Exclusion from Schools in England: A Review from an Educational Perspective of Policy, Practice and Research, 1997 to 2015*. Available at: www.education.ox.ac.uk/wordpress/wp-content/uploads/2015/02/MENTAL-HEALTH-AND-EXCLUSION-FINAL-DIGITAL-13-06-15.pdf (accessed 23 September 2016).

Cowie, H., Boardman, C., Dawkins, J. and Dawn, J. (2004) *Emotional Health and Wellbeing: A Practical Guide for Schools*. London: Paul Chapman Publishing.

Department for Education (2014) *National Curriculum in England*. Available at: www.gov.uk/government/collections/national-curriculum (accessed 12 November 2016).

Department for Education (2015) *Special Educational Needs and Disability Code of Practice: 0 to 25 Years*. Available at: https://assets.publishing.service.gov.uk/government/uploads/system/uploads/attachment_data/file/398815/SEND_Code_of_Practice_January_2015.pdf (accessed 12/9/18).

Department for Education (2016) *Mental Health and Behaviour in Schools*. Available at: www.gov.uk/ government/publications/mental-health-and-behaviour-in-schools—2 (accessed 12 September 2016).

Department for Education (2019) *Relationships and Sex Education (RSE) and Health Education. Draft Statutory Guidance for Governing Bodies, Proprietors, Head Teachers, Principals, Senior Leadership Teams, Teachers*. Available at: https://assets.publishing.service.gov.uk/government/uploads/system/uploads/ attachment_data/file/781150/Draft_guidance_Relationships_Education__Relationships_and_Sex_ Education__RSE__and_Health_Education2.pdf (accessed 27 June 2019).

Department of Health (2015) *Future in Mind: Promoting, Protecting and Improving Our Children and Young People's Mental Health and Wellbeing*. Available at: www.gov.uk/government/uploads/system/uploads/ attachment_data/file/414024/Childrens_Mental_Health.pdf (accessed 16 October 2016).

Department of Health and Social Care and Department for Education (2018) *Government Response to the Consultation on Transforming Children and Young People's Mental Health Provision: A Green Paper and Next Steps*. Available at: https://www.gov.uk/government/consultations/transforming-children-and- young-peoples-mental-health-provision-a-green-paper (accessed 11 September 2018).

Farrell, M. (2006) *Behavioural, Emotional and Social Difficulties: Practical Strategies*. London: David Fulton Publishers.

Frith, E. (2016) *Children's and Young People's Mental Health: Time to Deliver*. London: Education Policy Unit.

Glazzard, J. (2018) *Tackling Mental Health in the Classroom*. Available at: www.leedsbeckett.ac.uk/ news/1018-tackling-mental-health-in-the-classroom/ (accessed 15 October 2018).

Gov UK (2017 a) *Prime Minister Unveils Plans to Transform Mental Health Support*. Available at: https:// www.gov.uk/government/news/prime-minister-unveils-plans-to-transform-mental-health-support (accessed 12 October 2018).

Gov UK (2017 b) *Secondary School Staff Get Mental Health 'First Aid' Training*. Available at: https:// www.gov.uk/government/news/secondary-school-staff-get-mental-health-first-aid-training (accessed 12 October 2018).

Healthy Schools (2007) *Guidance for Schools on Developing Emotional Health and Wellbeing*. Available at: www.healthyschools.london.gov.uk/sites/default/files/EHWB.pdf (accessed 4 November 2016).

HM Gov (2017) *Internet Safety Strategy Green Paper*. Available at: https://assets.publishing.service.gov. uk/government/uploads/system/uploads/attachment_data/file/650949/Internet_Safety_Strategy_ green_paper.pdf (accessed 15 October 2018).

Mental Health First Aid England (2018) *Would You Know How to Help?* Available at: https://mhfaengland. org/individuals/youth/ (accessed 12 October 2018).

NCB/ASCL (2016) *Keeping Young People in Mind: Findings from a Survey of Schools Across England*. Available at: www.ncb.org.uk/sites/default/files/field/attachment/news/ascl_and_ncb_findings_from_ survey_briefing_final_footnotes.pdf (accessed 13 February 2017).

Newson, R. (2016) *School Leaders Voice Concerns over Children's Mental Health Care*. Available at: www. ncb.org.uk/news-opinion/news-highlights/school-leaders-voice-concerns-over-childrens-mental- health-care (accessed 12 November 2016).

Ofsted (2005) *Managing Challenging Behaviours*. Available at: www2.yorksj.ac.uk/pdf/managing_challenging_behaviour2.pdf (accessed 12 October 2016).

Ofsted (2006) *Inclusion: Does it Matter Where Pupils are Taught? Provision and Outcomes in Different Settings for Pupils with Learning Difficulties and Disabilities*. Available at: http://dera.ioe.ac.uk/6001/1/Inclusion%20does%20it%20matter%20where%20pupils%20are%20taught%20(pdf%20format)%20.pdf (accessed 17 November 2016).

Ofsted (2015) *School Inspection Handbook*. Available at: www.gov.uk/government/publications/school-inspection-handbook-from-september-2015 (accessed 12 November 2016).

Ofsted (2019) *School Inspection Handbook*. Available at: https://assets.publishing.service.gov.uk/government/uploads/system/uploads/attachment_data/file/805781/Relationships_Education__Relationships_and_Sex_Education__RSE__and_Health_Education.pdf (accessed 29 August 2019).

O'Reilly, M., Adam, S., Whiteman, N., Hughes, J., Reilly, P. and Dogra, N. (2018 a) Whose responsibility is adolescents' mental health in the UK? Perspectives of key stakeholders. *School Mental Health*, pp1–12. Available at: https://link.springer.com/content/pdf/10.1007%2Fs12310-018-9263-6.pdf (accessed 10 October 2018).

O'Reilly, M., Svirydzenka, N., Adams, S. and Dogra, N. (2018 b) Review of mental health promotion intervention in schools. *Social Psychiatric Epidemiology*, 53: 647–662.

PSHE Association (2015) *Teacher Guidance: Preparing to Teach about Mental Health and Emotional Well-being*. Available at: www.pshe-association.org.uk/sites/default/files/Mental%20health%20guidance.pdf (accessed 10 November 2016).

Public Health England (2014) *The Link Between Pupil Health and Wellbeing and Attainment*. Available at: www.gov.uk/government/uploads/system/uploads/attachment_data/file/370686/HT_briefing_layout vFINALvii.pdf (accessed 18 September 2016).

Public Health England (2015) *Promoting Children and Young People's Emotional Health and Wellbeing: A Whole School and College Approach*. Available at: www.gov.uk/government/uploads/system/uploads/attachment_data/file/414908/Final_EHWB_draft_20_03_15.pdf (accessed 5 October 2016).

Robert-Holmes, G., Mayer, S., Jones, P. and Fung Lee, S. (2018) *An Evaluation of Phase One of the Youth Mental Health First Aid (MHFA) in Schools Programme: 'The training has given us a vocabulary to use.'* Available at: https://mhfastorage.blob.core.windows.net/mhfastoragecontainer/5603f429f9cae811814fe0071b668081/Youth-MHFA-in-Schools-programme-UCL-evaluation-report.pdf?sv=2015-07-08&sr=b&sig=ymj3QDGof bxrqdRoqSnwmqGUet3Ed0So3j2IaSmYwI4%3D&se=2018-10-12T11%3A28%3A59Z&sp=r (accessed 13 October 2018).

Robinson, C. (2014) *Children, Their Voices and Their Experiences of School: What Does That Tell Us?* York: Cambridge Primary Review Trust: University of York.

Scottish Government (2017) *Mental Health Strategy 2017–2027*. Available at: https://beta.gov.scot/publications/mental-health-strategy-2017-2027/ (accessed 11 October 2018).

Stanley, J. (2018) *Teachers are at Breaking Point. It's Time to Push Wellbeing up the Agenda*. Available at: https://www.theguardian.com/teacher-network/2018/apr/10/teachers-are-at-breaking-point-its-time-to-push-wellbeing-up-the-agenda (accessed 12 October 2018).

Stirling, S. and Emery, H. (2016) *A Whole School Framework for Emotional Well-being and Mental Health*. Available at: www.ncb.org.uk/sites/default/files/field/attachment/NCB%20School%20Well%20 Being%20Framework%20Leaders%20Tool%20FINAL.pdf (accessed 9 August 2016).

Weare, K. (2015) *What Works in Promoting Social and Emotional Well-being and Responding to Mental Health Problems in School?* London: National Children's Bureau.

Weare, K. and Nind, M. (2011) Mental health promotion and problem prevention in schools: what does the evidence say? *Health Promotion International*, 26: 29–69. Available at: http://heapro.oxford journals.org/content/26/suppl_1/i29.full (accessed 21 November 2016).

Welsh Government (2017) *Written Statement: Providing for the Emotional and Mental Health Needs of Young People in Schools*. Available at: https://gov.wales/about/cabinet/cabinetstatements/2017/ mentalhealthneeds/?lang=en (accessed 10 October 2018).

Wyn, J., Cahill, H., Holdworth, R., Rowling, L. and Carson, S. (2000) *Mindmatters: A Whole School Approach Promoting Mental Health and Wellbeing*. Available at: www.researchgate.net/publications 12367371 (accessed 14 August 2016).

Young Minds (2017) *Wise Up: Prioritising Wellbeing in Schools*. Available at: https://youngminds.org.uk/ media/1428/wise-up-prioritising-wellbeing-in-schools.pdf (accessed 15 October 2018).

3

CHILDREN AND YOUNG PEOPLE'S BEHAVIOUR
WHAT IS BEING COMMUNICATED AND HOW SHOULD WE RESPOND?

CHAPTER OBJECTIVES

By the end of this chapter you should be aware of:

- the current issues relating to supporting positive behaviours in children and young people in an educational setting;
- the role professionals may play in understanding, promoting and supporting positive behaviour;
- the range of strategies and policy guidelines that can support children and young people who present with challenging behaviours in school;
- the barriers to supporting children and young people with behavioural difficulties;
- why it is important to always consider behaviour in a context of curiosity about what is being communicated;
- why unacceptable behaviours become a medium for acting out from a stress position.

TEACHERS' STANDARDS

This chapter supports the development of the following Teachers' Standards:

TS1: Set high expectations which inspire, motivate and challenge pupils

- Demonstrate consistently the positive attitudes, values and behaviour which are expected of pupils.

TS7: Manage behaviour effectively to ensure a good and safe learning environment

- Have clear rules and routines for behaviour in classrooms, and take responsibility for promoting good and courteous behaviour both in classrooms and around the school, in accordance with the school's behaviour policy.
- Have high expectations of behaviour, and establish a framework for discipline with a range of strategies, using praise, sanctions and rewards consistently and fairly.
- Manage classes effectively, using approaches which are appropriate to pupils' needs in order to involve and motivate them.
- Maintain good relationships with pupils, exercise appropriate authority, and act decisively when necessary.

Introduction

This chapter will focus on understanding the behaviour of children and young people in the class and wider school setting. Consideration will be given to potential links with mental health and well-being. It will also examine the risk factors that may generate negative behaviours and the challenges that practitioners may face. The impact of these behaviours on the child/young person themselves, their families and the individual's educational setting will also be explored. Finally, it will offer strategies to support children and young people within the educational setting so that they may successfully enjoy and participate appropriately in school life.

Why be concerned?

As children and young people develop and mature, managing changing emotions as a result of the maturation process can prove to be an understandable and unpredictable challenge. Physiological changes driven by hormonal activity alongside the child or young person's own personality and character can lead to issues around a range of positive and negative behaviours to be observed in any educational setting for many children and young people. For some children, allied to these normal maturation stages of development, are the additional issues centred on risk factors such as environmental and contextual considerations; for example, violence and poverty, the family, domestic abuse and child abuse. This may all in turn lead to the young person/child themselves developing attachment difficulties, neurodevelopmental difficulties and conditions (such as attention deficit hyperactivity disorder, or ADHD), and low self-esteem (Young Minds, 2016). All of these examples can lead to heightened levels of anxiety which is very difficult for children and young people to manage in a manner acceptable to the school environment. Sadly, it would not be uncommon for some children and young people to have experience of, and be subject to, many of these areas of difficulty. Government statistics (DfE, 2016 b) suggest that risk factors such as social disadvantage, family adversity and cognitive or attention problems have a cumulative impact upon children developing behaviour problems. Boys under the age of 10 who have five or more risk factors are almost 11 times more likely to exhibit conduct disorder compared to those with no risk factors. Girls similarly were also 19 times more likely to exhibit conduct disorder given five or more risk factors compared again to those with no risk factors. Statistics indicate that a minimum of three children per classroom have a potential mental health problem and that these can often be present through difficult and challenging behaviours; all teaching and school staff will therefore have an experience of this. It is through extrapolations by researchers such as Cole (2015) that we can start to appreciate the impact and scale of the issues faced by our schools with regard to managing children and young people who experience social, emotional and behavioural difficulties (SEBD).

It is really important to remember to try and re-frame behaviour in a psychological sense and try and understand what is being communicated. A child acting out in class, perhaps being the 'class clown', will distract the teacher and will often have a response that may be 'telling off' but the behaviour becomes re-enforced as other pupils may find the child popular. If we consider the child may not be able to manage or understand the classroom activity or task that has been set, then automatically anxiety levels become raised. As we discussed earlier, biologically, there has to be a response in order to be able to manage the anxiety at a level which can be tolerated. So being a 'clown' immediately relieves one from the anxiety-provoking task. Being 'told off' does not escalate anxiety to such a high level so relief is experienced and thus the behaviour unwittingly becomes re-enforced. It is estimated that 400,000–500,000 children will be faced with the risk of exclusion related to SEBD issues. Exclusion, despite it always being a last resort, is probably one of the most detrimental interventions for individual children and young people, further reinforcing a low sense of worth and removing contact with potentially the only professionals and a 'safe' setting in the young person's life. It should also be noted that punishment does not work for the majority of children who present with challenging behaviours; withholding play and break time activity is often counter-productive and therefore should be avoided.

Children who have attachment difficulties are likely to present with behaviour problems in the classroom. It is important to remember that attachment is the main mechanism for the regulation of relationships (Schore, 2005). The quality of attachment is determined by early experiences and these predict lifelong relationship patterns. Secondary attachment figures such as school staff can provide reliable sources of safety and comfort. In early years settings there are requirements for consistent key workers. Remember the principle of attachment is about internalising a sense of self and safety. The emotional activity within relationships becomes the supportive factor and children and young people develop hierarchies of attachment figures which would include school staff significant to them. Children and young people with an insecure attachment quality experience raised cortisol levels (the stress response hormone) even in fairly mild scary situations. Heightened anxiety initiates a stress response understood as fight, flight or freeze. Typically, a young person may take the fight response and become very challenging and confrontational in the classroom. The experience of 'rejection' following such an outburst, rather than a contained response, is likely to further escalate the attachment behaviour. Whilst this may not mitigate the behaviour or mean there should not be a proportionate response, it is necessary and helpful to understand the 'back story' and context.

Children and young people with a diagnosis of ADHD commonly have difficulties with the 'triad of impairments' which include:

- hyperactivity;
- difficulties with concentration;
- impulsivity.

It is easy, therefore, to appreciate how tricky the average classroom environment is to negotiate with this diagnosis. Yet, there is an expectation these children and young people will somehow manage. Many do but it can be helpful to include strategies such as time out cards and additional 1:1 support to help with classroom tasks. It can help to positively reframe ADHD as a child or young person with bags of energy and get up and go spirit. The traditional classroom can be a difficult and challenging place for many children. They often do remarkably well in alternative education settings that include more of an outside land-based curriculum.

The challenge for schools with regard to managing children and young people's behaviour would therefore seem more than evident given such figures. Researchers such as Weare (2015) indicate that 1 in 4 children and young people have a clinically identified mental health disorder and/or emotional behaviour problem that can limit their development and learning, whilst over 5 per cent of children, in particular boys, exhibit anti-social, behaviour and conduct disorder conditions. Furthermore, a survey by the Association of Teachers and Lecturers (ATL) reported that

> *the number of pupils in the UK with behavioural and mental health problems is on the rise.*

(Sellgren, 2013, p1)

It is important that appropriate provision is given to successfully support such pupils and young people and any of their associated challenging behaviours to reach their full educational potential. Given the expectations that schools are placed under with regard to securing suitable levels of behaviour (Steer, 2011; DfE, 2016 a) appropriate support and provision would seem to be of paramount importance if such individuals are to have a bright education in our school systems.

Whole school behaviour policy

Though there may be many triggers for a range of behaviours, which may include unacceptable mental or physical acts towards another child or adult, schools have a duty to manage such issues consistently using their mandatory whole school behaviour policy (DfE, 2012). The behaviour policy, though site-specific, may be underpinned by additional government advice such as 'Mental health and behaviour in schools' (DfE, 2016 b) which may serve to help schools understand how they can support children with disruptive behaviour. Children and young people who are depressed, anxious or withdrawn do not usually present with challenging behaviours in class; on the contrary their behaviour is often quiet and withdrawn and is less likely to attract concern, but nevertheless there should be equal concern and an appropriate response for these children.

Having a whole school behaviour policy will provide individuals with a template for behaviour and the provision for the promotion of a positive learning environment so that all staff and pupils can feel safe and that they belong. Any such policy, under its duty of care to promote equality and diversity, should promote fairness, equality and respect for every pupil no matter what the triggers may be for their behaviours. This policy will normally outline the different strategies to ensure that a pupil's treatment is equitable and consistent. However, it is important to note that despite such generic school policy guidance, as educators we will all react and operate differently when encountering what may often be seen as context-specific disruptive behaviours linked to an individual's emotional and social difficulties. For educators to be successful in such contexts, they should be

> *well organised, consistent, humorous, calm, enthusiastic, skilful in delivering their specialist subjects, set clear boundaries, flexible, understand 'behaviour' causation and empathetic.*

(Cole, 2015, p42)

More generic strategies that might be outlined in the policy to support positive behaviour may include, for example:

* individually and group agreed class or school and class rules;

* peer mentoring and buddying arrangements;

- a framework for rewards and sanctions;
- PSHE class-based intervention such as circle time;
- specific targeted interventions strategies such as the use of socially speaking and nurture groups;
- additional staffing.

However, for any behaviour policy to be successful in promoting class-based practice which best manages challenging behaviour, it is important that it is underpinned by professionals who know their children and young people well. That there are educators who will spend time to get to the root of any unacceptable behaviours rather than just reacting to what can understandably be a disruption to teaching and others being educated. For any education to be successful it should nurture a positive classroom ethos which is founded on good relationships, and where respect is underpinned by a genuine interest in the child or young person who is exhibiting the challenging behaviour (Ofsted, 2005).

Though only medical professionals can make a formal clinical diagnosis of a mental health diffi-culty that can influence a child's behaviour, schools are well placed to observe changes in a child's behaviour due to their daily contact with their children or young adults. Such observations may well provide clues and insight into the root causes of issues. Relationships will also provide the key to understanding a child's behaviour. For some of our most vulnerable of children, educational profes-sionals may be the only adult they may learn to trust and feel that they are understood by and have consistent contact with. Often knowledge of a child will be built up over time as will the strategies that support behaviour; however, in some situations mental health and behaviour may deteriorate quickly, perhaps triggered by an adverse external experience or factor. When noticing any changes in an individual's behaviour it is worth considering the following:

- Is their behaviour out of character compared to their normal actions and responses?
- Has the child appeared worried or starting talking to you about issues that are concerning them?
- Is there a particular time of day, group of individuals or relationship that triggers an adverse behaviour?
- Has the change in the behaviour been sudden or gradual?
- What has the responsible adult told you about the child recently and may that be causing a trig-ger for the behaviour, for example, a life change such as moving house, loss or separation such as birth of a sibling or a traumatic incident such as an accident?

KEY REFLECTIONS

- What factors may lead to issues around an individual's behaviour?
- How might a whole school behaviour policy lead to the support of behavioural inclusion?
- How might professional relationships support the behavioural inclusion of an individual?

━━━ CASE STUDY: PAULINE ━━━

Over the last couple of months Pauline, aged 10, has often come to school about 10 minutes after the school day has started. She is reluctant to come into the classroom and will often stand outside the door waiting to come in. When the teacher approaches Pauline she will be seen by other pupils backing away from the door and not wanting to engage with the teacher who is trying her best to coax Pauline into class. Pauline does, however, tell her class teacher that she does not want to be laughed at by the pupils when she comes in.

Case study reflections

- How long has this been happening for and is it an ongoing issue or something that may have happened to Pauline recently which might explain such a behavioural change?
- What does the class teacher need to do to start to understand Pauline's ongoing lateness?
- Why is Pauline reluctant to come into class?
- How might this lateness be affecting Pauline's mental health and well-being?

Though the teacher knows that Pauline is a sensitive child, the lateness issue has been brought on by her mother having to look after her elderly mother. The class teacher has not been told by the mother that she is finding routines difficult and that due to tiredness she is not waking up early enough in the morning to do all the things needed to get Pauline to school, which is making her late. Pauline's lateness is making her embarrassed and she does not like the other children laughing at her which is affecting her self-esteem and peer friendships. Pauline is also conscious that when she is late she has missed the start of the lesson which makes it hard for her to understand what is going on. The class teacher needs to be talking to both Pauline and her mother to see how the school can support her together with the school SENCo to see if she can access support through the school nurse or her doctor if necessary. Pauline's mother should also be advised to contact adult social care services to gain support with caring for her elderly mother. In the short term, the class teacher needs to find a strategy to help Pauline to come into class without her friends just thinking she is late again. Perhaps an arrangement may be made with another teacher or classroom assistant that Pauline appears to be late into class since she has been delayed by them on an errand and that she brings an item into class with the excuse collecting the item has made her late.

Barriers to relationships

As the Department for Education (2016 b, p24) suggests:

if parents/carers can be supported to better manage their children's behaviour, alongside work being carried out with the child at school, there is a much greater likelihood of success in reducing the child's problems, and in supporting their academic and emotional development.

It is important that, where possible, parents and carers work alongside the school to provide a cornerstone for you as an educational professional to support children and young people in your setting. Schools can offer not only someone who will listen but also they can provide sign-posting to agencies that can, for example, support them individually or as a family. The value of this partnership has been recognised in reports such as Ofsted (2009), where strong rela-tionships are seen as being fundamental to success. Parents and the extended family should be welcomed into school, and valued, and clear expectations set such as the value of a co-operative 'whole school' approach that embraces the child and young person, the school, families and the community.

However, in some situations, barriers will arise and you may find that parents or carers are very reluctant for you to get to know them and understand the root cause of behaviour in a child; they may also not take kindly to advice or signposting to parenting groups. This in itself may form fur-ther barriers to supporting the child or young person or to finding effective strategies or identifying other agencies who may support you with this issue. Individuals may be reluctant to engage with you for a range of reasons:

- a personal fear of engaging with an educational setting due to their own negative experiences;

- personal embarrassment or loss of pride due to an issue;

- child protection issues being identified;

- fear of intervention of other support services linked to their own personal experience or per-ceived impact upon the family.

Given a reluctance to engage, it may be hard to gain their confidence and consent. Such situations, however, can be overcome with time and patience. Strategies that may support and enable parents'/carers' engagement might include:

- letting parents know when their children have been successful, not just when there was a problem;

- the school's open-door policy;

- establishing firm links before the children started school, often visiting parents at home;

- the involvement of a school's learning mentor or a Parent Support Advisor who might be able to open up a dialogue given their lack of direct class-based link with the child;

- an induction meeting to review how the individual is settling into their new setting;

- targeting of pupil premium funding if there is a link to social disadvantage to support fun, non-academic activities with both the child and parent/carer that may promote a positive rela-tionship with the setting;

- signposting to outside agencies and resources such as MindEd, Relate or Women's Aid.

For some settings where there is a constant turnover of pupils on roll, getting to know an indi-vidual may prove challenging when managing behaviour which may be linked to mental health and well-being. This will often make it hard to initially assess what the issues are and to respond appropriately to the pupils' needs. If you receive a child or young person such as this, their school records from their previous setting will prove an excellent base to start your understanding of what are the triggers for the child's behaviour and what strategies are most effective and appropriate. If you find that the records do not really help you understand your new child, your next port of call could be to contact their last setting to talk to the head teacher or their prior class teacher about the child. This should be done in consultation with the head teacher and SENCo. Such a conversation will sometimes provide more detailed background knowledge on this child or young person's history, the issues they have faced and the most successful strategies to support them.

However, whatever the barriers and the trigger for behaviours relating to a child's mental health and well-being, for any approach to be successful it must be supported by an agreed whole school ethos which involves the head teachers, senior leaders and governors, creating a culture where the duty of care for safeguarding individuals is seen as of paramount importance. Such an approach is clearly supported by research which suggests that low exclusion rates may be achieved in schools that promote an inclusive whole school community approach both in their policy and practice when dealing with issues linked to individuals' mental health (Cole, 2015). As Cole (2015, p41) notes with regard to the establishment of an inclusive school climate:

> it requires a 'critical mass' of staff committed to inclusive values, who seek to avoid the exclusion of children, seeing this as failure on the part of their school. Their beliefs and practice influence colleagues around them ... Teamwork is the norm and a collegiate approach, frequently talking and listening to each other – as well as hearing the voices of young people.

In promoting an inclusive environment, it would be hoped that such a shared responsibility for the support of such individuals will be underpinned in an ethos where individuals can talk openly and honestly about the problems they encounter when dealing with the most challenging of behaviours. As Weare (2015) suggests, staying open-minded, calm and reflective helps the educational professional to allow for positive choices to be identified, to move the situation forward, and allows them to provide a positive role model for the child and young adult as well as helping them to manage their own emotional stress. Allied to this, it is also vital that professionals are allowed to engage in appropriate continued professional development if they are to best support our most vulnerable of children and young adults.

KEY REFLECTIONS

- What might be some of the key barriers that may stop parents and carers engaging with support for children and young people with behavioural issues?
- What strategies may be implemented to overcome these barriers to support?
- How might a setting maximise their knowledge of children and young people who join their setting with behavioural issues?

—— CASE STUDY: TYLER ——

Tyler has just started the new school year in Year 2. He has just celebrated his fifth birthday and is the tallest child in the class of 25 children. There is a teacher and teaching assistant, Mrs Brown and Miss Smith.

Tyler is often in trouble in class, usually for not staying on task and for getting up and walking around, looking at and often interrupting the other children, especially when the work involves writing practice and number work. Outside the classroom in the playground Tyler loves running around and playing tag, and he appears built for speed compared to some of his peers.

He can quickly get into arguments with the other children if they don't go along with his wishes around playing in a particular way. He gets angry very quickly if things are not going his way and will hit or kick the child he is having a disagreement with. Most of the other children (usually the other boys) will back off when challenged and some refuse to play or join in with him. Most of the children have known Tyler since pre-school so are used to his angry displays which erupt quickly and subside equally quickly.

Case study reflections

- For Tyler, this is not a new or a change in behaviour; he has always tended to behave in this way.
- What works in terms of managing his behaviour? How did his pre-school teachers deal with this?
- Could this be connected to ADHD perhaps? He does not sit still for long and struggles to concentrate in class-related tasks that involve writing or numbers.
- How does he get on in PE or other sports or outdoor activities?

Tyler is the tallest of his peers and appears as an older child of 7 so there often seems to be a general higher expectation of him around behaviour especially, but he is only just 5. He probably uses this to his advantage – it can be experienced by the others as intimidating, as he has quite a strong temperament and presence. So, he is both physically strong in appearance, but also psychologically in character, though he will not have the associated emotional maturity or strength.

Teaching staff are working closely with Mum and have a good relationship with her as Tyler can also be quite a challenge at home. At home Mum is often tired and Tyler is used to getting his own way and for things to be on his terms.

It is important for both school and Mum to work together to aim for a consistent approach as this will be the most effective. Mum may need additional support with this which could also include Granddad, who is close to Tyler.

Tyler and Mum are very close, which can lead to Tyler being quite omnipotent towards her so it is easy to see how this learnt behaviour becomes transferred to other situations, such as at school and with peers. Tyler had a poor start in life in terms of relationships. Dad left during the pregnancy and

Tyler has no contact with him. Mum has since had other relationships but is on her own again now. Tyler's father and one of his stepfathers had problems around emotional regulation and anger and were abusive towards Mum and Tyler. The maternal granddad helps out with looking after Tyler and does the school run when Mum is at work.

Tyler has experienced relationships that are unpredictable in terms of their behaviour and what will happen next, and people who leave and abandon him, which has led to anxiety in all of his future relationships. He may also feel it is his responsibility to 'protect' Mum – perhaps he has done so in the past? To do so requires a level of control-taking and omnipotence but it is not appropriate to continue in this way and can lead to trouble, as we have seen.

Children like Tyler are often misunderstood and in the desire to seek answers or provide a 'label' professionals may seek a medical explanation such as ADHD or attachment disorder, which is not a picture here. It is a combination of a child with a quick temperament (perhaps like his father), who appears older than his chronological age so there are greater expectations of him socially and cogni- tively, but who also actually appears as quite a presence. He has a good relationship with Mum and Granddad and despite his 'flare ups' remains popular. It is much easier to understand Tyler with the knowledge of his and his family experiences.

Given his athleticism, working with Tyler and providing opportunities for more physically based learning such as sports and outdoor work will give him an opportunity to channel his energies. Receiving praise for doing well will improve his self-esteem and lead to him feeling more able to trust other adults. Positive role models using male staff often succeed with children like Tyler.

Nurture groups

For some children and young people educational settings may use or have set up a nurture group as a means of supporting individuals who exhibit behavioural needs linked to issues surrounding their social and emotional development. Often such groups involve supporting children and young peo- ple who have damaged or insecure attachments with adults and their peers and as a result of this are vulnerable and therefore at risk of exclusion in an educational setting.

By using a Boxall Profile (Bennathan and Haskayne, 2007) settings can assess whether children and young people will need to be supported by a nurture group practitioner in a base room outside their normal classroom where they may be withdrawn for support. The Boxall Profile uses questionnaires to provide a means of assessing the negative and positive behaviours of children and young people who are displaying signs of social, emotional and behavioural difficulties (SEBD). Such an assess- ment can then be used to provide advice on how best to support and address any issue identified.

Often such children exhibit behavioural issues centred on:

- being quiet and withdrawn with poor relationships with adults and their peers;

- having friendship difficulties – keeping/making friends, accepting the rule of a game and sharing;

- finding it hard to listen to others or join in;

- having a low self-esteem;

- being disruptive towards others and whilst in lessons;

- bullying others.

Nurture groups often provide a time-limited intervention for children outside their normal school-based routines, supplying those development experiences often missed by the pupil which may have limited their ability to make trusting relationships with grown-ups or to relate appropriately to their peers. The success of this work centres on the positive, supportive role models that the staff can bring to these children and young people's lives. Role modelling and observations of these positive relationships provide an opportunity to practise and develop behaviours that are more socially acceptable, with such work being reinforced by the development of language and communications skills within the individual.

Examples of the type of successful strategies employed by nurture group practitioners may include having a clear start to the day by having the practitioner in the room which has been prepared prior to the pupil's arrival with a range of activities that they can choose from. Given the sometimes anxious state of some individuals on their arrival, this structure and its choice provides comfort and reassurance to the child or young person supporting their mental health and well-being. The structure and activities also prepares them for reintegration into a school day in the future when they re-join their class. Breakfast, or the creation of food, may help create a positive attachment to a member of staff as well as providing a loving and caring relationship where trust is formed. This can also enhance communications skills such as waiting to take one's turn as well as social skills such as sitting down and using cutlery. Something so simple may be alien to a child with a chaotic home life. Circle time may also be used to stimulate discussion and to build up their self-esteem. Personal literacy and numeracy targets will also be worked on during their day so as to reduce the likelihood of disruptive behaviour due to frustration of not being able to succeed in a whole class setting. Praise and rewards will be used to build up self-esteem as well as consistent and clear boundaries helping to reinforce the need to behave in an acceptable manner. Nurture groups generally end the day on a positive note or by reinforcing the knowledge that a fresh start is always available the next day. Using achievement books provides a means of sharing their achievements with their parent or carer. This can be a positive talking point for them, as well as a recognition that doing well is key in building self-esteem.

The organisation, commitment and work of nurture groups within educational settings has been investigated and recognised by organisations such as Ofsted:

> Nurture interventions involves a considerable investment from schools in terms of finance, time, planning and resources and staff training. However, the survey illustrates that, when successful, the impact on young children and their families can be highly significant and far-reaching.

> (Ofsted, 2011, p5)

CASE STUDY: CATHERINE

Catherine recently joined our school in Year 4 and was in foster care having been removed from her mother's and her stepfather's care due to an abusive home setting. She was placed in kinship foster care with her gran and was very frightened, anxious and withdrawn when she joined us.

She was very reluctant to share with others in her class and would often shout at them or not let them speak. She would often snatch things off them when they were working. Her vocabulary and social skills were very limited and her self-esteem was low. Catherine's gran was keen to help and support the school to help with Catherine's difficulties, health and well-being.

Case study reflections

- How might a nurture group benefit Catherine?
- What might a nurture group do to involve and support Catherine's gran?
- What aspects of Catherine's development will the staff at the nurture group have to focus on?

So what did the school do to help Catherine?

By working with the school SENCo and having her needs assessed using a Boxall Profile, it was agreed that Catherine should join the school's nurture group to help with her issues. This group provided an ideal opportunity for Catherine to feel supported and served as a place where caring relationships could be established. Catherine was invited to take turns in circle time activities, if she felt comfortable to do so, which was used to build up her self-esteem as well as creating opportunities for her to sit down and share and develop aspects of herself. When taking part in cooking activities she started to create more positive relationships and learnt when cooking with others to engage in conversation and social skills such as taking turns and listening and waiting. Catherine was encouraged to develop a sense of pride and achievement which helped her with her self-esteem. Catherine took the cakes she baked home so that the skills she had practised in her group could be reinforced when sharing them with her gran. This involved her gran in her school life and provided another opportunity for praise to be given to Catherine for her achievements. After a term in the nurture group it was felt that due to Catherine's progress she could return to some activities in her class.

If this topic has been new to you and you wish to gain more useful advice and support regarding nurture groups, you can visit the Nurture Group Network website at **www.nurturegroups.org/about-nurture**.

KEY REFLECTIONS

- How might a setting assess the SEBD of an individual?
- What behaviours might a child or young person with SEBD difficulties exhibit in their setting?
- How might a nurture group support and lead to the successful reintegration of an individual who has SEBD difficulties back into their classroom setting?

Special Educational Needs and Disability Code of Practice

For some children or young people exhibiting behavioural difficulties, it is important to real-ise that such issues may not always be caused by SEND issues linked to their mental health and well-being. However, when mental health and well-being issues are leading to consistent disrup-tive behaviour and this is having a direct impact upon the social, emotional and academic life of an individual, the setting must follow statutory regulations to support such children and young adults through the Special Educational Needs and Disability Code of Practice (SEND CoP; DfE, 2015). A range of mental health issues may require that special provision is made available. For some children, behavioural conditions such as autism spectrum disorder (ASD) will be identified and treated for prolonged periods of time using medication in their setting as part of a clinical diagnosis and treatment plan. However, for other children and young people, their behavioural difficulties may be linked to environmental or contextual issues with these conditions presenting themselves over a sustained or more sporadic or temporary length of time. However, whatever the cause or type of behaviour difficulties, such as aggression or anxiety, an individual may exhibit such conditions, which will no doubt impact upon the child's academic and social progress in schools with pupils often failing to meet their own rates of previous progress or to match up to that of their peers. Given such underperformance or types of trigger for unacceptable behaviours the educational setting will have a duty to support such children and young adults under the SEND CoP (DfE, 2015). This will be deemed as 'SEND Support' once parents have been consulted and their agreement secured for this intervention. It is important to remember that the SEND CoP (DfE, 2015) legislation clearly states that the majority of individuals (except for a limited number of exceptions) given their SEND must be accommodated and educated in the mainstream setting with this being accomplished by the important involvement of their carers or parents.

The SEND CoP (DfE, 2015, p98) clearly outlines in one of its broad areas of need that schools may need to support children who can be identified to have 'social, emotional and mental health' needs. This can include children who are withdrawn or isolated, as well as exhibiting disruptive, challeng-ing or disturbing behaviours, with these conditions in some cases being linked to underlying issues such as anxiety, depression, self-harm, substance abuse, eating disorders or physical symptoms that cannot be explained. Other conditions covered by this category include attention deficit disorder, attention deficit hyperactivity disorder or attachment disorders.

The Code of Practice (DfE, 2015) advocates that most children with special educational needs should be supported in their education through extra help provided in the educational setting and that they should be provided with high quality, differentiated provision in order to support the individual which will be co-ordinated by the school's special educational needs coordina-tor (SENCo). This person, often a teacher within the school, will be responsible for working with other teachers and parents to ensure that pupils with SEND get the appropriate level of support and the help that they need at school.

Such a SEND-based approach will be supported by the use of information such as school attainment, information gathered by other health and/or social care professionals, attendance data and by the knowledge gained by the setting pastoral support system. Depending on the severity of need, differ-ent levels of support may be provided through 'waves' of intervention or an Education, Health and Care (EHC) Plan. However, the success of any such support must be underpinned by a personalised assessment of the child's or young person's needs.

Through the use of 'Wave 1' interventions, class-based strategies to support improvements in behaviour can be used, this also being known as 'Quality First Teaching' (QFT). This may include class-based strategies such as visual timetables, group work to promote speaking and listening skills, the use of opportunities for personalised learning, the use of rewards and sanctions stickers and behavioural charts, for example, the use of zone boards. Such work will be complemented by the use of the SEAL programme to promote such positive behaviours both in the school and at home. This will help the development of emotional literacy so that individuals can communicate feelings, to help them manage their anger, anxiety and fear, as well as providing strategies for controlling their emotions. If individuals fail to make progress the SEND intervention may graduate onto a 'Wave 2' intervention.

'Wave 2' interventions will involve the identification of additional time-limited provision which may take the form of a small group intervention so as to enable pupils to make greater social and emotional progress and to help the child work at their age-related expectations. Such interventions may take the form of supporting social skills to help them in managing peer relationships, for example programmes such as socially speaking or help with their self-esteem through SEAL resources such as 'Good to be me'. If such interventions are unsuccessful then pupils can progress onto 'Wave 3' interventions which can include the school involving specialists or outside agencies such as educational psychologists or CAMHS, to help identify and support such settings. Highly personalised interventions used in Wave 3 programmes that may help with behaviour can include counselling sessions or the use of trained bereavement counsellors from organisations such as Winston's Wish. Interventions from trained individuals in the promotion of mindfulness can also help individuals manage issues around anger, stress and anxiety. For more information with regard to how literacy may be supported using a 'wave model' of intervention you can visit **www.interventionsfor literacy.org.uk/home/parents/sen-provision**.

Whatever the child's behaviourial needs or intervention programme, teaching assistants/learning support assistants/higher learning teaching assistants or school learning mentors can provide a vital academic and emotional support, wherever the child is placed on the SEND code of practice. Given their detailed knowledge of the child or young adult these professionals can often:

- effectively help plan and deliver effective interventions programmes;
- recognise and intervene before a brewing issue escalates;
- take the class so that an issue can be dealt with effectively by the teacher without learning time being affected;
- use their relationship with the child to promote their co-operation when needed.

For some children with complex education, health and care needs which are impacting on the individual's behaviour, the school-based SEND support may prove insufficient and additional provision can be provided to support the child through an Education, Health and Care (EHC) Plan. To obtain such support a detailed assessment to identify the child's special educational needs (if requested by the parents or educational setting) will be carried out. This will involve the educational setting evidencing the need and support given to the child as well as gaining information to support this application from individuals involved with the child or young person. This will include individuals such as the parent, teacher, educational psychologist, health professional/child's doctor, physiotherapist or health visitor and any social services based professionals. If successfully granted an EHC Plan will provide additional support from the local authority (LA) to enable the successful support of this child or young adult's needs. Through an agreed personal budget, families and the educational setting can decide and agree how provision is arranged and how the budget for a child/young person is to be spent.

When working with some children and young people a Family Common Assessment Framework (FCAF) can provide a strategy to help support an individual's needs. Though an FCAF is a voluntary process, it will allow the lead professional to bring together other support agencies such as health visitor, children's centre worker, teacher or school nurse so that they can help identify how a child or young person can receive the right support at an early stage before their needs increase. An action plan is then agreed to make sure that the individual can get the right sort of help to support their behaviour.

KEY REFLECTIONS

- How might behavioural issues relate to the SEND CoP?
- How might the 'waves' of interventions support individuals with behavioural issues?
- How might teaching assistants and outside agencies, rather than just teachers, support the provision of children and young people with behavioural issues?

CASE STUDY: AKIO

Akio is currently in a Year 2 class. His mother is now really struggling with his anger at home and is often coming to the class teacher at her wits' end saying that she can no longer cope. Father is no longer living with the family though he is involved in Akio's life and he is concerned his mental health issues are somehow related to his son's mental state of mind. Akio's behaviour is deteriorating in class with him shouting out constantly and hurting others when on the carpet. His constant mood swings and low self-esteem are now impacting on his progress. He is currently receiving Wave 2 support in terms of small group interventions to support his learning and behaviour by the class teaching assistant.

Case study reflections

- What risk factors does Akio have?
- How might the school continue to support Akio?

Since Akio's mother is engaging with the school they certainly should, given his issues, be looking to support him by moving onto Wave 3 levels of support. They could involve other agencies in helping to support his mother and father, Akio and the setting in dealing with his behavioural issues. This support may come through a referral to CAMHS or a child psychologist for an assessment alongside support from the school nurse and the family's GP. Interventions may include: provision of parenting/family-based interventions or possibly some one-to-one therapy for Akio in the form of counselling or cognitive behaviour therapy. The school could deploy a learning mentor, if they have one, to support Mum by providing a first point of contact for her to share her concerns in school. Certainly some Wave 3 interventions such as 'socially speaking' may help him consider his actions when on the carpet or when learning. If both Mum and Dad were willing, an FCAF certainly could progress a shared assessment of need and an action plan for how the agencies could work together to help support Akio and his parents. If Mum and Dad were willing they could have some family support through a health professional to help them with their current difficulties and help them to understand and manage Akio's behaviour at home. In the long term, if things continue to deteriorate despite the support offered, an EHC Plan could be applied for.

Levels of support

It is important to realise that though some issues around mental health and well-being are of ongoing concern, such issues can be triggered by a critical incident such as an unexpected death in the school. If this is the case, not only will perhaps the pupils be affected but if it is the loss of a close member of staff, the remaining staff and teaching team will be severely affected. These events are hard to plan for, but if this is the case support services may be accessed from voluntary organisations such as the Teacher Support Network (24 hours a day, throughout the year, support line) or through statutory agencies who can offer support such as bereavement counselling. Some educational settings will employ their own school-based counsellors or fund some shared arrangement with other schools. Such professionals will be important to support every aspect of an educational setting's mental health and emotional well-being, and their work may be supported by interventions such as play therapy or art/music therapy.

However, sometimes, despite high levels of school support, some children and young adults with high risk factors may find their mental health and well-being issues lead to behavioural issues and can ultimately lead to either temporary or permanent exclusion. Given a permanent exclusion, most pupils will end up attending a Pupil Referral Unit (PRU) which (under section 19 of the Education Act 1996) exists to provide education to children who are of compulsory school age who are unable to attend a maintained school for reasons of sickness, exclusion or other issues. A PRU will provide an academic education, and specially trained staff are on hand to respond to children's needs and to deal with and support any arising challenges to education.

KEY REFLECTIONS

- What are some of the key risk factors that can trigger behavioural issues around mental health and well-being?
- What strategies can educational professionals put in place to support the range of behavioural needs encountered?
- What outside agency support is available to support a school in addressing behavioural issues around mental health and well-being?
- What statutory requirements are placed on schools to support individuals who have behavioural issues?

CHAPTER SUMMARY

- A range of presenting behavioural issues can indicate a potential mental health and well-being problem.
- Schools have statutory duties to support and include pupils who have behavioural difficulties linked to their mental health and well-being needs.
- Appropriate supportive responses are crucial, including providing clear strategies to support individuals both in the classroom and through a range of provision linked to education, thus providing a climate in which children and young people with behavioural issues can flourish.
- Outside agencies can support teaching staff, schools and leaders who have concerns about children and young people's behaviour.
- The professionals who work in their settings have a clear role to play in identifying and supporting children with behavioural issues.

FURTHER READING

Blakemore, S.J. (2012) The mysterious workings of the adolescent brain: www.ted.com/talks/sarah_jayne_blakemore_the_mysterious_workings_of_the_adolescent_brain.

Bombèr, L.M. (2011) *What About Me? Inclusive Strategies to Support Pupils with Attachment Difficulties Make it Through the School Day*. London: Worth Publishing.

Geddes, H. (2005) *Attachment in the Classroom: The Links Between Children's Early Experience, Emotional Well-being and Performance in School*. London: Worth Publishing.

Goepel, J., Childerhouse, H. and Sharpe, S. (2015) *Inclusive Primary Teaching*, 2nd ed. Northwich: Critical Publishing.

Marshall, N. (2014) *The Teacher's Introduction to Attachment: Practical Essentials for Teachers, Carers and School Support Staff*. London: Jessica Kingsley Publishers.

Rogers, B. (2011) *Classroom Behaviour: A Practical Guide to Effective Teaching, Behaviour Management and Colleague Support*, 3rd ed. London: SAGE.

REFERENCES

Bennathan, M. and Haskayne, M. (2007) *What Is the Boxall Profile and How Effective Is It?* Available at: http://schools.bracknell-forest.gov.uk/sites/default/files/assets/what-is-the-boxall-profile-and-how-effective-is-it.pdf (accessed 11 October 2016).

Cole, T. (2015) *Mental Health Difficulties and Children at Risk of Exclusion from Schools in England: A Review from an Educational Perspective of Policy, Practice and Research, 1997 to 2015*. Available at: www.education.ox.ac.uk/wordpress/wp-content/uploads/2015/02/MENTAL-HEALTH-AND-EXCLUSION-FINAL-DIGITAL-13-06-15.pdf (accessed 23 September 2016).

Department for Education (DfE) (2012) *Behaviour and Discipline in Schools: Guidance for Governing Bodies*. Crown Copyright.

Department for Education (2015) *Special Educational Needs and Disability Code of Practice: 0 to 25 Years*. Available at: www.gov.uk/government/uploads/system/uploads/attachment_data/file/398815/SEND_Code_of_Practice_January_2015.pdf (accessed 26 August 2016).

Department for Education (2016 a) *Behaviour and Discipline in Schools: Advice for Headteachers and School Staff*. Available at: www.gov.uk/government/uploads/system/uploads/attachment_data/file/488034/Behaviour_and_Discipline_in_Schools_-_A_guide_for_headteachers_and_School_Staff.pdf (accessed 20 August 2016).

Department for Education (2016 b) *Mental Health and Behaviour in Schools*. Available at: www.gov.uk/government/publications/mental-health-and-behaviour-in-schools–2 (accessed 12 September 2016).

Ofsted (2005) *Managing Challenging Behaviour*. London: Ofsted.

Ofsted (2009) *The Exclusion from School of Children Aged Four to Seven*. London: Ofsted.

Ofsted (2011) *Supporting Children with Challenging Behaviours Through a Nurture Group Approach*. Available at: www.gov.uk/government/publications/supporting-children-with-challenging-behaviour (accessed 23 September 2016).

Schore, A. (2005) Attachment, affect regulation and the developing right brain: Linking development neuroscience to paediatrics. *Paediatrics in Review*, *26*(6). London: The British Library.

Sellgren, K. (2013) 'Disruptive behaviour rising, teachers say'. *BBC News*. Available at: www.bbc.co.uk/news/education-21895705 (accessed 19 August 2016).

Steer, A. (2011) *Learning Behaviours Lessons Learned: A Review of Behaviours Standards and Practices in Our School*. Available at: www.educationengland.org.uk/documents/pdfs/2009-steer-report-lessons-learned.pdf (accessed on 22 August 2016).

Weare, K. (2015) *What Works in Promoting Social and Emotional Well-being and Responding to Mental Health Problems in School?* London: National Children's Bureau.

Young Minds (2016) *About Self-esteem*. Available at: www.youngminds.org.uk/for_parents/whats_worrying_you_about_your_child/self-esteem/about_self_esteem (accessed 1 January 2016).

4

SELF-ESTEEM AND RESILIENCE

CHAPTER OBJECTIVES

By the end of this chapter you should be aware of:

- the definition of self-esteem;
- the impact of positive self-esteem on children;
- the impact of poor self-esteem on children;
- how self-esteem represents an aspect of the risk/resilience model;
- strategies that can support improving self-esteem both with children and young people and the school community.

TEACHERS' STANDARDS

This chapter supports the development of the following Teachers' Standards:

TS1: Set high expectations which inspire, motivate and challenge pupils

- Establish a safe and stimulating environment for pupils, rooted in mutual respect.

TS7: Manage behaviour effectively to ensure a good and safe learning environment

- Manage classes effectively, using approaches which are appropriate to pupils' needs in order to involve and motivate them.

TS8: Fulfil wider professional responsibilities

- Develop effective professional relationships with colleagues, knowing how and when to draw on advice and specialist support.
- Communicate effectively with parents with regard to pupils' achievements and well-being.

Introduction

This chapter will focus on the crucial role that the development of self-esteem can play in the lives of children and young people. It will examine how a developing sense of 'self' mediates the creation of self-esteem and the important role that social relationships and significant risk factors can have on its development. The link between 'self-efficacy' and self-esteem will be examined, along with its role in the feelings created towards a child's level of achievement. Consideration will be given to how positive and negative self-esteem may manifest itself in children's actions and influence their beliefs regarding their own abilities. Finally, the chapter will focus on what may be done in a school setting to promote positive self-esteem and to support its promotion within members of the school community.

What is self-esteem?

Self-esteem is how we think about ourselves and is reflective of our emotional evaluation of self-worth; this concept begins to grow and develop in a child's early years. Individuals with positive self-esteem will feel they are a good person, deserving of love and support, who can be successful. Low self-esteem leads to feelings of not being good enough, undeserving of love or support and a feeling that things will work out badly (Young Minds, 2019). Low self-esteem was the second highest reason for calls to Childline in 2014–15, accounting for more than 35,000 counselling sessions, citing children's struggles with friendship, impossible aspirations and the hazards of social media as contributing factors. The figures revealed self-esteem was the second highest concern for girls and the fourth for boys (NSPCC, 2016).

'Self' is the product of relationships with others according to what is happening and being experienced at the time. Nick Luxmoore (2008) discusses how saying 'hello' sounds simple but that it is the foundation from which a sense of self develops. This reminds us that we all exist in relation to others and with a sense of self developing through others' response and recognition of us. This is also in keeping with the role and importance of 'connectedness', cited as a resilience factor, in relation to school experiences (Weare, 2015).

All of us are born into a context of relationships, as well as what is happening within that context at the time. The development of babies' brains is influenced by relationships with other important people in their life. *The Brian Architecture Game* explains the importance and role of context and early experiences (see Further reading). Schore (2014) describes the effect of neglect on brain development, and discusses the neurobiology of secure attachment (Schore, 2013) (see Further reading).

Becoming a 'person' involves a large investment by others early in life, not only from family and friends but also communities and schools. Within any relationship, we will look to others for messages that provide us with a sense of our worth as a person. From this, an emerging sense of self becomes reflected back to us through the eyes and minds of others. As Music (2011, pp7 and 24) describes:

> a person's sense of self arises from being in the minds of others, without which it simply does not develop ... and that one's sense of self is socially and co-constructed ... human life develops from the

delicate interplay of nature and nurture, the meeting of a bundle of inherited potentials and the cultural, social and personal influences of the adults in an infant's life.

Positive self-esteem also has close links to, and can influence a child's feelings of, actual and perceived competence, or 'self-efficacy' (Bandura, 1977, 1989). This is the belief that we can do something and that we can influence events that affect our lives. Peter Fonagy's clip on mentalisation, *finding the meaning of their actions in your reactions,* is worth watching and demonstrates how individuals develop an emerging sense of self in relation to others and their reactions (see Further reading).

A child's level of self-efficacy can vary, according to individual temperament and how that has articulated with the child's environment, but it continues to evolve throughout childhood. A child with high self-efficacy will be more optimistic, less anxious and have a higher level of problem-solving skills, with the ability to persevere in times of difficulty, focusing less on the possibility of failure (Plummer and Harper, 2007). This is a concept that requires nurturing throughout childhood, especially within schools, as enabling a child to develop a sense of mastery and the ability to overcome a challenge will also, simultaneously, develop positive self-esteem, thus demonstrating that 'core self-evaluations' such as self-esteem and self-efficacy do not operate in isolation but can overlap with other dimensions of the 'self' (Bono and Judge, 2003).

Luxmoore (2008) makes the case for the 'self' being socially constructed and therefore with hope for repair, noting that 'self' is not a thing in itself but a way of understanding and describing our experience. This is in keeping with risk and resilience theories as being a dynamic and evolving process, as identified by Rutter (2012). If relationships get off to a poor start and are damaged there is the opportunity for reparation through future positive relationships. Self-esteem is an aspect of human development which is very sensitive to the quality of other relationships and so has a capacity for new possibilities and positive development. Relationships continue to be important and are at the heart of well-being and self-esteem. These develop in the school environment with friends, peers and teachers (The Children's Society, 2015).

There will be many children and young people in schools who have experienced their own 'self' (and thus their self-esteem) being adversely affected. This will be especially relevant for children in the care system. There were 75,420 looked-after children in England in 2018, an increase of 4 per cent on the previous year. Numbers of children looked after due to abuse or neglect are now the highest on record, representing over 60 per cent of all looked-after children (Rosa, 2019). There will be many other children in addition to these children also living in difficult circumstances who do not meet child protection thresholds. There will be significant proportions of these children in classrooms who will all have experienced loss, trauma and significant life events on multiple levels.

In addition, many other children may also have had similar experiences, all impacting on 'self' and identity. Young Minds (2014, cited in Weare, 2015, p8) reported that in an average classroom ten young people will have experienced parents separating, eight will have experienced severe physical violence, sexual abuse or neglect, one will have experienced the death of a parent and seven will have been bullied. Adverse childhood experiences (ACEs) were discussed in Chapter 1. Many children have experienced several ACEs with multiple impacts on several layers, including cognitive development, their sense of self, their self-esteem and ability to co-regulate.

Interestingly, refugee children can demonstrate remarkable resilience and are not necessarily likely to develop mental health problems. They may well have experienced early secure primary relationships and hold a secure attachment quality. An inner London primary school that included 90 refugee children had 14 identified with severe psychological problems or special educational needs. This showed that most of the refugee children were sufficiently resilient to be able to adapt to a new culture and did not have significantly more problems than typical primary schools in London (O'Shea et al., 2000, cited in Glen, 2002, p184).

Findings in *The Good Childhood Report 2015* (The Children's Society, 2015) indicated that children struggle with feelings and perceptions of themselves and about life at school and suggested this was an area for future prioritisation. Some of the other reasons cited are school pressures and stress from the increasing amount of testing and exams, together with peer pressure about looking a particular way, as explored in Chapter 5. Positive self-esteem and happiness are very closely linked, as are poor self-esteem and unhappiness.

KEY REFLECTIONS

- How would you define self-esteem?
- What part can relationships play in the construction of self-esteem?
- How might levels of self-esteem manifest themselves in a child?
- What can get in the way?

The importance of self-esteem

Self-esteem is a vital component to individuals and their lives since it affects their life choices and decision-making process. Children with high self-esteem are generally motivated and will seek to achieve well in life, whilst on the other hand children with lower self-esteem tend not to feel worthy and can lack the motivation to achieve.

Young Minds (2019) summarises positive self-esteem in children and young people as:

- have a positive image of themselves;
- are confident;
- can make friends easily and are not anxious with new people;
- can play in groups or on their own;
- will try and solve problems on their own, but if not able to will ask for help;
- can be proud of their achievements;

- can admit mistakes and learn from them;
- will try new things and adapt to change.

Low self-esteem is summarised by Young Minds (2019) as:

- have a negative image of themselves – they might feel bad, ugly, unlikeable or stupid;
- lack confidence;
- find it hard to make and keep friendships, and may feel victimised by others;
- feel lonely and isolated;
- tend to avoid new things and find change hard;
- can't deal well with failure;
- tend to put themselves down and may say things like 'I'm stupid' or 'I can't do that';
- are not proud of what they achieve and always think they could have done better;
- are constantly comparing themselves to their peers in a negative way.

The importance of resilience

As the risk and resilience model will show, low self-esteem is one of the risk factors in the development of poor mental health whereas positive or high self-esteem acts as a protective factor to mental health. Children and young people with low self-esteem are at a higher risk of developing mental health problems over their lifetime. Overall the model demonstrates that risk factors can predispose a child or young person to mental health problems. These are like ACEs and include features that sit in the domains of the family, the environment and the child him- or herself. What is important is understanding how resilience factors can be built on and therefore mitigate risk and help to redress the balance.

That said, defining resilience is not so straightforward. Is it about being strong when under stress and/or being able to 'bounce back'? Or is it more about the individual ability to manage stress and levels of positive feeling that make the difference? Children and young people need to have positive experiences but also the capacity to manage negative experiences without feeling overwhelmed (Music, 2017, pp 240, 244).

Self-esteem was defined by Pearce (1993) as one of the protective factors in terms of the likelihood of developing mental health problems. His risk and resilience model identified three areas of risk:

1.   environmental/contextual;

2.   the family;

3.   the young person/child him- or herself.

Examples of risk include:

- negative experiences in the *environment*, such as poverty, disaster, violence or being a refugee or asylum seeker;

- precipitating factors in the *family*, such as early attachment difficulties, domestic abuse, parental conflict and parental mental illness. Multiple family transitions can increase risk, with a cumulative effect on educational achievement, behaviour and relationships in general;

- for the *young person*, areas of risk include neurodevelopmental difficulties and conditions (such as attention deficit hyperactivity disorder (ADHD) or autistic spectrum conditions), low self-esteem, academic failure and poor school attendance, low IQ or learning difficulties, physical illness and genetic influences.

It is important to note that most factors are about context, extrinsic to the child, and not located within the child. Yet, in spite of major adversity, many young people and children cope well. The key is *resilience*, which acts as a protective factor. Rutter (1985) and again later (2006) described this as a dynamic evolving process and not just about static factors. The model of risk and resilience is not based on risk and protective factors in themselves but rather on how they interact. The flip side is the consideration of resilience factors which mitigate the risk factors. Having and acquiring resilience skills acts as a protective factor, and these can include:

- secure attachments;

- positive self-esteem;

- social skills;

- familial compassion and warmth;

- family stability;

- social support systems that encourage personal development and coping skills;

- having a skill or a talent.

The emphasis is on the process of resilience across developmental pathways. Studies have led theorists to suggest that all children inherit characteristics which make them both vulnerable (risk factors) and resilient (protective factors). There is a complex interplay between risk factors and promoting resilience. Resilience effects are shaped by social context. So, for children and young people, this includes educational settings. Even high-risk groups, as suggested above, are able individually to adapt and achieve against the odds and despite diversity (Rutter, 2012). A focus is often on risk or negative factors instead of positive attributes and resilience. In the following case study of Max, ADHD ticks a box as a risk factor but it is really important to know and practise reframing ADHD as a positive factor. It is most likely Max will have boundless energy, which can be wearing for those around him, but he will always be keen to participate in events outside the classroom where he could potentially do well. A 'state of mind' and improved self-esteem can come about through experiencing successes.

Where protective and resilience factors can be accessed, resourced and utilised, they can act as an important counterbalance, buffering risk factors (Department for Education, 2018 b). For example, a child may be genetically predisposed to developing ADHD. There may be other family members with a diagnosis. With the combination of a poor environment in terms of abuse or attachment difficulties, the child may be at greater risk of developing ADHD (Music, 2011). Similarly, a young person may be genetically predisposed to clinical depression or psychosis, which does not in itself mean the condition will necessarily develop. But if there is a combination of other poor external factors and negative experiences, as described above, depression, psychosis or other significant mental illness may emerge and develop into a clinical condition (Burton et al., 2014). Many children will experience an understandable knock to their self-esteem from these challenges; some are able to bounce back if there are other protective factors in place, or as Fuller (1998, p75) describes:

Resilience is the happy knack of being able to bungy jump through the pitfalls of life.

Resilience is a process and construct of individuals, families and communities, including schools, societies and groups. As Rutter (1987, cited in Werner and Smith, 2001, p3) describes, it is:

the end product of buffering processes that do not eliminate risk and adverse conditions in life but allow the individual to deal with them effectively.

Schools have an important role and can offer opportunities for supporting, promoting and improving children's resilience by using strength-based approaches, including positive praise and the use of circle time. Through these activities, schools have an important role in helping to reduce the risk of children developing mental health problems (Department for Education, 2018 b).

Alongside self-esteem, identifying a skill or a talent – also a protective factor – should not be underestimated. Mo Farah, the Olympic champion, was a migrant from Somalia, escaping the civil war and arriving in London aged 8 and speaking very little English. His potential athletic talent was spotted by his PE teacher at school and the rest, as we know, is history. The story had the potential to be so different (Burton et al., 2014).

CASE STUDY: MAX

Max is 8 and in Year 3 at primary school. Max has a diagnosis of ADHD, so he struggles with the 'triad of impairments' for ADHD (see Chapter 1), is easily distracted, finds it difficult to concentrate for very long and is sometimes impulsive. To support this, the school is trying to give him short tasks that have a clear structure and are differentiated to allow Max to succeed. At lunch time he finds it difficult to remain in the lunch queue so sometimes gets asked to keep still and stay in line by the dinner time staff and sometimes gets sent to the back of the queue if he doesn't comply.

Max also finds staying on task difficult in class. There are 29 other children in class. Max has a teaching assistant to support him. He is always pleased to receive praise and has some gold stars for being able to stay on task in class. Despite this support he sometimes gets into trouble with staff both in and outside the classroom. When this happens he can get very upset.

Life at home for Max is also difficult at times. He has an older brother, Tom, who is 16 and also has ADHD. The family have recently lost their father from the family home as the relationship between Tom and Max's parents has ended after an acrimonious time. Max and his family live in a two-bedroom flat on an inner-city estate. Mum has recently been diagnosed with clinical depression.

A favourite time of the school day is outside play. Max gets on well with his peers and has some good friendships. Max enjoys sports, particularly football. He attends after-school football club and plays football on Saturdays at a local sports centre.

Given this scenario there are many risk factors and ACEs that are linked to Max's issues.

- Environment: inner-city estate, two-bedroom flat, limited outside access to play as there is no garden. Opportunities for play can be reduced in schools where there has been a reduction in playtimes.
- Family: acrimonious parental relationship; father has left so significant event and loss. Brother has ADHD. Mum has a diagnosed mental health disorder.
- Child: Max has a neurodevelopmental difficulty (ADHD). Max finds it difficult to deal with being told off at school, which is more frequent for Max perhaps compared to other children, and this could contribute to low self-esteem, together with other factors as above.

However, despite these risk factors there are several potential resilience factors, which can improve Max's self-esteem. These include:

- enjoying and being good at sport (football);
- having friendships;
- attending after-school clubs and engaging at school;
- having quick thinking, boundless energy and an 'up for it' activist personality and attitude to life as results of his ADHD;
- home life for Max has the potential to settle down and be less acrimonious now the parents have separated.

The school is also trying to support Max by using different strategies such as focused tasks, positive praise and the support of a teaching assistant. By encouraging Max to join the school football club, the school is enabling him to taste success regularly and feel positive about his achievements outside the classroom, which will lead to improved self-esteem.

KEY REFLECTIONS

- How can high and low levels of self-esteem be characterised in a child?
- What risk and resilience factors can impact upon self-esteem?
- How can resilience be promoted within schools?

The value of self-efficacy

As mentioned earlier, self-efficacy is closely linked with self-esteem and develops from experiences throughout a child's life. It is the belief children or young people have that they can define a goal, persevere and see themselves as capable, and in this way self-efficacy provides the foundation for motivation, well-being and personal accomplishment. To build self-efficacy children and young people need opportunities to learn what their strengths are, helping to cultivate a belief that they can rely on these when facing a challenge. Within a whole school approach, children and young people need to feel they have influence, a 'voice' and involvement in decision making about their learning, classroom and school life (Weare, 2015). Ultimately, the more children or young people believe they can achieve, the more likely they are to generalise this to other areas of their lives, building self-efficacy in a wide range of activities.

Having a voice is also set out as an important right in Article 12 of the United Nations Convention on the Rights of the Child (1989). Many schools have taken part in the Rights Respecting Schools programme (**https://www.unicef.org.uk/rights-respecting-schools/**).

The case study below helps to demonstrate the importance of positive, trusting and empowering relationships and how schools can play a part in developing a child or young person's sense of mastery and the ability to persevere in times of difficulty, building self-efficacy. This was a vulnerable young person in difficult circumstances, and the end of the story could easily have been very different.

CASE STUDY: BECKY

Becky is 11, of dual-heritage ethnicity, and is in Year 6. Her family life is difficult; she has a volatile relationship with an overpowering mother and an absent father. Becky's mother (Rosie) struggles with her own mental health and finds it very difficult to put the needs of her children before her own. Becky's three older half-siblings have left home and her younger brother was, in her words, 'just annoying'. She lives in a three-bedroom house in an inner-city estate. Becky has struggled with low mood and anxiety since Year 4.

Becky has very low self-esteem and self-efficacy and was identified for increased support at school. Her school is very supportive of her and she has a particularly strong relationship with the deputy head teacher who is supporting the family with other professionals. Becky's and her family's needs were listened to and further thought was given as to how to meet them more effectively. Becky enjoyed school, was determined to attend school as much as possible and do as well as she could with her upcoming Key Stage 2 SATs, demonstrating hope and resilience.

Within counselling sessions at school Becky was supported to explore past and present relationships, how trust had been built and broken and how this affected her self-esteem and self-efficacy. Becky was given responsibilities within the classroom - lunch time monitor with other pupils, supporting a reading group of younger pupils - to encourage her sense of self-worth. Becky was very keen on drama but did not have the confidence to take part in lunch time rehearsals. With the support of the deputy head teacher, Becky was encouraged to attend and watch rehearsals, with a view to building on this.

The family support worker enabled Rosie to seek her own counselling and to work with her, reflecting on her relationship with Becky and possible strategies that may support them during difficult periods. With this support and encouragement Becky is developing into a more confident and capable young person and has a degree of control of her life. She is developing an improved relationship with her mum (Rosie) and is getting on better with her younger brother. Becky has strategies in place to help her manage difficult feelings in relation to her low mood and anxiety, increasing her sense of mastery.

The family support worker also supported Mum to get help with her own mental health problems, which she has done and Rosie is engaged with and supported by adult mental health services.

Becky is attending school regularly and her self-esteem and belief that she can achieve and overcome difficulties in her life (self-efficacy) have grown immensely.

Becky's case demonstrates the important role that relationships play with regard to the development of self-esteem and self-efficacy. Professionals within Becky's school, particularly the deputy head teacher and the school counsellor, play an important role in increasing Becky's motivation and personal achievement.

Case study reflections

- With regard to self-efficacy, what made the difference in Becky's case?
- What factors did relationships play in supporting Becky's self-esteem?
- How are factors in the classroom supporting Becky's self-esteem?
- Did you spot a potential skill or talent emerging (resilience factor)?

There are many factors that are making a difference for Becky.

- Verbal persuasion and constructive feedback (hearing positive feedback about the ability to accomplish a desirable activity): Becky is gaining this from the supportive professional relationships in her life, particularly the deputy head teacher, building her self-esteem through positive relationships with others. Hearing is believing!
- Performance accomplishments (successfully doing a desired activity): Becky is on track with her Key Stage 2 SATs targets and is relishing her increased responsibilities at school. She is developing a better relationship with her mum (Rosie). All Becky's accomplishments have led to a sense of mastery, which is influencing her perspective on her own abilities. Doing is believing!
- Physiological states (feelings about the behaviour): through positive relationships with others and the opportunity to think about the past with the school counsellor, Becky has been enabled to build her confidence and begun to control her low mood and anxiety. In turn, this is increasing her mood and positively impacting on her self-efficacy beliefs. Feeling is believing!
- Vicarious experience (seeing someone model the desired activity): Becky is observing other pupils within the drama group, younger pupils in the reading mentoring activity and her mother Rosie. She is looking at others and observing how they manage and whether they succeed or not, which is increasing her belief that she can indeed master her own situation. Seeing is believing!

It is important to note that desired activities and constructive feedback should not be unrealistic or grandiose as this can give children and young people the perception that they can accomplish an activity that they may not have the skills or knowledge to tackle. If children or young people are encouraged to make a change that they are not ready to attempt, there is the possibility they may fail, and this may mean they will be less likely to believe they can do it the next time, resulting in a diminished sense of self-efficacy. It is extremely important, therefore, that success in activities is within reach and feedback is appropriate. In Becky's case, being encouraged to watch drama activities initially and being fully supported within other responsibilities are slowly developing her confidence and self-belief, which will in turn feed into positive self-esteem and high self-efficacy.

Improving self-esteem with both children and young people within the school and its community

It is relevant to consider strategies for promoting resilience, and it has to be remembered that resilience can only develop through some exposure to risk or stress; as Rutter (1985) identified, resilience develops through this exposure occurring at a *manageable level of intensity* at developmental points where protective factors can operate. The major risk factors for children and young people tend to operate within chronic and transitional events such as continuing family conflict, chronic and persistent bullying, long-term poverty and multiple school and home changes. Children and young people seem to show greater resilience when faced with more single one-off acute risk and adversity events, such as bereavement (Coleman and Hagell, 2007). A good caregiving relationship can act as a protective factor and can mitigate other social and environmental factors such as poverty and disability. In addition, caregiving relationships for children and young people include relationships in school communities, thus becoming an important and additional resource.

Resilience can be grown and developed, which can be a challenge in an assessment-based society such as ours, as well as in our schools' current National Curriculum demands. There is a balance to be sought between the role of play as an asset and important tool for social development and subsequent development of resilience, and the pressure to achieve academic results, especially in early years settings (Joslyn, 2016). When positive experiences outweigh negative experiences, a child's 'scale' tips toward positive outcomes (Center on the Developing Child, 2015).

> *No matter the source of hardship, the single most common factor for children who end up doing well is having the support of at least one stable and committed relationship with a parent, caregiver, or other adult. These relationships are the active ingredient in building resilience: they provide the personalized responsiveness, scaffolding, and protection that can buffer children from developmental disruption. Relationships also help children develop key capacities – such as the ability to plan, monitor, and regulate behavior, and adapt to changing circumstances – that better enable them to respond to adversity when they face it. This combination of supportive relationships, adaptive skill-building, and positive experiences constitutes the foundation of resilience.*

(Center on the Developing Child, 2015)

Highly targeted therapeutic and educational support is required for identified at-risk groups including, for example, looked-after children. The National Institute for Health and Care Excellence (NICE, 2015) have guidance on looked-after children and young people.

When the term 'therapeutic' is considered, it is not only about its application in clinical and counselling work. It is also with reference to the importance of all relationships having a therapeutic element which therefore is a supportive relationship. All looked-after children in schools should have a personal education plan, although it is interesting to read in *Promoting the Education of Looked After Children and Previously Looked After Children* (Department for Education, 2018 b) that the focus is on behaviour and achievement, with little mention of mental health, apart from a requirement to work with local Child and Adolescent Mental Health Services (CAMHS) as necessary. This is curious, as looked-after children and care leavers have a fivefold increased risk of all the childhood mental, emotional and behavioural problems and a six- to sevenfold increased risk of conduct disorders (Department of Health, 2011). However, it does contain guidance and a case study example of the most appropriate use of Pupil Premium +. The Department for Education's *Mental Health and Behaviour in Schools* (2018 a) guidance acknowledges the lasting impact of ACEs throughout childhood, adolescence and adulthood, highlighting the importance for school staff to be aware of how this can impact on behaviour and education.

A school's role

Promoting resilience and building self-esteem to prevent mental health issues in schools are key areas of focus for teachers and educational professionals. Weare (2015) highlights that the real benefits for schools can be seen through *a whole school evidence informed approach* where a consistent group of approaches, programmes and interventions are designed and adopted so that all parts of the school work collaboratively towards building a safe and supportive school environment. When considering what 'good mental health' looks like, the Mental Health Foundation (2002) state that a child would have the ability:

- to develop psychologically, emotionally, intellectually and spiritually;
- to initiate, develop and sustain mutually satisfying personal relationships;
- to become aware of others and empathise with them.

Therefore, building on this from a whole school approach perspective, teachers need to think about the class and wider school environment. Does it build a sense of connectedness and purpose where all emotions and feelings are supported through a culture of warmth and respect? How are being and feeling differently celebrated?

There are a number of approaches, programmes and interventions that can be initiated which focus on the teaching of social and emotional skills, and which in turn help develop positive school environments. It has been shown that these programmes, which help children understand the challenges associated with growing up, transitions in life (such as Key Stages and schools) and change (such as separation, divorce and bereavement), can build resilience which may prevent the development of mental health problems in later life. Resilience is being able to cope with difficult situations, and children need to able to believe in their ability to cope through a positive image of themselves which can be developed through the delivery of high-quality programmes of social and emotional skills interventions.

One proposed structured programme in school could follow the wave model of intervention, as suggested by the National Children's Bureau (2014).

Wave 1	**Effective whole school framework for promoting emotional well-being and mental health** Quality-first teaching of social and emotional skills to all children through personal, social, health and economic-type programmes
Wave 2	**Skills-focused interventions** Small-group social and emotional aspects of learning (SEAL) for children who need help to develop social and emotional skills
Wave 3	**Therapeutic interventions** Individual and small groups Complementary to SEAL

All interventions would need to be informed by the evidence available through research, and mindful of a multiprofessional approach to practice in order for them to be successful and have an impact on children and families.

Schools can play a central role in supporting educational resilience given the number of hours and length of time children spend in school. Educational resilience is not only about academic and educational attainment, but is also about important relationships and social skills learnt in the process. This acts as a stabilising influence, particularly for vulnerable children (Joslyn, 2016).

In order to support children in a variety of educational settings, Newman (2004, p14) also suggests a three-point strategy to promoting resilience within children.

Strategy 1	Reduce the child's exposure to risk though means such as providing school meals to support a child's life, or attendance at an after-school club for children with no alternative but to play on the street
Strategy 2	Interrupt the chain reaction of negative events; if one risk factor increases, others will probably follow
Strategy 3	Offer the child or young person positive experiences, thus providing ways of enhancing self-esteem and developing relationships with positive adults

Alongside such an approach, a school may employ a strategy to help promote aspects of positive self-esteem, as outlined in the following section.

Personal, social, health and economic (PSHE)

Teaching children about mental health and emotional well-being should form part of a structured and personalised PSHE curriculum in order to ensure that it proves an effective vehicle to embed core skills across all areas of educational experience and is not viewed as a 'bolt-on' topic or theme. These sessions need to be tailored to the needs and ages of the children in your class but a whole school approach of key messages is vital – that children are provided with the knowledge, language, understanding and confidence to seek help when needed and to ask questions about mental health without fear of stigmatism or bullying.

A graduated approach to PSHE education as a whole school is vital. With younger children work begins on 'developing oneself', focusing on self-awareness, self-concept, self-efficacy and self-belief. An effective way to do this is through the development of emotional literacy using story books. Stories and storytelling help children to develop emotional literacy, to make sense of their world and appreciate different points of view. They enable children to develop social relationships through an experiential, familiar and safe learning approach and start to develop skills such as empathy, negotiation, compassion and difference and an understanding of what is right and wrong, kind and unkind.

The Department for Education has most recently worked with the PSHE Association to improve the quality of teaching of mental health and emotional well-being. This has resulted in fully updated guidance and lesson plans for 2019 to match the government's new statutory PSHE requirements regarding health education, relationships education and relationships and sex education. This can be found at **https://www.pshe-association.org.uk** on the resources page.

Key issues included in these lesson plans are:

- why it is important to teach about mental health and emotional well-being;

- building teaching about mental health into a planned PSHE programme;

- promoting well-being and resilience from an early age;

- ensuring teaching is appropriate to the age and maturity of pupils;

- key principles in teaching about mental health and emotional well-being safely and confidently;

- using visitors to the classroom to support lessons;

- addressing challenging mental health issues such as eating disorders, self-harm and suicide.

More recently the Department for Education has reviewed what must and should be covered as part of relationships education, relationships and sex education and health education in England (Department for Education, 2019). This has recommended that, from 2020, health education should become compulsory in all state-funded schools, with PSHE continuing to be compulsory within the independent sector. Such documentation outlines a need at both primary and secondary levels to study topics such as mental well-being, internet safety and harm, physical health and fitness, healthy eating, drugs, alcohol and tobacco, health and prevention and the changing adolescent body (Department for Education, 2019).

Recommendations around this new strategy have been conceived in part to help support and guard children and young people against the risk of online concerns and other factors that can endanger children and young people's mental health and well-being. It has also been suggested that such changes may help support individuals to become safer and healthier regarding their academic, personal and social lives. This work by the Department for Education is intended to support the teaching of good mental and physical health and well-being of children and young people to make them more resilient when they may be feeling, for example, unhappy, bullied or anxious. As the report suggests:

> *The focus in primary school should be on teaching the characteristics of good physical health and mental wellbeing. Teachers should be clear that mental wellbeing is a normal part of daily life, in the same way as physical health.*

> (Department for Education, 2019, p33)

Good practice: promoting positive mental health

The use of feedback boxes allows pupils to share a problem anonymously in the 'bullying box', or something good that another pupil did in the 'praise box'. These are sometimes managed by the personal, social, citizenship and health education coordinator, who may choose to file some comments and will pass safeguarding concerns on to the relevant staff member to follow up. This anonymous sharing allows teachers to pick up on common worries and problems which can then be discussed in weekly circle time sessions before they grow into more serious well-being or mental health risks. The teacher leads the discussion in a calm and respectful environment which allows the whole class to think together about what is happening without being judgemental or singling out the individuals involved. Reports from the boxes may also lead to referrals to Place2Be or CAMHS as well as other school-based interventions such as lunch time nurture clubs.

Social and emotional aspects of learning (SEAL)

For many schools the use of the SEAL initiative (DfES, 2005 b) gives them a practical resource of learning opportunities to help develop social, emotional and behavioural skills through a whole school approach. As with the PSHE Association framework, SEAL built on a spiral curriculum delivery through a themed approach which could be adapted and personalised to fit the needs of individual classes and children. The development of a skills- and values-based approach was core to this, and was reinforced in classroom-based activities, whole school assemblies and links to home and the community. Although these resources are now no longer freely available and have been archived, many schools still use these approaches in their PSHE and circle time activities and they are also used for professional development training for staff.

This work was originally promoted by the research of individuals such as Goleman (1996), linked to the notion of emotional intelligence, and was promoted by the government in publications such as *Social and Emotional Aspects of Learning (SEAL): Improving Behaviour, Improving Learning* (DfES, 2005 a) and *Excellence and Enjoyment: Social and Emotional Aspects of Learning* (DfES, 2005 b). Since the SEAL resources contained materials at their core which were designed to offer a selection of learning opportunities to achieve specific learning outcomes in the classroom, they can still provide advice and support for aiding the development of a child's self-esteem.

Materials linked to DfES (2005 b) continue to provide excellent activities for helping children to develop an improved sense of self through the development of self-awareness. As DfES (2005 b, p40) notes:

> Self-awareness enables children to have some understanding of themselves. They know how they learn, how they relate to others, what they are thinking and what they are feeling.

The materials linked to 'knowing myself' are particularly useful when considering how individuals can accept themselves for who and how they are, and in helping some individuals to be able to recognise when goals are hard to achieve. The unit linked to 'understanding my feelings' can help pupils recognise when they can become overwhelmed by their feelings and that it is alright to have feelings, but it is not alright to behave in any way they feel appropriate. 'Managing feelings' provides a range of strategies to recognise and accept feelings as well as managing and dealing with feelings.

Alongside SEAL materials, class-based strategies which involve listening to children and praising them for their effort will provide one means by which to promote a child's self-esteem. However, try to avoid generic praise – be specific and descriptive, show children by what is said that you value them and their efforts too.

Always try and make certain that pupils taste success by setting achievable targets. Encourage children through class-based opportunities to show their worth to the class. Ask them to talk about something they are knowledgeable about and successful in, or ask them to support their peers in a subject strength they have. Remember that all pupils have their own strengths and weaknesses, so avoid comparing children since it can lead to unrealistic expectations and often the propagation of failure.

Circle time

Circle time was originally developed by Jenny Mosley in order to promote respect for the individual as a whole and uses numerous practical activities for developing the whole person and his or her feelings of well-being (Mosley, 2001). Circle time sessions can also provide a possible vehicle for classroom delivery of the SEAL curriculum, as highlighted earlier. It centres on promoting positive relationships whilst seeking to nurture a sense of personal positivity and responsibility for others (Mosley, 2004). Circle time allows the school and its pupils to experience a supportive environment in which social, emotional and behavioural skills can be developed.

Circle time allows participants (usually sitting in a circle) to exchange ideas and feelings linked to a variety of issues important to the child along with behavioural and emotional items. The teacher who is involved in these sessions is there to facilitate the discussions and to provide activities to encourage participants to feel that their contributions are valued and included. Linked to circle time are what are called 'golden rules' which are displayed around the school to remind pupils of the agreed principles for positive aspects of social and moral behaviour. For example, these might include 'we do not hurt people's feelings'.

Through a supportive developmental framework of games, circle time allows pupils to consider aspects of their moral development involving their ideas supported by their peers. Games can include:

- asking all children to choose a positive adjective to describe themselves and others as the game moves around the circle;

- scenarios such as 'You see a child sitting on their own in the playground. They are upset by comments made by others about their football ability. What do you do?' helps to encourage pupils to think about the feelings of others and how they can promote a positive feeling of self-worth.

Working with parents

A school is often made aware of a child's low self-esteem as evidenced in the way they respond to praise and behave in school. Given this, the school should seek to work with the parents to try and promote improvements in a child's self-esteem both inside and outside school.

At a school level, remember that positive relationships with children are key to positive behaviour and regular attendance. Also remember that children behave well when they feel valued and that they belong, and that the school should try to create opportunities for children to experience and/or feel confident in a positive relationship with an adult. This will take time and may need to involve others in the process, such as the parents.

Contact with parents to discuss the school's concerns regarding a child's self-esteem can be made both formally on occasions, such as at parents' evening, or just when talking to a parent about a child's day when the child is picked up. If this is to be a positive meeting it is important that, whenever this is done, the member of staff makes certain that the parent does not in any way feel blamed or patronised regarding the child's behaviour. It is important that the parent is provided with help, support and strategies to deal with any behaviour at home in a consistent and positive way.

Such conversations will ensure that strategies and approaches used in school can form part of what is an agreed united approach between home and school when trying to make inroads into this aspect of a child's well-being. This may also form the basis of a support package for parents, helping them to promote positive parenting and attitudes at home. Remember that some parents too may not have had positive experiences when they were young, with their parents undermining their own feeling of self-worth. Given this, schools need to work with parents to make them also feel accepted and valued.

Strategies that can be employed both in school and at home
Identifying where the problem lies

Since children with poor self-esteem may find it difficult to articulate their feelings, try not to question them too much about why they are being negative. Often children will not be able to pin an exact reason on their feelings. Just try and gently, in conversation, ask questions such as 'Are you sure you are alright?' or 'If you want to tell me about your day, or the reason for your feelings, I am keen to listen'. A *TES* article on attachment and trauma and a primary teacher's response is insightful and explains children's behaviours that typically result in very negative outcomes, such as exclusion for the child. Taking a different approach can make all the difference in the world (Anonymous, 2019).

As discussed in Chapter 1, changing the language we use is all-important and makes a complete difference to the position we come from, as being much more empathetic, when engaging with a child. Instead of 'challenging behaviour' consider 'distressed behaviour'. Instead of 'What's the matter with you?' ask 'What has happened to you?'

Trying to acknowledge that we cannot all be good at everything, all the time

For children, feelings of being useless at their work are very real, so you should listen to how they feel and acknowledge that it is fine to feel this way and it is not uncommon to get cross, angry or sad from time to time. Tell them about moments you have struggled with issues to help them realise that it can happen to adults as well as children. If it is another child in the class that is denting the child's self-esteem, consider getting the child to think about negative points the other child may have as well as positive aspects. In this way the child can see that the other child may appear confident but has items s/he may feel vulnerable about, even though it is not shown. Try and to get to know the child's hopes and fears in a typical day and see if you can find a way to empathise with what the child is saying so you can support him or her more fully.

Concentrating on the positive points of the child

If children are unhappy or upset try and talk to them at an appropriate moment about what the issues are that are upsetting them. Try not to probe for answers if the child is not forthcoming. Give space and time to open up. Try not to get cross in these situations or criticise or blame the child. This will not help the situation and may even prove more problematic in the future. Remember to praise children for their own unique positive strengths. Avoid comparisons with siblings or other pupils since this may lead to resentment or the child not being able to compete with them.

Positive parenting

It is important that you help parents to make every effort to praise their child when the child has done well or tried hard. Little things will start having an impact upon self-esteem, for example, thanking children for tidying their bag away or hanging their coat up when they come into the house. If a parent is finding it difficult to accept the child's behaviour, try and encourage the parent to make certain that the child sees and hears that it is the behaviour the parent does not like and not the child, by making comments such as 'I like you but I do not like that behaviour'.

Teachers' self-esteem

Teachers often reflect on their own role in supporting a child with issues relating to self-esteem and often do not realise how these form part of being an effective teacher, as outlined by Part B of the Teachers' Standards (2014). In order for you to be effective when doing your job, you too must have high levels of self-esteem so that you act in a confident, relaxed and respectful manner towards the children in your school. Teachers' self-esteem may be influenced by many factors, such as feelings of inadequacy when dealing with school-based issues or due to their own personal lives. The question that must be asked, therefore, is 'Who is looking after the self-esteem of the teaching workforce in the school?' Authors such as Mosley (2001) have advocated that there is a need to build positive self-esteem within the teaching workforce and that it may be assessed when examining the responses to set questions such as 'Do you worry about your work when you are not in school?' Research by Weare (2015) notes that it is important that staff's successes and achievements are celebrated, but that there is also time for them to place realistic demands upon themselves professionally as well as to let go. A good work–life balance is needed to help staff recuperate and settings need to:

> find ways to make it safe for staff and leaders (as well as pupils) to acknowledge their human distress, weakness and difficulty and seek support and help for their mental health needs in non-stigmatised ways.

> (Weare, 2015, p7)

At a simple level, schools, teachers and leaders expressing gratitude and appreciation for the role that individuals can play in helping promote positive self-esteem within pupils can be a quick but effective way of building a teacher's self-esteem. Try and make a habit of telling your teacher colleagues how much they are appreciated since well-being must start with the staff as they are at the chalkface of any work with regard to promoting pupils' self-esteem.

- Remember that if you are trying to support self-esteem there are no quick fixes.

- Encourage staff to be realistic about what can be achieved and that this success will ebb and flow given that some of the good work achieved in schools can be quickly undone by risk factors at home.

- Consider that self-esteem is like a non-stick surface: most of what is tried will slide off.

- Small incremental gains can be made, so encourage your staff not to lose heart or patience.

- Make certain that there is always an open door so that teachers can share worries, concerns and disillusionment with regard to progress.

- Be there to reassure them that they are doing a good job and that any perceived failure is not down to them.

KEY REFLECTIONS

- What strategies can a school employ to improve resilience and the self-esteem of its pupils?
- What strategies might parents be told to use to support issues around self-esteem?
- What can colleagues do to support positive self-esteem amongst themselves?

CHAPTER SUMMARY

- Self-esteem is about how we think about ourselves in relation to others.
- Self-esteem is sensitive to the qualities of these systems such as families, schools and communities and thus can be negative or positive.
- Relationships are at the heart of well-being and self-esteem.
- Positive self-esteem is aligned with happiness.
- Low self-esteem is aligned with unhappiness.
- Positive self-esteem includes protective characteristics or 'resilience' factors, including a positive image of oneself, making friends easily, being able to solve problems and ask for help if needed, admitting mistakes and being able to adapt to change.
- Resilience factors can be influenced and improved through positive promotion of resilience in schools.
- Schools have opportunities to offer targeted support for at-risk groups and can play a key role in improving resilience factors and thus self-esteem.
- Educational resilience is not just about academic performance; it also includes development of relationships and social skills.

FURTHER READING

Anonymous (2019) How attachment theory helps behaviour. *TES*. Available at: https://www.tes.com/magazine/article/how-attachment-theory-helps-behaviour (accessed 25 July 2019).

Burke-Harris, N. (2018) *The Deepest Well: Healing the Long-Term Effects of Childhood Adversity*. London: Bluebird (Pan MacMillan).

Centre on the Developing Child at Harvard University has excellent resources on resilience including film clips, and explaining the science behind resilience and development and how we can actively improve and make a difference to children's lives. Available at: https://developingchild.harvard.edu/ (accessed June 2019).

Fonagy, P. (2016) *What is Mentalization?* Available at: https://youtu.be/MJ1Y9zw-n7U (accessed 25 July 2019).

Hunter, C. (2012) *Is Resilience Still a Useful Concept when Working with Children and Young People?* Child, Family, Community, Australia. Available at: https://aifs.gov.au/cfca/publications/resilience-still-useful-concept-when-working-child/export.

Schore, A. (2013) *Neurobiology of Secure Attachment*. Available at: https://www.youtube.com/embed/WVuJ5KhpL34 (accessed 25 July 2019).

Schore, A. (2014) *Attachment Trauma and Effects of Neglect and Abuse on Brain Development*. Available at: https://www.psychalive.org/video-dr-allan-schore-attachment-trauma-effects-neglect-abuse-brain-development/ (accessed 25 July 2019).

The Brain Architecture Game (2017) Available at: https://dev.thebrainarchitecturegame.com/ (accessed 25 July 2019).

The film *The Biology of Stress and the Science of Hope* (KPJR Films, 2015) is a must-watch. Here is a link to the trailer: https://www.bing.com/videos/search?q=resilience+the+biology+of+stress+and+science+of+hope+film+trailer&view=detail&mid=952A2BCE15771BBDBF0F952A2BCE15771BBDBF0F&FORM=VIRE (accessed June 2019).

Young Minds. *360 Degree Schools*. Available at: https://youngminds.org.uk/youngminds-professionals/360-schools/ (accessed June 2019).

━━ REFERENCES ━━

Bandura, A. (1977) *Social Learning Theory*. Englewood Cliffs, NJ: Prentice Hall.

Bandura, A. (1989) Human agency in social cognitive theory. *American Psychologist*, 44(9): 1175–1184.

Bono, J.E. and Judge, T.A. (2003) Core self-evaluations: a review of the trait and its role in job satisfaction and job performance. *European Journal of Personality*, 17: S5–S18.

Burton, M., Pavord, E. and Williams, B. (2014) *An Introduction to Child and Adolescent Mental Health*. London: SAGE.

Center on the Developing Child (2015) *In Brief: The Science of Resilience*. Available at: https://developingchild.harvard.edu/resources/inbrief-the-science-of-resilience/ (accessed June 2019).

Coleman, F. and Hagell, A. (2007) *Mental Health and Mental Disorders: Adolescence Risk and Resilience Against the Odds*. Chichester: John Wiley.

Department for Education (2015) *Special Educational Needs and Disability Code of Practice: 0 to 25 Years*. Available at: https://assets.publishing.service.gov.uk/government/uploads/system/uploads/attachment_data/file/398815/SEND_Code_of_Practice_January_2015.pdf (accessed 12/9/18).

Department for Education (2018 a) *Mental Health and Behaviour in Schools*. Available at: https://assets.publishing.service.gov.uk/government/uploads/system/uploads/attachment_data/file/755135/Mental_health_and_behaviour_in_schools__.pdf (accessed June 2019).

Department for Education (2018 b) *Promoting the Education of Looked After Children and Previously Looked After Children: Statutory Guidance for Local Authorities*. Available at: https://assets.publishing.service.gov.uk/government/uploads/system/uploads/attachment_data/file/683556/Promoting_the_education_of_looked-after_children_and_previously_looked-after-children.pdf (accessed June 2019).

Department for Education (2019) *Relationships and Sex Education (RSE) and Health Education. Draft Statutory Guidance for Governing Bodies, Proprietors, Head Teachers, Principals, Senior Leadership Teams, Teachers*. Available at: https://assets.publishing.service.gov.uk/government/uploads/system/uploads/attachment_data/file/781150/Draft_guidance_Relationships_Education__Relationships_and_Sex_Education__RSE__and_Health_Education2.pdf (accessed 27 June 2019).

Department of Health (2011) *No Health Without Mental Health: A Cross Government Mental Health Outcomes Strategy for People of All Ages*. Available at: www.gov.uk/government/uploads/system/uploads/attachment_data/file/213761/dh_124058.pdf (accessed June 2019).

DfES (2005 a) *Social and Emotional Aspects of Learning (SEAL): Improving Behaviour, Improving Learning*. Available at: http://webarchive.nationalarchives.gov.uk/20110809101133/nsonline.org.uk/node/87009 (accessed January 2016).

DfES (2005 b) *Excellence and Enjoyment: Social and Emotional Aspects of Learning*. Norwich: HMSO. Available at: http://webarchive.nationalarchives.gov.uk/20110809101133/nsonline.org.uk/node/87009 (accessed January 2016).

Fuller, A. (1998) *From Surviving to Thriving: Promoting Mental Health in Young People*. Camberwell: The Australian Council for Educational Research.

Glen, C. (2002) 'We have to blame ourselves': refugees and the politics of systemic practice, in Papadopoulos, R.K. (ed.) *Therapeutic Care of Refugees: No Place Like Home*. London: Tavistock Clinic Series.

Goleman, D. (1996) *Emotional Intelligence: Why it can Matter More Than IQ*. London: Bloomsbury.

Joslyn, E. (2016) *Resilience in Children: Perspectives, Promise and Practice*. London: Palgrave.

Luxmoore, N. (2008) *Feeling Like Crap: Young People and the Meaning of Self-esteem*. London: Jessica Kingsley.

Mental Health Foundation (2002) *A Bright Future for All: Promoting Mental Health in Education*. London: MHF.

Mosley, J. (2001) *Quality Circle Time in the Primary Classroom*, vol. 1. Cambridge: LDA.

Mosley, J. (2004) *More Quality Circle Time: Evaluating Your Practice and Developing Creativity Within the Whole School Quality Circle Time Model*. Cambridge: LDA.

Music, G. (2011) *Nurturing Natures: Attachment and Children's Sociocultural and Brain Development*. Hove, East Sussex: Psychology Press.

Music, G. (2017) *Nurturing Natures: Attachment and Children's Sociocultural and Brain Development*, 2nd ed. Hove, East Sussex: Psychology Press.

National Children's Bureau (2014) *Mental Health and Emotional Wellbeing in Schools*. Available at: https://www.ncb.org.uk/sites/default/files/uploads/documents/Health_wellbeing_docs/policy_context_briefing_pewmhs_mental_health_and_emotional_well-being_in_schools_ncb_nov_14_final%20%281%29.pdf (accessed 29/7/19).

National Institute for Health and Care Excellence (NICE) (2015) *Looked-after Children and Young People*. Available at: https://www.nice.org.uk/guidance/PH28/chapter/1-Recommendations (accessed 25 July 2019).

Newman, T. (2004) as cited in Coleman, F. and Hagell, A. (2007) *Mental Health and Mental Disorders, Adolescence Risk and Resilience Against the Odds*. Chichester: John Wiley, p14.

NSPCC (2016) *Children Plagued by Low Self Esteem and Loneliness*. Available at: https://www.nspcc.org.uk/what-we-do/news-opinion/children-plagued-by-low-self-esteem-and-loneliness/?_t_id=1B2M2Y8AsgTpgAmY7PhCfg%3d%3d&_t_q=self+esteem&_t_tags=language%3aen%2csiteid%3a7

f1b9313-bf5e-4415-abf6-aaf87298c667&_t_ip=86.139.120.151&_t_hit.id=Nspcc_Web_Models_Pages_ NewsPage/_c7184244-9430-4a66-8ec5-3e3d507de048_en-GB&_t_hit.pos=1 (accessed June 2019).

Pearce, J. (1993) as cited in HAS Report (1995) *'Together We Stand': The Commissioning, Role and Management of CAMHS*. London: HMSO, p23.

Plummer, D. and Harper, A. (2007) *Helping Children to Build Self-esteem: A Photocopiable Activities Book*. London: Jessica Kingsley.

Rosa, G. (2019) *State of Children's Rights in England 2018. Briefing Paper 4 Safeguarding Children*. Available at: http://www.crae.org.uk/media/126988/B4_CRAE_SAFEGUARDING_2018_WEB.pdf (accessed June 2019)

Rutter, M. (1985) Resilience in the face of adversity: protective factors and resistance to psychiatric disorders. *British Journal of Psychiatry*, 147: 589–611.

Rutter, M. (1987) as cited in Werner, E. and Smith, R. (2001) *Journeys from Childhood to Midlife: Risk, Resilience and Recovery*. New York: Cornell, p3.

Rutter, M. (2006) Implications of resilience concepts for scientific understanding. *Annals of the New York Academy of Science*, 1094: 1–12.

Rutter, M. (2012) Resilience as a dynamic concept. *Development and Psychopathology*, 24: 335–344.

The Children's Society (2015) *The Good Childhood Report 2015*. Available at: www.childrenssociety.org.uk/sites/default/files/TheGoodChildhoodReport2015.pdf (accessed June 2019).

United Nations Convention on the Rights of the Child (1989) *Article 12*. Available at: https://downloads.unicef.org.uk/wp-content/uploads/2010/05/UNCRC_PRESS200910web.pdf?_ga=2.195589615.2130650609.1561407161-1394268396.1528870769 (accessed June 2019).

Weare, K. (2015) *What Works in Promoting Social and Emotional Well-being and Responding to Mental Health Problems in School?* London: National Children's Bureau.

Werner, E. and Smith, R.S. (2001) *Journeys from Childhood to Midlife: Risk, Resilience and Recovery*. New York: Cornell University Press.

Young Minds (2019) *Supporting Your Child's Self-esteem*. Available at: https://youngminds.org.uk/find-help/for-parents/parents-guide-to-support-a-z/parents-guide-to-support-self-esteem/ (accessed June 2019).

5

BULLYING

CHAPTER OBJECTIVES

By the end of this chapter you should be aware of:

- what bullying is and the scale of bullying in schools today;
- the need to have a zero tolerance towards bullying;
- the importance of establishing a positive culture to enhance mental health and well-being;
- some examples of good practice in supporting children.

TEACHERS' STANDARDS

This chapter supports the development of the following Teachers' Standards:

TS1: Set high expectations which inspire, motivate and challenge pupils

- Establish a safe and stimulating environment for pupils, rooted in mutual respect.

TS5: Adapt teaching to respond to the strengths of all pupils

- Demonstrate an awareness of the physical, social and intellectual development of children, and know how to adapt teaching to support pupils' education at different stages of development.

TS7: Manage behaviour effectively to ensure a good and safe learning environment

- Have clear rules and routines for behaviour in classrooms, and take responsibility for promoting good and courteous behaviour both in classrooms and around the school, in accordance with the school's behaviour policy.
- Have high expectations for behaviour, and establish a framework for discipline with a range of strategies, using praise, sanctions and rewards consistently and fairly.

S8: Fulfil wider professional responsibilities

- Make a positive contribution to the wider life and ethos of the school.
- Communicate effectively with parents with regard to pupils' achievements and well-being.

Part 2: Personal and professional conduct

- Having regard for the need to safeguard pupils' well-being, in accordance with statutory provisions.

Introduction

The chapter will consider the impact of external factors on a child or young person's mental health and well-being, specifically looking at the impact of bullying. The role of the school will be considered.

What is bullying?

The Anti-Bullying Alliance (2017) defines bullying as:

> 'the repetitive, intentional hurting of one person or group by another person or group, where the relationship involves an imbalance of power'. It can happen face-to-face or through cyberspace.

There is no legal definition of bullying. However, according to government guidance, it should be understood as *behaviour by an individual or group, repeated over time, that intentionally hurts another individual or group either physically or emotionally* (Department for Education, 2014, p6).

Bullying and having an experience of being bullied is extremely detrimental to well-being and will be one of the adverse childhood experiences we know to have lifelong effects. It must also be regarded as a safeguarding issue; an immediate and appropriate proportionate response is required when a bullying incident occurs. Camila Batmanghelidjh (2007), in her book *Shattered Lives: Children Who Live with Courage and Dignity*, states that no one hurts someone else who has not been hurt themselves, which is a useful rule of thumb to bear in mind when considering children who bully others.

Bullying in schools

All schools are legally required to try and prevent bullying. According to section 89 of the Education and Inspections Act 2006, maintained schools must adopt measures with a view to preventing bullying; they should form part of their behavioural polices and should be communicated to parents and students. The Education (Independent School Standards) Regulations 2014 deal with academies or other independent schools, and require proprietors of these schools to devise equivalent plans to prevent bullying (The Centre for Social Justice, 2016, p8).

The Centre for Social Justice (2016, p3) found that over 16,000 children between the ages of 11 and 15 are absent from state schools where bullying is the main reason for absence, a figure that rises to over 77,000 where bullying is cited as one of a number of reasons given for absence. Absenteeism leads to further isolation and compounds the damage caused by bullying, making it even harder to return to school. Almost a third of depression experienced by young adults in the UK is linked to bullying in teenage years. The psychological consequences of bullying can still manifest themselves almost 40 years after the event.

There has been a significant increase in the number of school exclusions over racist behaviour. Although this demonstrates that schools are tackling the problem, it shows an alarming reflection of our current society since the EU referendum in 2016 and continued anti-immigration rhetoric. NSPCC Childline has reported an increase in faith- and race-based bullying towards Muslim, Jewish, Christian, Black and Sikh children following terrorist attacks against children as young as 9.

Children reported they had resorted to self-harming and changing their appearance to manage the constant abuse and negative stereotyping (NSPCC, 2017). Race hate crime against children reached a 3-year high in 2019 according to Childline, with children aged 12–15 more likely to get in touch (NSPCC, 2019). Figures are no doubt the tip of the iceberg, with only a percentage of children seeking help.

It is vital that children and young people have the right to feel safe to attend school and to focus on their studies free from disruption and the fear of bullying. This will help them flourish not only academically but socially too. Schools and police have powers to stop bullying and have a responsibility to ensure children and young people are safe.

The Good Childhood Report 2016 (Children Society, 2016) gives us an indication of the scale of bullying and how it affects children, young people, parents, carers and teachers in school. From just under 6,000 respondents it became clear that a bullying culture can have a significant impact on the mental health and well-being of children and young people. Of those surveyed:

- 42 per cent had to take time off school because of bullying;

- 67 per cent felt depressed as a result of bullying;

- 90 per cent of the bullying took place at school;

- 57 per cent were bullied on Facebook;

- 38 per cent were bullied on Instagram;

- 32 per cent were bullied on Snapchat;

- 50 per cent of young people were bullied about their appearance.

The Department for Education (2018) *Bullying in England April 2013–March 2018 Analysis on 10–15 Year Olds from the Crime Survey for England and Wales* includes concerning up-to-date statistics. It reports that one in six children have been bullied, with verbal bullying being the most common type. Groups of children most likely to be bullied include:

- younger children (those aged 10–12 years);

- those of a white ethnic origin;

- those with a long-term illness or disability;

- those who received extra help at school;

- those living in the most deprived areas;

- those who had truanted from school in the previous 12 months;

- those who had been suspended or excluded from school in the previous 12 months;

- those living in one-adult households;

- those living in rented accommodation;

- those living outside London.

A total of 72 per cent of respondents felt their schools had dealt with the bullying well, which is promising, but still leaves a significant proportion that had not done so. It also shows a reduction from 78 per cent in 2014 and therefore remains a cause for concern and it is clearly an area for continued vigilance and improvement.

Are schools doing enough?

During Anti-bullying Week in November 2018, at an event hosted by Kidscape, children and parents made poignant remarks and noted that:

> *But the overriding, unanimous concern is that schools are not doing enough. Specifically, these parents feel their schools are downplaying the issue.*
>
> *Some don't even use the word bullying – one mother asked her school if they were doing anything for Anti Bullying Week and she was told they didn't like the word.*
>
> *An argument can be made for this in terms of focusing on kindness or highlighting positive behaviour. But it is dangerous to speak in euphemisms.*
>
> *A refusal to use the 'B' word can be very damaging for the victims. Framing things as a 'falling out' rather than bullying – resolutely refusing to call it what it is – denies the child's experience. You're effectively gaslighting them.*
>
> *It also puts an unreasonable onus on the child to prove it's happening. An example being that one victim was brought face to face with their perpetrator, who then denied it all, and the matter was concluded. The result here is the child in question feels like they made it up, and the school is effectively mirroring the bullying behaviour.*
>
> *But it's never the victim's fault.*
>
> *If anyone who was bullied at school could change one thing, it would be not blaming themselves. The danger is if you deny a child's experience, if you erase the word 'bullying', you erase the truth for that victim, and the child is left with no one to blame but themselves.*
>
> *Schools have a responsibility to grasp the nettle. Admitting that bullying happens does not mean they have failed as school. But by denying its existence they are failing the victims, and they are perpetuating a culture of fear, denial and blame.*

There clearly remains a lot of work to do, and as Gemma noted at the event:

> *There's no quick fix. Today is the start of a journey.*

> (Thompson, 2018)

The State of Children's Rights in England 2018 report recommends an intensification of efforts to tackle bullying, including through teaching human rights, building capacities of students and staff members to respect diversity and involving children in initiatives aimed at eliminating bullying (King, 2019, p4).

Serious concerns have also been raised about aspects of the Prevent strategy and its impact on education. There is now a statutory duty on teachers and many public servants to report signs of radicalisation and that this is stifling fundamental rights and freedoms of children, including freedom of expression and belief. It has been demonstrated that Muslim children have been disproportionately impacted and fear being reported for expressing political and religious views. The National Union of Teachers passed a motion rejecting the Prevent strategy in 2016 (Children's Rights Alliance for England, 2016).

Bullying and mental health

The Royal College of Psychiatrists (2017) suggests bullying can have a direct impact on mental health and well-being, leading to depression, feelings of loneliness and lack of confidence in individuals. Given all this concerning evidence, it seems vital that all schools have robust systems for identifying and dealing with bullying because of the negative effect it has on individuals. Sadly, in cases of self-harm and completed suicides amongst children and young people, bullying is frequently cited as a trigger or a reason and is often a significant contributing factor, as discussed in Chapter 1. The sad death of Molly Russell aged 14 was such an example; her father identified bullying on social media as the cause (BBC News, 2019).

Each setting should have a zero acceptance policy of any such type of bullying if we are to help our children and young people deal with such a serious issue.

Bullying and the teacher workforce

With the release of the Department for Education (2010) White Paper, *The Importance of Teaching*, the government made it clear that poor discipline is responsible for decreased levels of retention within the teaching workforce. Linked to staff leaving the profession, with good teachers being forced out of the classroom, is the lack of respect towards teaching staff in general and the impact it has on their health and well-being. The White Paper led to a number of key recommendations to ensure schools create a:

culture of respect and safety, with zero tolerance of bullying, clear boundaries, good pastoral care and early intervention to address problems

and an expectation that head teachers

take a strong stand against bullying – particularly prejudice-based racist, sexist and homophobic bullying.

(Department for Education, 2010, p32)

Bullying and Ofsted

The new Ofsted *School Inspection Handbook* (2019) focuses on 'behaviour and attitudes' as a core area:

The behaviour and attitudes judgement considers how leaders and staff create a safe, calm, orderly and positive environment in the school and the impact this has on the behaviour and attitudes of pupils.

(Ofsted, 2019, p51)

When judging schools' performance on 'behaviour and attitudes', Ofsted will consider factors that have been shown (through research evidence) to contribute most strongly to the development of positive attitudes and behaviours in school children. These include:

> An environment in which pupils feel safe, and in which bullying, discrimination and peer-on-peer abuse – online or offline – are not accepted and are dealt with quickly, consistently and effectively whenever they occur.

(Ofsted, 2019, p51)

Ofsted continues to assess whether children feel safe in school and are protected from bullying in the playground, corridors and classroom. Record keeping of bullying incidents will be monitored as well as, more importantly, how the school has responded to these incidences to ensure a zero-tolerance approach. Evidence will also be reviewed from parents and carers. The grade descriptors for a school to obtain 'outstanding' for 'behaviour and attitudes' mean that schools need to meet all criteria and, beyond that, have to make certain that:

- *Pupils behave with consistently high levels of respect for others. They play a highly positive role in creating a school environment in which commonalities are identified and celebrated, difference is valued and nurtured, and bullying, harassment and violence are never tolerated.*
- *Pupils consistently have highly positive attitudes and commitment to their education. They are highly motivated and persistent in the face of difficulties. Pupils make a highly positive, tangible contribution to the life of the school and/or the wider community. Pupils actively support the well-being of other pupils.*
- *Pupils behave consistently well, demonstrating high levels of self-control and consistently positive attitudes to their education. If pupils struggle with this, the school takes intelligent, fair and highly effective action to support them to succeed in their education.*

(Ofsted, 2019, pp54–55)

The importance of creating a positive culture

In 2012 Ofsted produced a document entitled *No Place for Bullying* to give schools guidance on how to create a positive culture and prevent and tackle bullying. It is appreciated the guidance is now over 6 years old (2012) at the time of writing (2019/20). Yet it remains entirely relevant and even more urgent for schools to act appropriately and swiftly, given the information and the more recent statistics mentioned above. The document outlined a national survey which looked at how effective schools were in tackling bullying through a whole school approach.

The document's Executive Summary outlines the breadth of the survey:

> Between September and December 2011, Her Majesty's Inspectors visited 37 primary schools and 19 secondary schools for the main part of the survey. The schools were located in both urban and rural areas and varied in size and type. At their previous Ofsted inspection none had been judged to be inadequate. Altogether, inspectors held formal discussions with 1,357 pupils and 797 staff.

(Ofsted, 2012)

It goes on to highlight that school inspectors found that the schools visited fell into three distinct groups.

Group one

In the best schools, the culture and ethos in the school were very positive. The schools' expectations and rules clearly spelled out how pupils should interact with each other. Respect for individual differences had a high profile. In these schools pupils developed empathy, understood the effect that bullying could have on people, and took responsibility for trying to prevent bullying.

(Ofsted, 2012)

It is clear that the approach schools in this group had to planning and delivering the curriculum supported the development of these positive attitudes. Pupils had numerous opportunities to build their understanding of diversity, and to work through strategies to prevent bullying.

The way in which these schools dealt with bullying was also important:

These schools recorded bullying incidents carefully and analysed them to look for trends and patterns. They then used this information to plan the next steps. The action they took was firm and often imaginative. If pupils had been bullied then they felt very confident that action was taken and it stopped promptly. Governors were well informed and questioning about bullying.

(Ofsted, 2012)

Group two

The largest number of schools fell into the second group.

These schools had a positive culture and most pupils were considerate of each other. Many of the schools had developed a range of effective strategies for pupils to learn about moral and social issues. However, their practice was not as consistent as that of the strongest schools and on occasion had areas of relative weakness.

(Ofsted, 2012)

It was this lack of consistency that meant that their practice in this area fell short. The report also mentions that the curriculum offered in these schools did not include the same opportunities for pupils to learn about diversity. They also differed in the way in which they dealt with bullying. Their approach was less robust and consistent so they were not able to plan and implement next steps in the same way.

Group three

In this smaller third group of schools the curriculum did not develop pupils' understanding of diversity. Schools in this group also lacked a positive whole school culture and ethos. Incidents of bullying were dealt with reactively and thus there was little planned preventative work.

Key to ensuring a positive culture was an embedded high-quality behaviour policy which was consistently and regularly used by staff and teachers. There was also sufficient training for staff on the policy, its implementation and bullying in general.

Training for staff

Training for teachers and support staff is essential in order to:

- build expertise, knowledge and confidence in using inclusive language;

- develop skills in how to deal effectively with negative behaviours.

Ofsted analysed responses from a survey (questionnaire) in which 305 teachers and 160 support staff were asked about the training on bullying (see Table 5.1).

Table 5.1 *Table showing the responses from 305 teachers and 160 support staff who met with inspectors and completed a brief questionnaire about the training they had received on the issue of bullying*

	Teachers (%)		Support staff (%)	
	Primary (129)	Secondary (176)	Primary (104)	Secondary (56)
Bullying in general	80	95	82	88
Racism and related bullying	55	56	33	66
Homophobia and related bullying	29	41	21	55
Aspects of disability and bullying	44	45	28	48
Sexist language and behaviour	30	32	27	50
Sexual bullying	27	30	15	45
Cyberbullying	64	77	51	63
Other prejudice-based actions and related bullying	27	27	15	36

Source: Ofsted, 2012.

The table shows that not all members of staff had training in bullying since beginning working in schools. It also shows that training, when it had been provided, did not cover all areas of bullying consistently. The training of staff is key to ensuring the development and embedding of a positive culture across the school.

The importance of a clear vision shared by all in the school, with clear values permeating through the curriculum and school environment, is clear. Not only should a behaviour policy underpin such a positive school culture for dealing with and preventing bullying and the effects it has on mental health and well-being, it should be remembered that such a policy is a statutory requirement for all schools (Department for Education, 2012).

Establishing the culture and communicating expectations

Evidence from the National Children's Bureau (2016), *A Whole School Framework for Emotional Well-Being and Mental Health*, reinforces the importance of a whole school approach in order to embed a culture of acceptance and respect for children and young people. The Senior Management Team in a school are responsible for ensuring that shared values are made clear to all stakeholders, including children, young people, staff, parents, governors and the wider community, and that all buy into ensuring that these are manifested in the life of the school. This may be achieved by establishing a clear vision of what the school stands for. Doing so will ensure that children and young people feel part of a safe community and that they understand what is acceptable and not acceptable behaviour, with such expectations being continually reinforced by staff. Clear school policies for behaviour linked to bullying should be consistently embedded across the whole school and shared with parents on the school website.

As part of the United Nations Convention on the Rights of the Child (UNCRC, 1989) Article 12 and as part of good practice, schools should ensure that the pupil voice is valued as policy through school councils so that issues can be voiced in a supportive way. This ensures that children and young people are active participants in their own educational experience. Pupils who are vulnerable should be identified and a clear strategy for support highlighted and embedded in the Special Educational Needs and Disability policy.

Research shown in the Department for Education (2014) document *Mental Health and Behaviour in Schools* clearly identifies factors that put children and young people at greater risk of mental health issues (see Table 5.2). One of these factors is low self-esteem, which in a school environment could be due to bullying, discrimination, peer pressure or breakdown in friendship groups (see Chapter 4). The report identified that schools could put protective factors in place such as clear behaviour and bullying policies as well as a whole school approach to promoting positive mental health and well-being, as discussed in Chapter 1.

Bullying is a sad and concerning aspect for many children and young people in our schools and the same could be said for staff too. We all have a responsibility to provide schools that are safe and engaging environments for our young people where they can flourish. Part of that responsibility includes a whole school approach with a zero-tolerance policy towards bullying and where perpetrators are dealt with and appropriately supported to change. Protection against bullying, and support of victims where it has occurred, is of utmost importance given its detrimental lifelong effects.

KEY REFLECTION

- How is your school vision being effectively translated into meaningful learning experiences for all the pupils and what factors impact on these in your school?
- How up to date and relevant are your policies given the changing face of bullying?

Table 5.2 Table showing the risk and protective factors that are believed to be associated with mental health outcomes

	Risk factors	Protective factors
In the child	• Genetic influences	• Secure attachment experience
	• Low IQ and learning disabilities	• Outgoing temperament as an infant

(Continued)

Table 5.2 (Continued)

	Risk factors	Protective factors
	• Specific development delay or neuro-diversity • Communication difficulties • Difficult temperament • Physical illness • Academic failure • Low self-esteem	• Good communication skills, sociability • Being a planner and having a belief in control • Humour • A positive attitude • Experiences of success and achievement • Faith or spirituality • Capacity to reflect
In the family	• Overt parental conflict including domestic violence • Family breakdown (including where children are taken into care or adopted) • Inconsistent or unclear discipline • Hostile and rejecting relationships • Failure to adapt to a child's changing needs • Physical, sexual, emotional abuse, or neglect • Parental psychiatric illness • Parental criminality, alcoholism or personality disorder • Death and loss – including loss of friendship	• At least one good parent–child relationship (or one supportive adult) • Affection • Clear, consistent discipline • Support for education • Supportive long-term relationship or the absence of severe discord
In the school	• Bullying including online (cyber) • Discrimination • Breakdown in or lack of positive friendships • Deviant peer influences • Peer pressure • Peer on peer abuse • Poor pupil to teacher/school staff relationships	• Clear policies on behaviour and bullying • Staff behaviour policy (also known as code of conduct) • 'Open door' policy for children to raise problems • A whole school approach to promoting good mental health • Good pupil to teacher/school staff relationships • Positive classroom management • A sense of belonging • Positive peer influences • Positive friendships • Effective safeguarding and Child Protection policies • An effective early help process • Understand their role in and be part of effective multi-agency working

	Risk factors	Protective factors
		• Appropriate procedures to ensure staff are confident to raise concerns about policies and processes, and know they will be dealt with fairly and effectively
In the community	• Socio-economic disadvantage	• Wider supportive network
	• Homelessness	• Good housing
	• Disaster, accidents, war or other overwhelming events	• High standard of living
	• Discrimination	• High morale school with positive policies for behaviour, attitudes and anti-bullying
	• Exploitation, including by criminal gangs and organised crime groups, trafficking, online abuse, sexual exploitation and the influences of extremism leading to radicalisation	• Opportunities for valued social roles
		• Range of sport/leisure activities
	• Other significant life events	

Source: Department for Education, 2014.

KEY REFLECTIONS

- How does your school promote a culture where bullying is not accepted?
- What strategies do you currently have in place to support children and young people's well-being?
- How can the school curriculum be used to support aspects of individuals' resilience?

CHAPTER SUMMARY

- Bullying is a serious safeguarding issue and is highly likely to have a lasting impact on children and young people's mental health and well-being.
- Schools should have a zero-tolerance approach to bullying in whatever form.
- Schools have a responsibility to protect and support victims of bullying and act appropriately in tackling perpetrators.
- There needs to be a whole school approach to bullying with clear expectations for individuals' behaviour.

FURTHER READING

Anti-Bully Alliance (2014) *Bullying at School*. Available at: http://www.anti-bullyingalliance.org.uk/media/7468/bullying-and-the-law-may-14.pdf (accessed 12 January 2017).

Anti-Bullying Alliance (no date) *Bullying and Mental Health: Guidance for Teachers and Other Professionals: SEN and Disability: Developing Effective Anti-bullying Practice*. Available at: https://www.anti-bullying alliance.org.uk/sites/default/files/field/attachment/Mental-health-and-bullying-module-FINAL.pdf (accessed June 2019).

Government Equalities Office (2014) *Body Confidence: Findings from the British Social Attitude Survey – October 2014*. Available at: https://www.gov.uk/government/publications/body-confidence-a-rapid-evidence-assessment-of-the-literature (accessed 5 February 2017).

Gov.UK (2016) *Bullying at School*. Available at: https://www.gov.uk/bullying-at-school/bullying-outside-school (accessed 12 January 2017).

Gov.UK (2016) *Keeping Children Safe in Education: Statutory Guidance for Schools and Colleges*. Available at: https://www.gov.uk/government/publications/keeping-children-safe-in-education--2 (accessed 2 August 2019).

━━ REFERENCES ━━

Anti-Bullying Alliance (2017) *Bullying and the Law Briefing*. Available at: https://www.anti-bullying alliance.org.uk/sites/default/files/field/attachment/Bullying%20and%20the%20Law%20FINAL_0.pdf (accessed June 2019).

Bandura, A. (1977) Self-efficacy: towards a unifying theory of behavioural change. *Psychology Review*, 84(2): 191–215.

Bandura, A. (1997) *Self-efficacy: The Exercise of Control*. New York: W.H. Freeman.

Batmanghelidjh, C. (2007) *Shattered Lives: Children Who Live with Courage and Dignity*. London: Jessica Kingsley.

BBC News (2019) Focus: Instagram 'helped kill my daughter'. Available at: https://www.bbc.co.uk/iplayer/episode/p06z00z8/focus-instagram-helped-kill-my-daughter (accessed 25 July 2019).

Bloom, B.S., Engelhart, M.D., Furst, E.J., Hill, W.H. and Krathwohl, D.R. (1956) *Taxonomy of Educational Objectives: The Classification of Educational Goals. Handbook 1: Cognitive Domain*. New York: David McKay.

Bunting, M. (2006) *Looking After Looked After Children, Sharing Emerging Practice*. London: Young Minds. Available at: https://issuu.com/philayres/docs/lacmentalhealth (accessed June 2019).

Children's Rights Alliance for England (2016) *State of Children's Rights in England 2016. Briefing 6, Education, Leisure and Cultural Activities*. Available at: http://www.crae.org.uk/media/118310/crae_scr2016_b6_education-web.pdf (accessed June 2019).

Children Society (2016) *The Good Childhood Report 2016*. Available at: http://www.childrenssociety.org.uk/sites/default/files/pcr090_mainreport_web.pdf (accessed June 2019).

Claxton, G. (2002) *Building Learning Power: Helping Young People Become Better Learners*. Bristol: TLO.

Department for Education (2010) *The Importance of Teaching: The Schools White Paper*. Available at: https://www.gov.uk/government/uploads/system/uploads/attachment_data/file/175429/CM-7980.pdf (accessed 1 January 2017).

Department for Education (2012) *Ensuring Good Behaviour in Schools: A Summary for Head Teachers, Governing Bodies, Teachers, Parents and Pupils*. Available at: http://dera.ioe.ac.uk/14113/1/Ensuring%20 Good%20Behaviour%20in%20Schools%20-%20A%20summary%20for%20heads%20governing%20 bodies%20teachers%20parents%20and%20pupils.pdf (accessed June 2019).

Department for Education (2013) *The National Curriculum in England*. Available at: https://www. gov.uk/government/uploads/system/uploads/attachment_data/file/425601/PRIMARY_national_ curriculum.pdf (accessed June 2019).

Department for Education (2014) *Mental Health and Behaviour in Schools*. DFE-00435-2014. Available at: https://www.gov.uk/government/uploads/system/uploads/attachment_data/file/508847/Mental_ Health_and_Behaviour_-_advice_for_Schools_160316.pdf (accessed 8 February 2017).

Department for Education (2018) *Bullying in England April 2013–March 2018: Analysis on 10–15 Year Olds from the Crime Survey for England and Wales*. Available at: https://assets.publishing.service.gov.uk/ government/uploads/system/uploads/attachment_data/file/754959/Bullying_in_England_ 2013-2018.pdf (accessed June 2019).

Gonzales-DeHass, A.R. and Willems, P.P. (2013) *Theories in Educational Psychology: Concise Guide to Meaning and Practice*. Plymouth: Rowman & Littlefield Education.

Grotberg, E. (1995) *A Guide to Promoting Reslience in Children: Strengthening the Human Spirit*. Available at: http://www.bibalex.org/Search4Dev/files/283337/115519.pdf (accessed June 2019).

Hewitt, S., Buxton, S. and Thomas, A. (2017) *Teacher Education Advancement Network Journal University of Cumbria* 9(1): 22–35. Available at: file:///C:/Users/burm1/AppData/Local/Packages/Microsoft. MicrosoftEdge_8wekyb3d8bbwe/TempState/Downloads/345-Article%20Text-827-1-10-20170112%20 (1).pdf (accessed July 2019)

Jennings, S. (1992) *Dramatherapy with Families, Groups and Individuals: Waiting in the Wings*. London: Jessica Kingsley Publications.

King, L. (2019) *The State of Children's Rights in England 2018. Briefing 6, Education, Cultural and Leisure Activities*. Available at: http://www.crae.org.uk/media/126994/B6_CRAE_EDUCATION_2018_WEB.pdf (accessed June 2019).

National Children's Bureau (2016) A whole school framework for emotional well-being and mental health NCTL (2014) *Closing the Gap with the New Primary National Curriculum*. Reference DFE-374. Available at: https://www.gov.uk/government/uploads/system/uploads/attachment_data/file/349288/ closing-the-gap-with-the-new-primary-national-curriculum.pdf. (accessed 28 January 2017).

NSPCC (2017) *Childline Sees Spike in Counselling Sessions About Race and Faith-based Bullying*. Available at: https://www.nspcc.org.uk/what-we-do/news-opinion/childline-spike-counselling-sessions-race-faith-based-bullying/?utm_source=twitter_nspcc&utm_medium=nspccsocialmedia&utm_ campaign=owntwitter_tweet (accessed June 2019).

NSPCC (2019) *Race Hate Crimes Against Children Reach 3 Year High*. Available at: https://www.nspcc.org. uk/what-we-do/news-opinion/race-hate-crimes-against-children-reach-3-year-high/ (accessed June 2019).

Ofsted (2012) *No Place for Bullying: How Schools Create a Positive Culture and Prevent and Tackle Bullying*. Ref: 110179. Available at: https://www.gov.uk/government/uploads/system/uploads/attachment_ data/file/413234/No_place_for_bullying.pdf (accessed 12 January 2017).

Ofsted (2015) *School Inspection Handbook*. Available at: https://www.gov.uk/government/publications/school-inspection-handbook-from-september-2015 (accessed June 2019).

Ofsted (2019) *School Inspection Handbook*. Available at: https://www.gov.uk/government/publications/school-inspection-handbook-eif

Royal College of Psychiatrists (2017) *The Emotional Cost of Bullying: Information for Parents, Carers and Anyone who Works with Young People*. Available at: http://www.rcpsych.ac.uk/healthadvice/parentsandyouthinfo/parentscarers/bullyingandemotion.aspx (accessed June 2019).

The Centre for Social Justice (2016) *Bullying and Self-exclusion: Who Cares?* Roundtable report. Available at: https://www.centreforsocialjustice.org.uk/core/wp-content/uploads/2016/11/Bullying-RT-Report-1.pdf (accessed June 2019).

Thompson, C. (2018) *The Children's Commissioner for England, Anti-bullying Week: The B Word*. Available at: https://www.childrenscommissioner.gov.uk/2018/11/16/anti-bullying-week-the-b-word/ (accessed June 2019).

UNCRC (1989) *Convention on the Rights of the Child*. Available at: https://www.unicef.org/crc/files/Rights_overview.pdf (accessed June 2019).

Yeager, D. and Dweck, C. (2012) Mindsets that promote resilience: when students believe that personal characteristics can be developed. *Educational Psychologist*, 47(4): 302–314.

6

SOCIAL MEDIA, CYBERBULLYING AND BODY IMAGE

CHAPTER OBJECTIVES

By the end of this chapter you should be aware of:

- the importance of establishing a positive culture to enhance mental health and well-being;
- the influence (both positive and negative) of social media on children and young people's mental health and well-being;
- the need to have a zero tolerance towards cyberbullying and the impact of cyberbullying on children and young people;
- using personal, social, health and economic (PSHE) education to promote positive body image in classrooms.

TEACHERS' STANDARDS

This chapter supports the development of the following Teachers' Standards:

TS1: Set high expectations which inspire, motivate and challenge pupils

- Establish a safe and stimulating environment for pupils, rooted in mutual respect.

TS5: Adapt teaching to respond to the strengths and needs of all pupils

- Demonstrate an awareness of the physical, social and intellectual development of children, and know how to adapt teaching to support pupils' education at different stages of development.

TS7: Manage behaviour effectively to ensure a good and safe learning environment

- Have clear rules and routines for behaviour in classrooms, and take responsibility for promoting good and courteous behaviour both in classrooms and around the school, in accordance with the school's behaviour policy.
- Have high expectations for behaviour, and establish a framework for discipline with a range of strategies, using praise, sanctions and rewards consistently and fairly.

TS8: Fulfil wider professional responsibilities

- Make a positive contribution to the wider life and ethos of the school.
- Communicate effectively with parents with regard to pupils' achievements and well-being.

Part Two: Personal and professional conduct

- Having regard for the need to safeguard pupils' well-being, in accordance with statutory provisions.

Introduction

This chapter will examine the issues and challenges around children and young people's use of social media and its contribution to their mental health and well-being. The chapter will also consider the impact of external factors on a child or young person's mental health and well-being, specifically looking at the impact of cyberbullying and how body image can influence individuals' feelings towards a sense of positive well-being. The role of the school will be considered and links will also be made to the role of teachers, parents and carers in the positive use of social media sites and the use of phones and tablets.

Children and young people's use of social media and its influence on mental health and well-being

Social media use is now an integral part of children and young people's lives and is felt by many of them to be as important as breathing. Research indicates that 91 per cent of 16–24-year-olds use social media (Office for National Statistics, 2016) and the most common platforms they use are Facebook, Google+, LinkedIn, Pinterest, Instagram and Snapchat (Royal Society for Public Health, 2017), although this changes and updates constantly. Primary school children, by Years 5 and 6, usually have access to their own mobile phone and use social media as a way of cementing their friendships (Glazzard and Mitchell, 2018). The most common social media sites used by this age range are Snapchat, Instagram, Musical.ly and WhatsApp (Children's Commissioner, 2018). There is a need for teachers and parents alike to keep abreast of technology development to support children and young people's learning, to embrace the opportunities of the internet and to identify and mitigate the dangers in order to keep safe online.

Young people's use of technology in particular is felt to be affected by industry, advertising and the media. These stakeholders all play a critical role in promoting positive mental health (Glazzard and Mitchell, 2018). Social media is not often thought about in a positive way and it is important to balance out the positives of the internet and social media use with the negatives.

Recent research has suggested that social media and the internet should be used in a positive way to target young people in promoting well-being, prevent mental illness and support those with diagnosed conditions (O'Reilly et al., 2018). An example of this is an NHS-approved app called Calm Harm, created to combat the urge to self-harm, which has been downloaded more than 124,000 times; four out of five downloads during the last 18 months have been by young women aged 10–23 (Krause, 2019). However, an app cannot replace face-to-face pastoral care or the benefits of communicating with an understanding adult at school. It also ultimately increases screen time and this is at odds with wider and emerging issues (*The Lancet*, 2019).

Celebrity culture can promote ideas and provide thought-provoking material that encourages young people to seek out further positive mental health information, e.g. Zoella and her video blog about anxiety; Stormzy and his thoughts and experiences of depression.

In relation to the way social media is used by children and young people, research suggests that passive social media use (browsing other people's online content) may decrease well-being, whereas active social media use (posting content and interacting with others) may actually increase well-being (Lin et al., 2016).

Self-harm rates are high and rising, particularly among young girls, and the combination of social media's incentives to be noticed and a lack of effective regulation can be toxic and may be contributing to this rise (Davie, 2019 as cited by Hymas, 2019). The suicide of a 14-year-old British girl in 2017 (see Chapter 5) highlighted concerns regarding the ease of access to explicit self-harm images on Instagram and other platforms.

The UK government's White Paper *Online Harms* puts forward plans for a regulatory framework for online safety to keep children and young people safer online with clear safety standards, reporting requirements and enforcement powers (HM Government, 2019).

Fardouly and Vartanian (2016) suggest that more time spent on social media by young people can be linked to poorer body image and more depressive symptoms (McCrae et al., 2017) and that girls in particular are twice as likely to show signs of depressive symptoms linked to the use of social media compared to boys at age 14 (UK Millennium Cohort Study, 2019). However, there are less consistent links with other mental health symptoms, including anxiety (Prizant-Passal et al., 2016). A recent study examining links between parental control over the time preadolescents spend on social media demonstrated that greater parental control may be associated with better preadolescent mental health; however further longitudinal research is needed (Fardouly et al., 2018).

Cyberbullying

Bullying is behaviour by an individual or group, repeated over time, that intentionally hurts another individual or group either physically or emotionally. It can take many forms (for instance, cyberbullying via text messages, social media or gaming, which can include the use of images and videos) (Department for Education, 2017). Evidence suggests cyberbullying is on the rise, with Childline reporting an increase of 12 per cent of cases relating to cyberbullying in 2016–17 compared to the previous year (NSPCC, 2017). In addition, the number of children and young people who have experienced bullying online has increased by 88 per cent in 5 years (NSPCC, 2016).

Research into whether trends in relation to age, gender, race and sexuality found in offline bullying are mirrored in cases of cyberbullying is limited. However, a survey by the Health and Social Care Information Centre (HSIC) revealed that twice as many girls (19 per cent) than boys (10 per cent) reported being a victim of cyberbullying in 2014 (HSCIC, 2015). One explanation offered is that: *Boys are more overt on social media, whereas girls bully by exclusion, which means there is an elevated chance for girls to be perpetrators and victims* (Papadopoulos, 2018). Li (2006) explains that this may be due to differences in conversational styles and gender roles in society; males tend not to ask for help or discuss problems, viewing this as a sign of weakness, whereas girls are not likely to take this into consideration.

It is important to bear in mind that the majority of children and young people do not experience cyberbullying and this is across the age groups. However the likelihood of experiencing cyberbullying appears to increase with age; in younger age groups cruel comments are more common (The Royal Foundation Taskforce on the Prevention of Cyberbullying, 2017). The increased availability of new technologies has also been associated with a rise in cyberbullying (Young Minds, 2016) and research demonstrates an increase in the use of group messaging services (WhatsApp, Instagram, Facebook Messenger) for bullying and harassment (Ofcom, 2016).

Currently there is an upward trend in internet usage amongst children and young people; this correlates with the increasing concern regarding the dangers of the internet (Subrahmanyam and Greenfield, 2008; Ofcom, 2013). These dangers are particularly related to exposure to inappropriate content, cyberbullying and making harmful contacts online (Valkenburg and Peter, 2010). Research also demonstrates that there is a need to balance the opportunities of the internet with the dangers as well as to educate parents and carers regarding the positive aspects of the internet, rather than purely sensationalising the dangers (Tynes, 2007).

Given the recent rise in ownership of mobile devices by children, and their involvement in aspects of social media, it seems inevitable that statistics such as those detailed earlier are unlikely to improve immediately. As the Department for Education (2017, p8) suggests:

> *Cyber-bullying is a different form of bullying and can happen at all times of the day, with a potentially bigger audience, and more accessories as people forward on content at a click.*

Sharples et al. (2009) suggest that children are well aware of internet dangers such as cyberbullying but are not trusted to self-regulate their behaviour. Parents are out of date and unable to impose appropriate safeguards, and schools are balancing the use of the internet for creativity, community and personal learning with their pupils' safety. Therefore children and young people's online activity becomes a tool for attributing blame and can be viewed with a sense of unease and distrust by adults, leaving children and young people to negotiate this themselves (Duerager and Livingstone, 2012). With these perspectives in mind, children and young people can either be seen as vulnerable, with the internet posing a risk to their cognitive and social development, or as competent and creative, IT-literate and in need of a rich, stimulating online environment. Livingstone (2009) argues that it is these historical changes to childhood that reposition children in society and can even impede their passage to adulthood.

> *Excessive use of social media when combined with bullying has been linked to poor mental health problems. Felix Alexander was a 17-year-old who took his life after years of relentless bullying. Social media takes away the boundaries that school, social groups or communities used to provide. Online bullying that no longer stops at the end of the school day can seem relentless and 24/7 in nature when it happens.*
>
> (Children's Commissioner, 2016)

For schools, professionals and children and young people, cyberbullying can be linked to threats and intimidation, harassment, unwanted peer pressure and unauthorised access to accounts. As Childnet International (2016) suggests, a disproportionate number of individuals with special education needs and disabilities and learners identifying as gay, lesbian, bisexual or transgender are affected by cyberbullying.

For schools, cyberbullying can be at the root of issues allied to children and young people's feelings of positive self-worth and well-being, and can also be linked to safeguarding issues such as downloading inappropriate web content and sexting (sending an individual explicit images or messages via a mobile device). Research demonstrates that children and young people's attitudes to sexting varies, from those who do not see it as a major issue to those who deem it potentially damaging or illegal (Lenhart, 2009). The issue is not helped by unclear terminology, exaggerated findings and less emphasis on reasons for sexting (Lounsbury et al., 2011).

Cyberbullying content and activities may be illegal given they may involve the inclusion and distribution of indecent materials. Such illegal usage may fall under the Communications Act 2003, Section 127, where it is considered a crime to send an electronic message which is of a grossly offensive nature or is indecent, obscene or even of a menacing character (NSPCC, 2017). Should any school believe that the content or activity linked to the internet in schools is illegal, then they should contact the police for help and support as soon as possible, as well as following any suitable safeguarding practices. The Professionals Online Safety Helpline can provide schools with free advice and guidance relating to any cyberbullying concerns. Importantly, schools should remember that they also have powers under the Education Act 2011 for teaching professionals to tackle cyberbullying by providing them with the authority to search for inappropriate content on electronic devices.

Childnet International (2016, p12) suggests that in order to start dealing with such issues, schools should consider the following proactive measures:

- promote a shared understanding and awareness about cyberbullying;

- keep policies up to date and current;

- make reporting easier so as to stop the incident from escalating and to remove the items from circulation;

- promote the positive uses of technology;

- work with key safeguarding authorities such as the police and the local authority to gain support in terms of guidance and training;

- in England, use the Computing Programmes of Study for primary and secondary schools to promote internet safety;

- use the citizenship curriculum, PSHE, as well as religious education;

- make individuals aware of school sanctions that may follow if cyberbullying is found to be present in such settings;

- involve parents so that they too can support the promotion to eradicate such behaviours.

Research by Phippen (2016) identified, when examining online policy and practice, that almost 60 per cent of schools had no engagement regarding online safety issues with respect to their community and that 55 per cent of school governors had not been trained in online safety issues. Clearly, schools should work to involve other stakeholders so that they too can help educate children and young people as well as promote online safety for the children and young people in their care. In order to make the right decisions, children and young people need to feel empowered with the correct knowledge and confidence to act accordingly. Katz (2012) suggests that internet safety educators should build on the child or young person's self-efficacy and autonomy and find out what they know in order to be successful.

In relation to supporting parents and carers in keeping their child safe online, research demonstrates that children and young people who talked about internet safety with their parents were more knowledgeable and confident regarding appropriate action (Fleming et al., 2006). Therefore parents and carers should be encouraged to talk with their child about the internet and usage and promote the positives whilst being mindful and vigilant of the dangers.

The South West Grid for Learning has produced free to access support materials, along with curricular guidance, linked to supporting and improving digital literacy. This encourages individuals to think critically, as well as to promote safe, responsible participation in our digital world. The materials may be found at **https://digital-literacy.org.uk/**. Such material may also support schools' work in their computing curriculum, which will no doubt aim to provide online safety education as part of its delivery. Further information regarding online safety linked to the computing curriculum may be found at **https://www.childnet.com/resources/online-safety-and-computing**.

KEY REFLECTIONS

- What is cyberbullying?
- How can cyberbullying affect mental health and well-being?
- What strategies and powers can schools use to support children and young people who have encountered cyberbullying?

Impact of social media: body image

Due to the increased pressures of social media, the prevalence of the printed image and their access to film and television, children and young people can now more easily access imagery and messages that not only reflect the way they 'should' look but also how they 'should' behave in order to satisfy the norms of what society portrays as being socially acceptable.

Major findings from the report *Somebody Like Me* (BEREAL, 2017, pp4–5) worryingly indicate that:

- Four in five young people (79 per cent) said how they look is important to them.

- Nearly two-thirds of young people (63 per cent) said what others think about the way they look is important to them.

- More than half of young people (52 per cent) said they often worry about the way they look.

- More than a third of young people (36 per cent) agreed they would do whatever it took to look good.

- Almost three in five young people (57 per cent) have gone on a diet, or would consider going on a diet, to change the way they look.

- One in ten young people (10 per cent) said they would consider plastic surgery to change the way they look.

It is also important not to assume that body image issues linked to an individual's well-being and mental health will be centred on girls alone. As the PSHE Association (2019, p7) suggests:

- Over half of girls and a quarter of boys think their peers have body image problems.

- One-third of young boys aged 8–12 are dieting to lose weight.

The Good Childhood Report (Children's Society, 2018) also provides an overview of variations and trends through an 8-year longitudinal study linked to the state of children's subjective well-being. One of the aspects being researched is the gender differences in satisfaction with appearance. A key finding was that since 2002 there has been a long-term trend of divergence in satisfaction with appearance for boys and girls, with girls becoming increasingly unhappy with their appearance, friends and marginally with life as a whole. Children were asked to talk about their feelings and the research found that a main theme was that how they looked was an important factor in determining their well-being.

With the proliferation of the use of social media such as Instagram, Snapchat, selfies and the growth of vloggers, girls in particular have access to images and videos presenting the rise of unattainable 'perfection' – how to have the perfect body, lifestyle, friends, clothes, make-up and beauty products.

Subscriptions to some of these vloggers on YouTube are increasing rapidly, with popular vloggers like Zoella having over 11 million followers. Linked to the influence that celebrities like Zoe Sugg (Zoella) have with young girls, MindEd unveiled her as one of their digital ambassadors in 2014 due to her videos talking about her own struggles with anxiety and panic attacks.

The attempt to dispel the myth of perfection is a positive way forward, allowing an opportunity for children and young people, particularly girls, to see that everyone has insecurities and problems; the important thing is that it is crucial to talk about them. However, as teachers, it is important to note when considering issues around body confidence that your use of language is crucial, and you should avoid commenting on changes to an individual's body, behaviour and appearance, even if such comments are of a positive nature. It is important that individuals are happy with their own personal qualities rather than constantly considering how others view them. As the National Advisory Group (2009, p43) suggests:

> *Teachers are important models for students and their language about their own body image or comments about others can inadvertently communicate negative body image messages to students.*

PSHE as a curriculum vehicle

School settings can play a significant role in supporting children and young people in the growth of improved body confidence and self-esteem as part of their current PSHE curriculum. This can be allied to aspects of schools' work on healthy lifestyles and the need to engage in physical activities.

The Ten Principles of PSHE Education (available at **www.pshe-association.org.uk**) show that good practice applied to any work relating to issues around body image should include:

- Plan a 'spiral programme' which introduces new and more challenging learning, while building on what has gone before, which reflects and meets the personal developmental needs of the children and young people.

- Start from where the children and young people are. For maximum impact involve them in the planning of your PSHE programme.

- Take a positive approach which does not attempt to induce shock or guilt.

- Provide opportunities for children and young people to make real decisions about their lives.

- Provide a safe and supportive learning environment where children and young people can develop the confidence to ask questions, challenge the information they are offered, draw on their own experience, express their views and opinions and put what they have learnt into practice in their own lives.

Due to body image being an area of increasing concern for children, young people, parents and teachers, the PSHE Association (2019) has updated teacher guidance in relation to the key standards in teaching about body image. This guidance offers teachers advice about the safe and confident teaching of body image within the PSHE curriculum.

As previously mentioned in this chapter, the values embedded throughout the school are vital for children to feel safe and happy. A culture of openness in the classroom, where children feel comfortable to talk about their feelings and worries, is the duty of the whole school. The language that we use in front of children needs careful consideration to ensure we are acting as positive role models and not reinforcing negative and unrealistic perceptions. Conversations that can easily occur in the classroom or corridors amongst adults about dieting, comments about particular parts of the body – 'fat shaming' – or talking about celebrities in the press can send mixed messages to children if we are working towards a positive body image programme in the school.

Consider the following case study and begin to establish ideas for practice and strategies your school might use to support the issue of positive body image.

CASE STUDY: PROMOTING POSITIVE BODY IMAGE

Oak Cottage Primary School was recently highlighted by Ofsted as a good-practice case study for teaching about body image as part of PSHE education. The case study is detailed by the PSHE Association (2019) with links to the school's approach and detailed lesson plans for Years 1–5.

The project began with training for staff and parents to highlight the impact of social media on perceptions of body image on children. From this a programme of work was developed with the option of additional staff training, if needed, linked to specific topics.

In Years 1 and 2, pupils begin to recognise similarities and differences between themselves and others. By encouraging positive self-esteem, they develop an appreciation of these differences. Pupils are taken on a journey with the support of a robot. They are asked to identify individual features about themselves and their peers and how to celebrate their originality. The robot supports the pupils by guiding them to recognise the importance of differences. They enjoy discussing what makes them 'special' and sharing this with others.

In Year 3, pupils discuss positive role models and the influence they have on them. This introduces the topic of the media. In Year 4, pupils begin to look more closely at how images of celebrities are changed using digital enhancement and airbrushing. They also begin to define what beauty means to them and how this may differ according to culture, race or religion. In Year 5, pupils begin to recognise the importance of physical appearance and become more aware of the differences between themselves and those around them. They openly discuss the influence the media has on them and identify celebrities that they would like to look like.

Children were encouraged to talk about their own experiences, expressing their own views and opinions in a safe learning environment. Work was encouraged to be shared with parents and carers at home to enable parents to be able to talk confidently about some of these issues with their children. Feedback from the children, staff and parents about this programme was extremely positive and children felt empowered to accept their own bodies and confident to challenge any negativity or stereotypical language.

Case study reflections

- What training has your staff had around body image?
- Does promoting issues around body image feature in your PSHE curriculum?
- How does your school communicate with parents around issues to do with body image?

The PSHE Association strongly recommends that when talking about body image in your classrooms this should dovetail with teaching around healthy eating and lifestyle in order for children to associate both together as a lifestyle choice. The PSHE Association (2019) has produced detailed guidance in terms of their Key Standards in Teaching about Body Image with this guidance linking to programmes of study around the themes of 'health and well-being', 'relationships' and 'living in the wider world' in Key Stages 1–4 (**https://www.pshe-association.org.uk/system/files/PSHE%20%E2%80%93%20Key%20standards%20in%20teaching%20about%20body%20image%2022nd%20April.pdf**). The importance of the pupil voice and the personalisation of the teaching content are crucial to the success of the programme – helping children to talk about things that are important to them without fear of bullying or embarrassment is a skill that teachers need to master. This links to the Ofsted/PSHE case study above where the first part of the programme was an intensive staff training session to ensure all adults were confident and equipped for the teaching programme.

Knowing your class will inform your decisions about content, but there are also other factors to consider, such as whether to teach single- or mixed-gender sessions and also whether there are children in your class who you know are affected by some of the issues being discussed. Ground rules about behaviour and a regular reinforcement of class and school values, as discussed earlier, will be crucial at this point to establish a safe and respectful environment.

Teachers have a duty to safeguard children, and one of the biggest concerns is around disclosure. Creating an open and honest environment needs to be balanced by clear rules which ensure children and young people understand that we do not discuss our own personal or private lives in the session, use names or put any peers or teachers on the spot. All children have the right to decide not to participate if they do not feel comfortable. Teachers cannot promise that information would not be shared if we felt a child was at risk of harm. Teachers should ensure they follow the school safeguarding policy.

As well as promoting this topic through the vehicle of PSHE there are various other ways in which children and young people can provide input into the content of the teaching programme. These include, for example, the use of worry boxes in classrooms, corridors or toilets, use of the school council or pupil leadership team and the use of Clickers using interactive whiteboards and completion of anonymised questionnaires. Curriculum subjects can be used to promote reflection on aspects of body image and confidence such as science linked to evolution, inheritance and history, and how, through diet and lifestyle, our appearance and bodies have changed. In addition to this, much valuable advice and support for schools can be found from BEREAL, who have produced an extremely useful toolkit for schools to help support and tackle issues around body confidence. This can be found at **www.berealcampaign.co.uk/schools**.

CHAPTER SUMMARY

- Cyberbullying is an increasingly worrying concern for schools and children and young people.
- Cyberbullying can lead to criminal acts as well as having a negative influence on children and young people's mental health and well-being.
- Social media and societal expectations are resulting in issues of mental health and well-being centred on body image.
- Schools need clear strategies to support individuals with the teaching and understanding of issues centred around body image.
- The positives and negatives of social media need to be kept in balance. Teachers and parents need to keep abreast of technology development to support learning, embrace the opportunities of the internet and identify and mitigate dangers in order to keep safe online.

REFERENCES

BEREAL (2017) *Somebody Like Me: A Report Investigating the Impact of Body Image Anxiety on Young People in the UK*. Available at: www.berealcampaign.co.uk/somebody-like-me (accessed 20 June 2019).

Childnet International (2016) *Cyberbullying: Understand, Prevent and Respond – Guidance for Schools*. Available at: www.childnet.com/ufiles/Cyberbullying-guidance2.pdf (accessed 17 June 2019).

Children's Commissioner (2016) *Children with Mental Health Problems Need Help to Recover and Thrive*. Available at: www.childrenscommissioner.gov.uk/news/children-mental-health-problems-need-help-recover-and-thrive (accessed 18 June 2019).

Children's Commissioner (2018) *Life in 'Likes': Children's Commissioner Report into Social Media Use Among 8–12 Year Olds*. Available at: www.childrenscommissioner.gov.uk/wp-content/uploads/2018/01/Childrens-Commissioner-for-England-Life-in-Likes.pdf (accessed 2 February 2019).

Children's Society (2018) *The Good Childhood Report*. Available at: https://www.childrenssociety.org.uk/sites/default/files/the_good_childhood_report_full_2018.pdf

Department for Education (2017) *Preventing and Tackling Bullying: Advice for Head Teachers, Staff and Governing Bodies*. Available at: https://assets.publishing.service.gov.uk/government/uploads/system/uploads/attachment_data/file/623895/Preventing_and_tackling_bullying_advice.pdf (accessed 25 June 2019).

Duerager, A. and Livingstone, S. (2012) *How Can Parents Support Children's Internet Safety?* London: EU Kids Online.

Fardouly, J. and Vartanian, L.R. (2016) Social media and body image concerns: current research and future directions. *Current Opinion in Psychology*, 9: 1–5. https://doi.org/10.1016/j.copsyc.2015.09.005.

Fardouly, J., Magson, N., Johnco, C., Oar, E. and Rapee, R. (2018) Parental control of the time pre-adolescents spend on social media: links with preadolescents' social media appearance comparisons and mental health. *Journal of Youth and Adolescence*, 47. Available at: https://link-springer-com.apollo.worc.ac.uk/content/pdf/10.1007%2Fs10964-018-0870-1.pdf (accessed 20 June 2019).

Fleming, M., Greentree, S., Cocotti-Muller, D., Elias, K. and Morrison, S. (2006) Safety in cyberspace: adolescents' safety and exposure online. *Youth & Society*, 38(2): 138–154.

Glazzard, J. and Mitchell, C. (2018) *Social Media and Mental Health in Schools*. London: Critical Publishing.

Health and Social Care Information Centre (HSCIC) (2015) *Health and Well-being of 15 Year Olds in England: Finding Out from the What About YOUth?* Survey 2014. Available at: http://content.digital.nhs.uk/catalogue/PUB19244/what-about-youth-eng-2014-rep.pdf (accessed 20 June 2019).

HM Government (2019) *Online Harms*, White Paper. Available at: https://assets.publishing.service.gov.uk/government/uploads/system/uploads/attachment_data/file/793360/Online_Harms_White_Paper.pdf (accessed 20 June 2019).

Hymas, C. (2019) Children as young as 12 'competing to become better self-harmers'. *The Telegraph*, 2 February. Available at: https://www.telegraph.co.uk/news/2019/02/02/children-young-12-competing-become-better-self-harmers/ (accessed 2 February 2019).

Katz, A. (2012) *Cyberbullying and E-safety*. London: Jessica Kingsley Publishers.

Krause, N. (2019) App to combat self-harm urge downloaded more than 124,000 times. *British Journal of School Nursing*, 14(1): 6.

Lenhart, A. (2009) *Teens and Sexting. Pew Internet & American Life Project*. Available at: www.pewinternet.org/files/old-media/Files/Reports/2009/PIP_Teens_and_Sexting.pdf (accessed 20 June 2019).

Li, Q. (2006) Cyberbullying in schools: a research of gender differences. *School Psychology International*, 27: 157–170.

Lin, L, Sidani, J.E., Shensa, A., Radovic, A., Miller, E., Colditz, J.B. and Primack, B.A. (2016) Association between social media use and depression among U.S. young adults. *Depression and Anxiety*, 33(4): 323–331. Available at: https://doi.org/10.1002/da.22466 (accessed 20 June 2019).

Livingstone, S. (2009) *Children and the Internet: Great Expectations, Challenging Realities*. Cambridge: Polity Press.

Lounsbury, K., Mitchell, K. and Finkelhor, D. (2011) *The True Prevalence of 'Sexting'*, pp1–4. Crimes against Children Research Center. Available at: http://cola.unh.edu/sites/cola.unh.edu/files/research_publications/Sexting_Fact_Sheet_4_29_11.pdf (accessed 20 June 2019).

McCrae, N., Gettings, S. and Purssell, E. (2017) Social media and depressive symptoms in childhood and adolescence: a systematic review. *Adolescent Research Review*, 2(4): 315–330. Available at: https://doi.org/10.1007/s40894-017-0053-4 (accessed 20 June 2019).

National Advisory Group (2009) *A Proposed National Strategy on Body Image*. Available at: www.eatingdisorderhope.com/pdf/Proposed-National-Strategy-on-Body-Image_australia.pdf (accessed 20 June 2019).

NSPCC (2016) *What Children are Telling us About Bullying: Childline Bullying Report 2015/16*. Available at: https://www.nspcc.org.uk/globalassets/documents/research-reports/what-children-are-telling-us-about-bullying-childline-bullying-report-2015-16.pdf (accessed 20 June 2019).

NSPCC (2017) *Childline Counselling for Cyberbullying Continues to Rise*. Available at: https://www.nspcc.org.uk/what-we-do/news-opinion/cyberbullying-rise-reported-during-anti-bullying-week-2017/ (accessed 20 June 2019).

Ofcom (2013) *Children and Parents: Media Use and Attitudes Report*. Available at: http://stakeholders.ofcom.org.uk/binaries/research/media-literacy/october-2013/research07Oct2013.pdf (accessed 20 June 2019).

Ofcom (2016) *Children and Parents Media Use Attitudes Report*. Available at: https://www.ofcom.org.uk/__data/assets/pdf_file/0034/93976/Children-Parents-Media-Use-Attitudes-Report-2016.pdf (accessed 20 June 2019).

Office for National Statistics (2016) *Measuring National Well-being: Insights into Children's Mental Health and Well-being*. Available at: www.ons.gov.uk/peoplepopulationadncommunity/wellbeing/articles/measuringnationalwellbeing/2015-10-20 (accessed 2 February 2019).

O'Reilly, M., Dogra, N., Hughes, J., Reilly, P., George, R. and Whiteman, N. (2018) *Potential of Social Media in Promoting Mental Health in Adolescents*. Available at: https://academic-oup-com.apollo.worc.ac.uk/heapro/advance-article/doi/10.1093/heapro/day056/5061526 (accessed 20 June 2019).

Papadopoulos, L. (2018) *Safety Net: Cyberbullying's Impact on Young People's Mental Health*. Inquiry Report, YoungMinds. Available at: https://youngminds.org.uk/media/2189/pcr144b_social_media_cyberbullying_inquiry_full_report.pdf (accessed 20 June 2019).

Phippen, A. (2016) *360safe – The E-safety Self Review Tool: UK Schools Online Safety Policy and Practice Assessment 2016*. Available at: www.swgfl.org.uk/360report2016.aspx (accessed 20 June 2019).

Prizant-Passal, S., Shechner, T. and Aderka, I.M. (2016) Social anxiety and internet use – a meta-analysis: what do we know? What are we missing? *Computers in Human Behavior*, 62: 221–229. Available at: https://doi.org/10.1016/j.chb.2016.04.003 (accessed 20 June 2019).

PSHE Association (2019) *Teacher Guidance: Key Standards in Teaching About Body Image*. Available at: https://www.pshe-association.org.uk/system/files/PSHE%20%E2%80%93%20Key%20standards%20in%20teaching%20about%20body%20image%2022nd%20April.pdf (accessed 20 June 2019).

Royal Society for Public Health (2017) *hashtagStatusOfMind: Social Media and Young People's Mental Health and Wellbeing. Royal Society for Public Health*. Available at: www.rsph.org.uk/uploads/assets/uploaded/62be270a-a55f-4719-ad668c2ec7a74c2a.pdf (accessed 2 February 2019).

Sharples, M., Graber, R., Harrison, C. and Logan, K. (2009) E-safety and web 2.0 for children aged 11–16. *Journal of Computer Assisted Learning*, 25: 70–84.

Subrahmanyam, K. and Greenfield, P. (2008) Online communication and adolescent relationships. *The Future of Children*, 18: 119–146.

The Lancet (2019) *Editorial: Social Media, Screen Time, and Young People's Mental Health*. Available at: https://www.thelancet.com/journals/lancet/article/PIIS0140-6736(19)30358-7/fulltext (accessed 20 June 2019).

The Royal Foundation Taskforce on the Prevention of Cyberbullying (2017) *National Action Plan to Tackle Cyberbullying*. Available at: http://www.royalfoundation.com/duke-cambridge-launches-national-action-plan-tackle-cyberbullying/ (accessed 20 June 2019).

Tynes, B. (2007) Internet safety gone wild. *Journal of Adolescent Research*, 22: 575–584.

UK Millennium Cohort Study (2019) *Kelly, Zilanawala, Booker & Sacker, EClinicalMedicine*. Available at: http://bit.ly/2Qub4DG (accessed 22 June 2019).

Valkenburg, P. and Peter, J. (2010) Online communication amongst adolescents: an integrated model of its attraction, opportunities and risks. *Journal of Adolescent Health*, 48: 121–127.

Young Minds (2016) *Resilience for the Digital World*. Available at: https://youngminds.org.uk/media/1490/resilience_for_the_digital_world.pdf

7

THE INFLUENCE OF FAMILY MENTAL HEALTH

CHAPTER OBJECTIVES

By the end of this chapter you should be aware of:

- the definition of a family in this new millennium and how the child functions as an individual within a family;
- the impact of maternal mental health in pregnancy and the early years and the potential impact on the family and specifically the developing child and young person and their emotional well-being;
- paternal mental health and the possible impact on the family and specifically the child or young person's mental health and emotional well-being;
- how family mental health difficulties can be translated into the classroom setting;
- how to develop an interagency approach to support families with mental health difficulties and the advantages of this approach to children and young people and the whole school;
- ways schools can engage with parents, significant others and the community within a supportive framework.

TEACHERS' STANDARDS

This chapter supports the development of the following Teachers' Standards:

TS8: Fulfil wider professional responsibilities

- Develop effective professional relationships with colleagues, knowing how and when to draw on advice and specialist support.
- Take responsibility for improving teaching through appropriate professional development, responding to advice and feedback from colleagues.
- Communicate effectively with parents with regard to pupils' achievements and well-being.

Introduction

This chapter will focus on the influence of family mental health in pregnancy, the early years and beyond in order to seek to understand the impact on the developing child/young person. It will begin by defining a family in the twenty-first century and reflect on how the child functions as an individual within such a family. How family mental health affects the child and then how this becomes translated into the classroom will also be explored. It will also consider the importance of engaging and working with parents, significant others and the community (especially families affected by mental health issues), demonstrating how an interagency approach could support family mental health. Further thought will be given to what an interagency approach could look like and the advantages to the family and the school of using such an approach, in order to achieve high levels of engagement.

What is a family in this new millennium and how can the child function as an individual in such a family?

Families are undergoing considerable change; many children are raised in single-parent families, with same-sex parents, blended families, step families and foster or adoptive families. The importance of extended families also plays a significant part in how the family system functions. When reflecting on the functionality of families it is important to consider that a family is usually but not always multigenerational, and can include aunts, uncles, cousins and grandparents (Geldard et al., 2018). Grandparents and older family members give families and communities a sense of belonging and build a sense of who they are in relation to others; they are often an important source of wisdom and stability in the family system.

As children grow they incorporate values, beliefs and attitudes from the world around them and they may find as adults that some of these are not as appealing as others. Some family members will have similar values, beliefs and attitudes and some will be very different and this is dependent on personality and experiences (nature and nurture).

As the primary provider of the child's emotional, intellectual and physical environment the family and the family environment will impact on the child's view of the world and ability to function in that world. Each adult family member will have his or her own history that inevitably influences how the child is raised, how the family will develop and mature and how the family will function. It is important within the context of this chapter to acknowledge that family connectedness and structure will impact on children's later adjustment to the world around them.

We are who we are in relation to others (Cecchin, 1987); each individual family member's thoughts, behaviours and perception of the family are influenced by the behaviour of other family members alongside developmental changes within the family and external events. Children will ultimately demonstrate thoughts and behaviours that help them survive in the family unit and to get their needs met – these ways may or may not be appropriate or adaptive and may even be problematic but it is important as professionals we understand that children will behave in the best way they know how in the family and community system.

The prevalence and most common mental health difficulties within the family and the potential impact on the child

When considering the 'family' within this chapter, reference will be made, in the main, to parents. With one in four adults in the UK experiencing some form of mental illness in any given year (McManus et al., 2016) and many of these being parents, it is important that as professionals working with families we are aware of the impact of mental distress or illness on the family. Parental mental illness can make parenting difficult but not impossible. Wherever possible, promoting the welfare and safeguarding of children should be the responsibility of parents, with appropriate support if necessary.

The concept of 'burden of care' has been used extensively to describe the emotional, psychological, physical and economic effects on families caring for a person with mental illness (Awad and Voruganti, 2008). Families may also be subjected to negative stereotypes, which may lead to discrimination, a sense of shame and families being blamed for their relatives' mental health problems (Corrigan and Miller, 2004). In addition experiences of stigma and difficulties navigating the mental health services may contribute further to family difficulties and potentially further impact on the child (Keogh et al., 2017).

As professionals working with families it is important to be aware of the most common types of mental illness in order to understand their impact on parents, children and young people. It is also important to consider that parental mental illness can vary in impact and the way that it presents itself and that the effect on the child is influenced by the type, severity and duration of the illness (Henry and Kumar, 1998, as cited by Aldridge and Becker, 2003). It can be evidenced that families from poorer and more disadvantaged backgrounds are more likely to be affected by common mental health difficulties (such as those detailed within the web link below) and their adverse consequences (Campion et al., 2013). With approximately 17,000 children and young people in the UK living with parents with severe and enduring mental illness (Mental Health Foundation, 2016 a), the need to support the family within an interagency approach has never been greater.

According to the National Institute for Health and Care Excellence (NICE, 2011), the most common adult mental health illnesses include depression and anxiety disorders (generalised anxiety disorder, social anxiety disorder, panic disorder, obsessive-compulsive disorder and post-traumatic stress disorder). In order to understand the impact on children and young people there is a need for an awareness of how mental health difficulties affect parents; you can find a brief synopsis and further information regarding specific common adult mental health difficulties at **https://www.time-to-change.org.uk/about-mental-health/types-problems**.

Siblings of children or young people with a mental illness are individuals who have largely gone unrecognised and can remain invisible to statutory services. These children and young people will have unique experiences shaped by this relationship, and their mental health and well-being can be negatively affected by a number of factors (Greenberg et al., 1997). These negative factors include:

* increased responsibility within the family unit;

* possible loss of support from their sibling;

- changes in role (such as taking on new supportive roles);

- intense and conflicting emotions (for example, confusion, despair, hopelessness, anger and grief);

- interpersonal and intrapersonal difficulties;

- difficulties in trying to deal with the mental health system.

(Griffiths and Sin, 2016)

Stigma can also contribute negatively to siblings; if they tell others about their sibling's mental health they may receive support or they may be shunned, lose friends and experience discrimination – this makes for a difficult choice for those so young. Many siblings find that having a brother or sister with a mental illness is not always an exclusively negative experience. They can find great strength and compassion within their relationship that they can then apply to others; they also gain coping skills and knowledge that can benefit their own lives. These experiences can lead to new opportunities and life directions (Jewell, 2000; Sin et al., 2008).

In terms of gender difference within parental mental health, women are more likely than men to have a common mental health difficulty (19.1 per cent or one in five women as opposed to 12.2 per cent or one in eight men) (McManus et al., 2016). Women are also twice as likely as men to be diagnosed with anxiety disorders (Martin-Merino et al., 2009). However, men are over three times more likely to commit suicide than women (Oliffe et al., 2011) and men tend to exhibit mental health difficulties more indirectly, for example through alcohol and substance misuse, aggression towards themselves or others and risk taking in general (Courtenay, 2000; Wilkins, 2010; Department of Health, 2012). Evidence suggests that larger numbers of men have undiagnosed mental health problems, due to stigma regarding mental health, societal constraints of masculinity, differences in presentations of mental illness and inappropriate services to support men (Devon, 2016).

This is particularly the case when we consider the impact of mental health stigma towards black and minority ethnic communities, with 93 per cent of people surveyed indicating that they face discrimination because of their mental ill health (Owen, 2013). To consider further gender differences and the impact of family mental health difficulties on children and young people, the next few subsections will separate paternal and maternal mental health and highlight the impact on the family.

KEY REFLECTIONS

- What influence does the family system have on the child?
- Why is it important that we have some awareness of the most common adult mental health difficulties?
- How can we ensure that the needs of siblings of children/young people with mental health difficulties are considered?
- How significant is the impact of mental health stigma on all family members, and in particular black and minority ethnic families?

Paternal mental health and the possible impact on the child/young person

To explore paternal mental health fully we initially need to think about what it is to be a father and how that role has changed dramatically over the past three decades from an all-powerful patriarch to a new nurturant father, who plays an active role in his children's lives (Lamb, 2004; O'Brien, 2005). Whereas previously, societal expectations would demand that the primary responsibility of childcare would fall to the mother, 69 per cent of parents now believe childcare is the responsibility of both parents (Ellison et al., 2009). As demonstrated within a large European study, Britons were found to be increasingly receptive to the idea that fathers are just as capable as mothers of caring effectively for young children; only 13 per cent of the British population felt it is the *man's role to earn and the woman's to care* (Scott and Clery, 2013). Expectations of fatherhood can also be different according to different cultural contexts (Khan, 2017). According to Kan and Laurie (2016), African Caribbean men hold the most egalitarian attitudes and within Bangladeshi Muslim and Pakistani Muslim (among other black and minority ethnic) communities there is now strong support by both sexes for high levels of early father involvement (Chowbey et al., 2013).

Since 2003, unmarried fathers jointly registering their child's birth have the right to full parental responsibility; parental leave for fathers has also been extended (Gov.UK, 2014 a). The changing landscape of fatherhood is also further evident within UK policy context; for example, the introduction of shared parental leave (Gov.UK, 2014 b). The need for health professionals to support fathers during childbirth and the transition to parenthood is clear in several UK policies (NICE, 2006, 2008; Department of Health/Partnerships for Children, Families and Maternity, 2007; Department for Children, Schools and Families, 2010). *The Healthy Child Programme* (Department of Health, 2009) is of key relevance for health visitors, emphasising the need to support and engage fathers. These changes are an indicator of a growing acknowledgment and recognition of the important role of a father in children's lives.

Research demonstrates that active and regular engagement of fathers in a child's life predicts a range of positive outcomes for children, including reducing behavioural problems and psychosocial problems, enhancing cognitive development and decreasing the likelihood of involvement in crime (Sarkadi et al., 2008). There is a need, therefore, to support fathers in their role, to help them be prepared for changes to come and to support them in managing their own and their children's emotions and uncertainties, whether at home or in school.

Changes in the family structure and functioning alongside increasing numbers of women in the workforce have raised questions about fathers' parenting-related stress and their mental health and how it may affect their children. There are numerous studies that suggest negative influences on parent–child interactions and children's development. It is important to note, however, that the majority of these studies focus on mothers. Harewood et al. (2016) indicate small to moderate effects of fathers' parenting-related stress on cognitive and language development in children aged 2–3 years with specific detrimental effects on boys' language development, even though the majority of fathers in the study were not primary carers. This study indicates that fathers have a direct effect on their children's development and suggests that interventions should address both mothers' and fathers' parenting-related stress and emotional health so they can better support their children's development (Harewood et al., 2016).

A campaign by Time to Change (2016) uncovered how teenage boys' own attitudes to mental health are influenced by their father's behaviour and his ability to talk about his feelings, with half of teenage boys feeling they cannot open up to their dads about their mental health. The emphasis of the campaign is to encourage fathers to talk more openly to their sons to empower them to manage their own mental health successfully (Censuswide, 2016).

In relation to the early years there is a growing interest in understanding how a father's postnatal mental health influences outcomes for children in childhood. Ramchandani et al. (2005) associate fathers' postnatal depressive symptoms with emotional and behavioural difficulties for children aged 3–7 years and Fletcher et al. (2011) report that children whose fathers reported postnatal depressive symptoms were more likely to experience social, emotional and behavioural difficulties by age 5.

These studies demonstrate the need for specific strategies and support for both parents in the postnatal and early years period for long-term investment in the well-being of their children throughout their lives and educational career.

Parental mental health is frequently cited as a feature in Serious Case Reviews, together with domestic abuse and substance misuse (frequently alcohol). This is often referred to as the 'toxic trio' and was evident in the Serious Case Review of Daniel Pelka. Daniel's mother had been diagnosed with clinical depression. She was also admitted to hospital and seen by mental health professionals following an overdose (Coventry Safeguarding Children Board, 2013). Serious Case Reviews like Daniel's indicate that professionals sometimes lack awareness of the extent that a mental health problem can impact on parenting capacity and how this can result in a failure to identify potential safeguarding issues. Therefore, learning from case reviews indicates that professionals, importantly those in education settings, must be able to recognise the relationship between adult mental health and child protection, maintaining focus on the child but also listening to parents, to be able to recognise risk. It is also important to recognise other issues such as drug or alcohol dependency, domestic violence and little or no family/community support in addition to mental health problems that can exacerbate the risk presented by mental health issues (Brandon et al., 2013). The majority of parents with mental health issues present no risk to their children but even in low-level concern cases the needs of the children must be paramount. The following case study can help you to think further about the impact of paternal mental health on children and supportive ways of working and services that may help.

CASE STUDY: JAMAL

Jamal is 9 years old and is currently in Year 4 at the local primary school. He lives with his dad, Tyrone, and his 5-year-old brother, Saul (in reception class). Tyrone struggles with depression, which can affect his parenting capacity and his ability to care for himself. The family are supported by Grandma Jean (Tyrone's mother) who lives nearby and visits daily to offer practical and emotional support to both boys and Tyrone. The family have a good relationship with the school and both boys' teachers, and Tyrone attends parents' evenings and assemblies when he and Grandma Jean are able to.

Teachers have noticed that, over the past few weeks, both boys have been arriving to school late, appear hungry and are dishevelled, wearing unwashed and creased clothing. Jamal has said that

(Continued)

(Continued)

Dad is sleeping lots and Grandma Jean has been ill so not able to come as often to see them. During class the boys are tired and irritable, which is very different to how they usually behave. When Tyrone collects the boys from school at the end of the day he swiftly takes them away and does not want to engage with anyone.

Case study reflections

- What are the major changes that have put the boys at risk?
- What should be the school's response to this situation?
- What can the school do to support the family at this time?

Jamal and Saul are vulnerable to their father's mental health and as such their recent behaviours and appearance are a significant concern and a sign that the family is not coping. Grandma Jean being ill and unable to help also means that the boys and Tyrone are subjected to further distress and uncertainty. The school has built up a good relationship with the family and should specifically try to engage Tyrone in a conversation urgently, either by phone or in person, to discuss their concerns regarding the children, the school's statutory role in supporting the children's health and well-being and the effects on the children's education. The children are at risk of neglect and there is an ongoing concern regarding their health and well-being whilst their father is ill and Grandma Jean is not well. Initially the school should try to meet with the family and engage them within an Early Help assessment to think further with them about interagency support that would help the situation. If this is not possible then a safeguarding referral needs to be made to children's social care services to undertake an assessment to think further about support for the family and specific help needed now and possibly in the future.

It would be good practice in this case to talk to Tyrone first to discuss the family situation and the Early Help assessment and potential safeguarding referral, but if he refuses to engage or disagrees with the referral it should still go ahead as the children's safety and well-being must always come first, in accordance with safeguarding legislation and policy. Both Jamal and Saul need to be told that the teachers are worried about them and their dad, and are going to help and will be asking other professionals to help also. Jamal and Saul will need to be reassured that they have someone they can share their worries with, that they are being heard and things will get better, as they will be worried about their dad and missing their grandma and are doing the best they can in an uncertain environment. The school could invite the children to breakfast club and ensure their nutritional needs are met through the day. If this family is in receipt of pupil premium monies this could be used by the school to support the children's well-being as well as other aspects of their educational needs. Both Jamal and Saul should be given space and time to express their feelings and ask questions within a contained, supportive and safe environment.

Maternal mental health and the possible impact on the child/young person

Becoming a mother is a time of heightened emotions, and while most of these are positive, some women will experience temporary feelings of low mood, and for some women these feelings may be severe and long-lasting. The mental health of women during pregnancy and within a year of giving birth (perinatal mental health) is a public health priority due to its impact on both the mother and the child's health. Statistics demonstrate around 50 per cent of perinatal mental health problems are untreated or undetected and this can have a devastating impact on women and their families (Mental Health Foundation, 2016 b). There are several common mental health conditions during pregnancy, with depression being the most common. While most women experience 'baby blues' following delivery, postnatal psychological distress is highly prevalent across a variety of cultures (Satyanarayana et al., 2011). Research has also demonstrated a link between disadvantaged socioeconomic status and postnatal depression (Tannous et al., 2008).

The main impact of maternal mental health is on the attachment relationship between baby and mother and it is important to consider that bonding between a mother and her baby begins fairly early in pregnancy (Sedgmen et al., 2006). Maternal and paternal depression has been found to predict a difficult child temperament at 6–8 months and 21–24 months within a large cohort study (Avon Longitudinal Study of Parents and Children) and the effects were found to be more significant for boys than girls (Hanington et al., 2010). Murray et al. (2011) also reported an increased risk of depression by age 16 in children and young people whose mothers suffered from postnatal depression. Anxiety in mothers has also been found to predict a difficult infant temperament, such as clinging behaviour, frequent crying and irritability (Austin et al., 2005).

Some studies have demonstrated a link between maternal depression and cognitive and language difficulties as the child gets older (Sohr-Preston and Scaramella, 2006); others, however, have found no evidence of such a relationship (Tse et al., 2010). Psychological distress and mental illness, including depression and anxiety, influence a child's emotional, cognitive and behaviour development (Hollins, 2007), with maternal depression that occurred when the child was 2–3 years old being a risk factor for anxiety in 10–11-year-olds (Letourneau, 2013). Studies have also demonstrated a link between maternal antenatal anxiety and attention deficit hyperactivity disorder (ADHD) in children, showing that if a mother is stressed whilst pregnant this significantly increased the average number of child symptoms, ranging between 3.8 per cent for ADHD and 8.7 per cent for anxiety (Bendiksen et al., 2015).

There is also a well-established link between mental ill health and domestic violence and abuse, and both men and women, across all diagnoses, are more likely to have experienced domestic violence than the general population (Howard, 2012). The most prevalent cause of depression and other mental health difficulties in women is domestic violence and abuse, and it is estimated this is the case in 50–60 per cent of women mental health service users (Trevillion et al., 2012). Research such as this highlights the need for professionals to recognise the increased vulnerability of men and women with mental health difficulties to domestic violence and the implications of this for their children. Professionals require training and supervision to be able to identify and address these issues. Children and young people's needs remain paramount and it is important that:

organisations must ensure that staff working with children always focus on the needs of the child, and never allow themselves to be distracted by the problems of the adults.

(Brandon et al., 2010)

Whilst reflecting on the possible effects of family mental health difficulties on a child/young person, as detailed above, it is also important to be aware of protective factors that can help to mediate some of these effects, such as:

- the mental ill health being mild or short-lived;

- there being another parent or family member who can help;

- there being no other family disharmony;

- the child/young person having wider support from extended family, friends, teachers or other adults;

- a secure base – the child/young person feeling a sense of belonging and security;

- the child/young person having good self-esteem – an internal sense of worth and competence;

- the child/young person having a sense of self-efficacy – a sense of mastery and control, along with an accurate understanding of personal strengths and limitations;

- there being at least one secure attachment relationship;

- there being access to wider supports such as extended family and friends;

- there being positive nursery, school and or community experiences.

(Greater Manchester Safeguarding Partnership, 2014)

The role of teachers, teaching staff and the school is evident within most of the above protective factors, offering a unique opportunity to support the child/young person and family. Other chapters also examine how schools can support children and young people who have, or who may exhibit, issues around mental health and well-being. The following subsection will help you to think further as to how teaching staff in particular could engage the family and work together with other agencies to support the child/young person and family.

Engaging families and encouraging a positive school climate

One protective factor to encourage good mental health in children and young people is the creation of a positive school environment that enhances a sense of belonging and connectedness (Public Health England, 2016). Weare (2015) promotes the importance of engaging the 'whole community' and building a supportive school with a sense of connectedness, focus and purpose, the acceptance of respect, warm relationships and positive communication and the celebration of difference. These concepts need to be applied to families, especially those with family mental health needs. Naomi (a parent of two, who struggles with anxiety) blogs about her experiences at her children's school:

School found out about my mental health difficulties when social services got involved. At the time I was humiliated and my mental health deteriorated but the school was amazing – without their gentle kindness and support my mental health would have remained unmanageable. They asked me how they could help and did all they could to reduce my anxiety and stress. They helped me meet with the local parenting programme where we sat with our knees against the tiny infant table. They agreed I could drop off and pick up ten minutes early. It made a huge difference to my anxiety and with that reduced I began thinking more clearly and began working on different ways to manage the playground situation and began making connections with other parents.

(Mind, 2015)

We can see from Naomi's blog post how valuable a positive and non-stigmatising approach can be in a school setting and how building a relationship with teaching staff based on kindness and support with small thoughtful changes and suggestions can make a big difference to families.

Working with families has been shown to have a significant impact on children and young people's mental health, both by helping family life reinforce the messages of the school and by helping parents to develop their own parenting skills and approaches (Weare, 2015). When working with families with mental health difficulties the 'whole school' should promote a non-stigmatising, non-judgemental approach so that parents do not feel blamed for their children's difficulties; schools must look for strengths in families and try to build on them.

Because of the changing demographic of modern parenting (Centre for Longitudinal Studies, 2010), traditional approaches to parental involvement have been largely unsuccessful. Working and single parents, in particular, have little time to attend school activities and workshops during school hours, which would help support them with the skills they need to assist their children with academic tasks, yet parents and family background remain the biggest influence on a child's development and life chances (Campbell, 2011).

Some parents will have had a negative experience of school as children, so teachers will need an empathetic and thoughtful approach in order to encourage an accepting, trusting relationship to be established between the school and parents. Campbell (2011) explored attitudes towards home–school partnerships with 'hard to reach parents'; 75 per cent of the parents cited negative relationships with school being linked to their experience of unfriendly or unwelcome encounters with school staff or indeed other parents. Therefore it is vitally important that schools nurture a connectedness with parents or carers. This must be done very carefully, however, and sometimes very slowly.

Strategies identified by school leaders to enhance parental engagement with 'hard to reach' families and build trusting and meaningful relationships with parents were identified as:

- parenting support strategies: drop-in parenting workshops, home liaison workers, home visits from school staff related to new intakes, 'stay and play' days, 'come and see my work' days;

- communicating: contact at the school gate, social events, parent–teachers' association, parents' evenings, school leaders displaying openness and striving to embed community cohesion;

- volunteering: projects (developing a garden, school fair, etc.) – anything that will break down barriers and tap into the hidden expertise of parents;

- family learning: after-school clubs, parent–child homework sessions, opportunities particularly for fathers to get involved, e.g. fathers' storytelling weeks and offering these on Saturday morning sessions to maximise availability, themed days (ICT, cooking, sport);

- decision making: joining school governing body, parent council, seeking parental contributions to the school development plan and gaining feedback using regular parental questionnaire. Initially, non-threatening tasks that are not at a high level may be more appropriate and these could be fence painting, washing water bottles, and so forth;

- collaborating with the community: involvement in specific projects, e.g. Healthy Schools, sustainability agenda, increasing parent-friendliness of the school building to create a welcoming environment. Using a buddy system by drawing on parents to support other parents who want to come in but are not at ease or confident enough to come alone;

- remote involvement: school blogs, podcasts, school website with online questionnaires and resources, text messaging alerts.

(Campbell, 2011)

Parental engagement with families with mental health difficulties may start with schools or a class teacher encouraging parents to give up time to hear readers or help with cooking or craft sessions. This can be, for many, a non-threatening way to support building bridges between the work of the school and class and a parent. When parents are involved in the school they can see all the good work that is done to support children and young people. They can start to build trusting relationships with professionals, which in the long term may prove invaluable in getting a family to accept and engage with support.

The importance of an interagency approach to support family mental health

Inter- or multiagency approaches and ways of working have received much attention over the years, especially within the area of child protection. It has also been the focus of political agendas; *Every Child Matters* (HM Treasury, 2003), for example, set out a model of practice that involved a range of professionals working together in order to promote positive outcomes for children and young people. Even though this White Paper is no longer current governmental policy, the principles of using an inter- or multiagency approach to encourage best practice and best outcomes for the family still stand. In the context of education and family mental health in particular, an example of multiagency working is the collaboration of services under an Early Help assessment. This framework encourages schools and all services involved to work together to meet the needs of a child/ young person and family to ensure they have the opportunity to fulfil their potential. Effective multiagency working can be a significant challenge; it is time consuming and can lead to conflict. However, it significantly contributes to putting together different parts of the jigsaw and can lead to more effective services and joint problem solving to the benefit of the child/young person and family (Atkinson et al., 2007). This way of working supports a family from a holistic perspective and can ensure that all parties involved contribute to a plan of action and work together with the family towards a care plan which meets all of the child or young person's needs (Welsh Government, 2014).

Living in a household where parents or carers have mental health problems does not mean a child will experience abuse or negative consequences as most parents are able to give their children safe and loving care. However when working with families with multiple and complex problems and needs connected to parental mental health and safeguarding, professionals should maintain a focus on the child's well-being at all times.

The Think Family agenda (Department for Children, Schools and Families, 2009) is a useful framework to ensure a joined-up approach to these needs. This framework aims to give clarity to the roles and responsibilities of agencies to ensure cooperation and collaborative working. It works with family strengths, providing tailored support needs. Based on the Crossing Bridges Family Model (Falkov, 1998), the Think Family agenda helps professionals to consider the parent, the child and the family as a whole, and how the mental health and well-being of the family where a parent has a mental illness are linked in at least three ways:

1. Parental mental health problems can adversely affect the development, and in some cases, the safety of children.

2. Growing up with a parent with a mental illness can have a negative impact on a person's adjustment in adulthood, including that person's transition to parenthood.

3. Children, particularly those with emotional, behavioural or chronic physical difficulties, can precipitate or exacerbate mental ill health in their parents/carers.

This framework is now considered ex-government policy but is still being used within many local authorities within England as a concept to recognise and promote the importance of a whole-family approach, particularly within the agenda of parental mental health and child welfare.

Children and young people's household and caring responsibilities can increase within such families when the parent is ill. This can place additional burdens on children/young people in vulnerable situations, and have adverse effects on family relationships. Furthermore, because mental illness is often a variable condition, caring and household responsibilities can be unpredictable and intermittent, fostering inconsistent boundaries and child–parent roles (Gatsou et al., 2015). There are approximately 700,000 young carers in the UK (Raws, 2016) and some of these children/young people will be within families where their parents or siblings have mental health difficulties. It is important for schools and teachers to be aware of this group of children and the impact that caring responsibilities can have on the child; children can find helping someone very rewarding, but the child also has the right to be looked after and there is a duty of care for professionals to ensure families gain the support they need.

Being able to talk with teachers or a member of the pastoral team regarding their lives, worries and concerns is really important for young carers and the school can be a real lifeline for these families. As further support for the child/young person there is a network of young carers' groups that run all over the UK that offer support and advice for families and children/young people. Groups can be sourced via the Carers Trust webpages (**https://carers.org/**). The Children's Society also supports schools with young carers and their families with free resources and information within their web-pages (**https://www.childrenssociety.org.uk/back-to-school/young-carers**). Schools can also make a referral for a young carer's assessment via their local authority.

KEY REFLECTIONS

- What could be the possible impacts on the child/young person when a parent has a mental illness? Will all children/young people be affected in the same way?
- What protective factors mediate the effects of family mental illness? How could the school encourage these? What would that look like?
- Why might families with mental health difficulties find it difficult to engage with their children's school? How can a positive partnership between the school, the family and the community be encouraged?

CHAPTER SUMMARY

- A range of common mental health difficulties can exist within the family and these can have a significant impact on children and young people.
- Adhering to statutory requirements with regard to safeguarding children and young people is important, and professionals need to be vigilant to the impact of changes within the family.
- All teaching staff should be encouraging and supportive to parents within a 'positive community', encompassing a non-stigmatising and non-judgemental strength-based approach.
- Building trusting and supportive relationships between school and family is key to fostering family resilience and raising parental self-esteem, thus enhancing family coping strategies and improving the family's relationship with help and support.

FURTHER READING

Common Assessment Framework. Available at: www.education.gov.uk/consultations/downloadable Docs/ACFA006.pdf

Early Help Assessment (2018) *Keeping Children Safe in Education: Statutory Guidance for Schools and Colleges*. Available at: https://assets.publishing.service.gov.uk/government/uploads/system/uploads/attachment_data/file/741314/Keeping_Children_Safe_in_Education__3_September_2018_14.09.18.pdf

Family Action. Available at: www.family-action.org.uk/what-we-do/adult-mental-health-and-well being.

REFERENCES

Aldridge, J. and Becker, S. (2003) *Children Caring for Parents with Mental Illness: Perspectives of Young Carers, Parents and Professionals*. Bristol: The Policy Press.

Atkinson, M., Jones, M. and Lamont, E. (2007) *Multi-agency Working and its Implications for Practice: A Review of the Literature*. Available at: www.nfer.ac.uk/publications/MAD01/MAD01.pdf

Austin, M.P., Hadzi-Pavlovic, D., Leader, L., Saint, K. and Parker, G. (2005) Maternal trait anxiety, depression and life event stress in pregnancy: relationships with infant temperament. *Early Human Development*, 81: 183–190.

Awad, A.G. and Voruganti, L.N. (2008) The burden of schizophrenia on caregivers. *Pharmacoeconomics*, 26(2): 149–162.

Bendiksen, B., Aase, H., My Diep, L., Svensson, E., Friis, S. and Zeiner, P. (2015) The associations between pre- and postnatal maternal symptoms of distress and preschooler's symptoms of ADHD, oppositional defiant disorder, conduct disorder, and anxiety. *Journal of Attention Disorders*. Available at: https://doi.org/10.1177/1087054715616185

Brandon, M., Sidebotham, P., Bailey, S. and Belderson, P. (2010) *A Study of Recommendations Arising from Serious Case Reviews 2009–2010*. Available at: www.gov.uk/government/uploads/system/uploads/attachment_data/file/182521/DFE-RR157.pdf

Brandon, M., Bailey, S., Belderson, P. and Larsson, B. (2013) *Neglect and Serious Case Reviews: A Report from the University of East Anglia*, commissioned by NSPCC. Available at: www.nspcc.org.uk/global assets/documents/research-reports/neglect-serious-case-reviews-report.pdf

Campbell, C. (2011) *How to Involve Hard-to-reach Parents: Encouraging Meaningful Parental Involvement with Schools*. National College for School Leadership. Available at: http://dera.ioe.ac.uk/12136/1/down load%3Fid%3D156367%26filename%3Dhow-to-involve-hard-to-reach-parents-full-report.pdf

Campion, J., Bhugra, D., Bailey, S. and Marmot, M. (2013) Inequality and mental disorders: opportunities for action. *The Lancet*, 382(9888): 183–184.

Cecchin, G. (1987) Hypothesizing, circularity, neutrality revisited: an invitation to curiosity. *Family Process*, 26: 405–413.

Censuswide (2016) *Time to Change*. Available at: https://www.time-to-change.org.uk/news/half-teenage-boys-dont-feel-they-can-open-their-dads-about-mental-health

Centre for Longitudinal Studies (2010) *Millennium Cohort Study*. London: Institute of Education. Available at: www.cls.ioe.ac.uk/text.asp?section=000100020001

Chowbey, P., Salway, S. and Clarke, L. (2013) Supporting fathers in multi-ethnic societies: insights from British Asian fathers. *Journal of Social Policy*, 42(2): 391–408. doi: http:// dx.doi.org/10.1017/S004727941200102X

Corrigan, P.W. and Miller, F.E. (2004) Shame, blame, and contamination: a review of the impact of mental illness stigma on family members. *Journal of Mental Health*, 13(6): 537–548.

Courtenay, W. (2000) Constructions of masculinity and their influence on men's well-being: a theory of gender and health. *Social Sciences and Medicine*, 50: 1385–1401.

Coventry Safeguarding Children Board (2013) *Daniel Pelka: Serious Case Review*. Available at: http://moderngov.coventry.gov.uk/documents/s13235/Daniel%20Pelka%20Serious%20Case%20 Review%20SCR.pdf

Department for Children, Schools and Families (2009) *Think Family Toolkit: Improving Support for Families at Risk: Strategic Overview*. Available at: https://webarchive.nationalarchives.gov.uk/20130323053534/ https://www.education.gov.uk/publications/eOrderingDownload/Think-Family.pdf (accessed 2 August 2019).

Department for Children, Schools and Families (2010) *Support for All: The Families and Relationships Green Paper Summary*. London: HMSO. http://webarchive.nationalarchives.gov.uk/20130401151715/ http://www.education.gov.uk/publications/eOrderingDownload/CM-7787.pdf

Department of Health (2009) *The Healthy Child Programme*. https://www.gov.uk/government/uploads/ system/uploads/attachment_data/file/167998/Health_Child_Programme.pdf

Department of Health (2012) *Statistics from the National Drug Treatment Monitoring System: Vol 1, The Numbers*. Available at: www.nta.nhs.uk/uploads/statisticsfromndtms201112vol1thenumbersfinal.pdf

Department of Health/Partnerships for Children, Families and Maternity (2007) *Maternity Matters: Choice, Access and Continuity of Care in a Safe Service*. London: HMSO. http://webarchive.nationalarchives. gov.uk/20130107105354/http:/www.dh.gov.uk/prod_consum_dh/groups/dh_digitalassets/@dh/@en/ documents/digitalasset/dh_074199.pdf

Devon, N. (2016) The male mental health crisis is real – so why is it still being ignored? *The Telegraph*, 4 February. Available at: www.telegraph.co.uk/men/thinking-man/the-male-mental-health-crisis-is-real–so-why-is-it-still-being/

Ellison, G., Barker, A. and Kulasuriya, T. (2009) *Work and Care: A Study of Modern Parents*. Manchester: EHRC.

Falkov, A. (1998) *Crossing Bridges: Training Resources for Working with Mentally Ill Parents and their Children – Reader for Managers, Practitioners and Trainers*. Brighton: Pavilion Publishing.

Fletcher, R., Freeman, E., Garfield, C. and Vimpani, G. (2011) The effects of early paternal depression on children's development. *Medical Journal of Australia*, 195: 685–689.

Gatsou, L., Yates, S., Goodrich, N. and Pearson, D. (2015) The challenges presented by parental mental illness and the potential of a whole-family intervention to improve outcomes for families. *Child and Family Social Work*, 22(1). Available at: https://doi-org.apollo.worc.ac.uk/10.1111/cfs.12254

Geldard, K., Geldard, D. and Yin Foo, R. (2018) *Counselling Children: A Practical Introduction*. 5th edn. London: Sage Publishing.

Gov.UK (2014 a) *Parental Rights and Responsibilities*. Available at: www.gov.uk/parental-rights-responsibilities/who-has-parental-responsibility

Gov.UK (2014 b) *New Shared Parental Leave Regulations Come into Effect*. Available at: www.gov.uk/ government/news/new-shared-parental-leave-regulations-come-into-effect

Greater Manchester Safeguarding Partnership (2014) *Children of Parents with Mental Health Difficulties*. Available at: http://greatermanchesterscb.proceduresonline.com/chapters/p_ch_par_mental_health_ diff.html

Greenberg, J.S., Kim, H.W. and Greenley, J.R. (1997) Factors associated with subjective burden in siblings of adults with severe mental illness. *American Journal of Orthopsychiatry*, 67: 231–241.

Griffiths, C. and Sin, J. (2016) Rethinking siblings and mental illness. *British Psychological Society*, 26: 808–811.

Hanington, L., Ramchandani, P. and Stein, A. (2010) Parental depression and child temperament: assessing child to parent effects in a longitudinal population study. *Infant Behaviour and Development*, 33: 88–95.

Harewood, T., Vallotton, C. and Brophy-Herb, H. (2016) More than just the breadwinner: the effects of fathers' parenting stress on children's language and cognitive development. *Infant and Child Development*, 1–19. DOI: 10.1002/icd.1984

HM Treasury (2003) *Every Child Matters* (Cm5860). Available at: www.gov.uk/government/publications/every-child-matters

Hollins, K. (2007) Consequences of antenatal mental health problems for child health and development. *Current Opinions in Obstetrics and Gynecology*, 1: 568–572.

Howard, L. (2012) *People with Mental Disorders More Likely to Have Experienced Domestic Violence*. Available at: www.kcl.ac.uk/ioppn/news/records/2012/December/Domestic-violence.aspx

Jewell, T.C. (2000) Impact of mental illness on well siblings: a sea of confusion. *Journal of the National Alliance on Mental Illness*, 11(2): 34–36.

Kan, M.-Y. and Laurie, H. (2016) *Gender, Ethnicity and Household Labour in Married and Cohabiting Couples in the UK*. Cheltenham: Institute for Social and Economic Research, University of Essex. Available at: https://www.iser.essex.ac.uk/research/publications/working-papers/iser/2016-01.pdf

Keogh, B., Skärsäter, I., Doyle, L., Ellilä, H., Jormfeldt, H., Lahti, M., Higgins, A., Meade, O., Sitvast, J., Stickley, T. and Kilkku, N. (2017) Working with families affected by mental distress: stakeholders' perceptions of mental health nurses' educational needs. *Issues in Mental Health Nursing*, 38(10): 822–828. DOI: 10.1080/01612840.2017.1341587

Khan, L. (2017) *Fatherhood: The Impact of Fathers on Children's Mental Health*. Centre for Mental Health. Available at: https://www.eani.org.uk/sites/default/files/2018-10/The%20Impact%20of%20Fathers%20on%20Child%20Mental%20Health.pdf

Lamb, M. (2004) *The Role of the Father in Child Development*. Hoboken, NJ: John Wiley.

Letourneau, N. (2013) Maternal depression, family functioning and children's longitudinal development. *Journal of Pediatric Nursing*, 28(3): 223–234.

Martin-Merino, E., Ruigomez, A., Wallander, M., Johansson, S. and Garcia-Rodriguez, L. (2009) Prevalence, incidence, morbidity and treatment patterns in a cohort of patients diagnosed with anxiety in UK primary care. *Family Practice*, 27(1): 9–16.

McManus, S., Bebbington, P., Jenkins, R. and Brugha, T. (eds.) (2016) *Mental Health and Wellbeing in England: Adult Psychiatric Morbidity Survey 2014*. Leeds: NHS Digital. Available at: http://webarchive.nationalarchives.gov.uk/20180328130852tf_/http://content.digital.nhs.uk/catalogue/PUB21748/apms-2014-full-rpt.pdf/

Mental Health Foundation (2016 a) *Parents*. Available at: www.mentalhealth.org.uk/a-to-z/p/parents

Mental Health Foundation (2016 b) *Mums and Babies in Mind*. Available at: www.mentalhealth.org.uk/projects/mums-and-babies-mind

Mind (2015) *Naomi (20 January): Mental Health and the School Playground*. Available at: www.mind.org.uk/information-support/your-stories/mental-health-and-the-school-playground/#.WIEk7ztxvV4

Murray, L., Arteche, A., Pasco Fearon, D., Halligan, S., Goodyer, I. and Cooper, P. (2011) Maternal postnatal depression and the development of depression in offspring up to 16 years of age. *Child & Adolescent Psychiatry*, 50(5): 460–470.

NICE (2006) *Routine Postnatal Care of Women and their Babies*. Clinical Guideline 37. Available at: https://www.nice.org.uk/guidance/cg37

NICE (2008) *Antenatal Care: Routine Care for Healthy Pregnant Woman*. Clinical Guideline 62. Available at: https://www.nice.org.uk/guidance/cg62

NICE (2011) *Common Mental Health Disorders: Guidance and Guidelines*. Available at: www.nice.org.uk/guidance/cg123

O'Brien, M. (2005) *Shared Caring: Bringing Father into the Frame*. London: Equal Opportunities Commission.

Oliffe, J., Kelly, M.M., Bottorff, J.L., Johnson, J.L. and Wong, S.T. (2011) 'He's more typically female because he's not afraid to cry': connecting heterosexual gender relations and men's depressions. *Social Science and Medicine*, 73(5): 775–782.

Owen, D. (2013) *Mental Health Survey of Ethnic Minorities*. Ethnos Research and Consultancy. Available at: www.time-to-change.org.uk/sites/default/files/TTC_Final%20Report_ETHNOS_summary_1.pdf

Public Health England (2016) *The Mental Health of Children and Young People in England*. Available at: www.gov.uk/government/uploads/system/uploads/attachment_data/file/575632/Mental_health_of_children_in_England.pdf

Ramchandani, P., Stein, A., Evans, J. and O'Connor, T. (2005) Paternal depression in the postnatal period and child development: a prospective population study. *The Lancet*, 365: 2201–2205.

Raws, P. (2016) *Just How Many Young Carers are There?* The Children's Society. Available at: https://www.childrenssociety.org.uk/news-and-blogs/our-blog/just-how-many-young-carers-are-there

Sarkadi, A., Kristinsson, R., Oberklaid, F. and Bremberg, S. (2008) Fathers' involvement and children's developmental outcomes: a systematic review of longitudinal studies. *Acta Paediatrica*, 97: 153–158.

Satyanarayana, V., Lukose, A. and Srinivasan, K. (2011) Maternal mental health in pregnancy and child behaviour. *Indian Journal of Psychiatry*, 53(4): 351–361.

Scott, J. and Clery, E. (2013) *Gender Roles: An Incomplete Revolution?* London: National Centre for Social Research. Available at: http://www.bsa.natcen.ac.uk/latest-report/british-socialattitudes-30/gender-roles/introduction.aspx

Sedgmen, B., McMahon, C., Cairns, D., Benzie, R. and Woodfield, R. (2006) The impact of two-dimensional versus three-dimensional ultrasound exposure on maternal-fetal attachment and maternal health behavior in pregnancy. *Ultrasound in Obstetrics & Gynecology*, 27: 245–251.

Sin, J., Moone, N. and Harris, P. (2008) Siblings of individuals with first-episode psychosis: understanding their experiences and needs. *Journal of Psychosocial Nursing*, 46(6): 34–38.

Sohr-Preston, S. and Scaramella, L. (2006) Implications of timing of maternal depressive symptoms for early cognitive and language development. *Clinical Child Family Psychology Review*, 9: 65–83.

Tannous, L., Gigante, L.P., Fuchs, S.C. and Busnello, E.D. (2008) Postnatal depression in Southern Brazil: prevalence and its demographic and socioeconomic determinants. *BMC Psychiatry*, 8(1). DOI: 10.1186/1471-244X-8-1

Time to Change (2016) *Half of Teenage Boys Don't Feel They Can Open Up to Their Dads About Mental Health*. Available at: https://www.time-to-change.org.uk/news/half-teenage-boys-dont-feel-they-can-open-their-dads-about-mental-health (accessed 2 August 2019).

Trevillion, K., Oram, S., Feder, G. and Howard, L. (2012) Experiences of domestic violence and mental disorders: a systematic review and meta-analysis. *Public Library of Science ONE*, 7(12). DOI: 10.1371/journal.pone.0051740

Tse, A.C., Rich-Edwards, J.W., Rifas-Shiman, S.L., Gillman, M.W. and Oken, E. (2010) Association of maternal prenatal depressive symptoms with child cognition at age 3 years. *Paediatric Perinatal Epidemiology*, 24: 232–240.

Weare, K. (2015) *What Works in Promoting Social and Emotional Well-being and Responding to Mental Health Problems in Schools?* London: National Children's Bureau.

Welsh Government (2014) *Developing Community Partnerships and Multi-agency Working*. Available at: http://dera.ioe.ac.uk/23239/4/150615-face-theme5-en.pdf

Wilkins, D. (2010) *Untold Problems: A Review of the Essential Issues in the Mental Health of Men and Boys*. London: Men's Health Forum.

THE NEED FOR INCLUSION

CHAPTER OBJECTIVES

By the end of this chapter you should be aware of:

- the concept of inclusivity in relation to children and young people's mental health and well-being in schools;
- the importance of applying inclusivity to a child or young person's mental health and well-being;
- the benefits of inclusivity to the child/young person, the school, staff and the wider community;
- the benefits of promoting an inclusive ethos towards children and young people's mental health and well-being in school;
- strategies that can support the promotion of an inclusive ethos within schools.

TEACHERS' STANDARDS

This chapter supports the development of the following Teachers' Standards:

TS1: Set high expectations which inspire, motivate and challenge pupils

- Establish a safe and stimulating environment for pupils, rooted in mutual respect.
- Set goals that stretch and challenge pupils of all backgrounds, abilities and dispositions.

TS2: Promote good progress and outcomes by pupils

- Be aware of pupils' capabilities and their prior knowledge, and plan teaching to build on these.

TS5: Adapt teaching to respond to the strengths and needs of all pupils

- Know when and how to differentiate appropriately, using approaches which enable pupils to be taught effectively.
- Have a secure understanding of how a range of factors can inhibit pupils' ability to learn, and how best to overcome these.
- Demonstrate an awareness of the physical, social and intellectual development of children, and know how to adapt teaching to support pupils' education at different stages of development.
- Have a clear understanding of the needs of all pupils, including those with special educational needs; those of high ability; those with English as an additional language; those with disabilities; and be able to use and evaluate distinctive teaching approaches to engage and support them.

Introduction

This chapter will focus on the need to promote an inclusive ethos within schools when supporting children and young people's mental health and well-being. It will make links to the existing principle of inclusivity laid out within the *Special Educational Needs and Disability (SEND) Code of Practice* (Department for Education, 2015 a). It will examine the current concept of inclusivity within schools, both as an ethos in itself and in relation to legislation and guidance from both the Department for Education and Department of Health, and explore what this means for the promotion of children's mental health and well-being in schools. Consideration will be given to the benefits of inclusivity to the child or young person and the impact of this on the relationship with their school, staff and the wider community. Finally, the chapter will explore strategies that can support the promotion of an inclusive ethos for children and young people's mental health and well-being.

Defining inclusion and practice

The journey to define and understand the concept of inclusion has long been considered a lengthy and complex task. This has resulted in claims being made that inclusion forms a 'bewildering concept' which can allow for a range of applications and interpretation (Avramidis et al., 2002, p158). The task to define this notion has also been complicated by its inextricable link to our drive for understanding the concept of special educational needs and disabilities (SEND), especially given that such a concept has long been associated with that of a learning difficulty or a disability in line with the definition as set out by the Education Act 1996. This has meant that the mental health and well-being of children and young people have historically been somewhat marginalised when considering the notion of inclusion. This is surprising given that reports and authors such as the *National Service Framework: Children, Young People and Maternity Services* (Department of Health, 2004 a), Brown et al. (2012, cited in Department for Education, 2015 b, p34) and *Future in Mind* (Department of Health, 2015) have all highlighted a considerable range of need in terms of children and young people's mental health issues in schools. Most recently authors such as Gee (2018) have suggested that, at any one point, one-sixth of the UK population will be experiencing a mental health problem, which indicates that at least ten million children and adults have concerns around their mental health and well-being, and that one in ten school children have a mental health condition which is diagnosable, with 75 per cent of all mental health issues being embedded in individuals' lives by the time they are 18.

The notion that inclusive education has developed from what may be seen as a social model of disability, which recognises the difference in children, has led to this term's constant evolution in an attempt to reflect such differences (Save the Children, 2002). What seems important is not so much a definition of what is inclusion but the need to understand that inclusion is an ongoing process. This involves educators continually striving to meet such diverse needs through what may be seen as a constantly evolving and responsive set of pedagogies. Through our attempts to explore inclusive practice there has been more recently a greater impetus to explore the notion of inclusion in terms of what it means for the educational practice of children and young people. This has been driven by Acts of Parliament such as the Equality Act 2010, which made it unlawful for any education provider, including a private or independent provider, to discriminate between children and young people on the grounds of disability, race, sex, gender reassignment, pregnancy and maternity, religion or belief, or sex (known as 'protected characteristics'). Mental health difficulties are therefore now a protected characteristic under the 'disability' section of the Act, with its application being linked to whether the individuals have a physical or mental impairment that has a substantial, adverse and long-term effect on their normal day-to-day activities. It is important to note that without a clinical diagnosis it may be unclear if a child falls under such a 'protected characteristic'. However, frequently nowadays children in schools are diagnosed with neurodevelopmental conditions such as attention deficit hyperactivity disorder (ADHD), autistic spectrum condition or even perhaps a mental health condition such as depression or anxiety.

More recently with the Children and Families Act (2014) and the *SEND Code of Practice: 0 to 25 Years* (Department for Education, 2015 a), inclusive policy and practice now truly acknowledges the importance of social, emotional and mental health difficulties within pupils in our schools. Whole school approaches aimed at promoting good mental health with all learners are now highlighted as best practice within government guidance, such as *Mental Health and Behaviour in Schools* (Department for Education, 2015 b) and *Government Response to the Consultation on Transforming Children and Young People's Mental Health Provision: A Green Paper and Next Steps* (Department of Health and Social Care and Department for Education, 2018). All such documents signal the vital importance of looking at mental health as a whole school inclusive approach with regard to children and young people's mental health and well-being. Such an approach ensures an inclusive ethos to supporting mental health. It seeks to emphasise a preventive universal provision, rather than one which may been seen as reactive and targeted (Vostanis et al., 2012).

It is worth noting, however, that there has been a historic profile of a separation between school and health and that child health has been a matter for local decision. In addition, conflicts and challenges have been posed by those who are responsible for health on an individual level, for example *Choosing Health* (Department of Health, 2004 b), rather than that of the whole community. This includes families and schools, who have a responsibility as set out in the Extended Schools and Health Services programme (Department for Education and Skills/Department of Health, 2006; DeBelle et al., 2007).

Despite the journey we have been on to promote and establish inclusive practice, there will no doubt be future hurdles to overcome to establish best practice. However, as the United Nations Educational, Scientific and Cultural Organization (UNESCO) notes, it is important that we are:

> *proactive in identifying the barriers and obstacles learners encounter in attempting to access opportunities for quality education, as well as in removing those barriers and obstacles that lead to exclusion.*

> (UNESCO, 2005, p13)

KEY REFLECTIONS

- How has the notion of inclusion developed over time?
- How would you now define inclusion?
- Will the definition of inclusive practice continue to develop?

The importance of schools for the inclusion of children and young people's mental health and well-being

It is worth remembering that 'child and adolescent mental health' is a relatively new health care specialism following the *Together We Stand* document in 1995 (Health Advisory Service, 1995). Prior to that date, children in schools were often identified as problematic largely from a behaviour-based position, which still continues in part today. Teachers and support staff routinely study and take courses in behaviour management, yet children and young people's needs are very much more complex, especially those of children with mental health problems. Therefore there is a need, as promoted by the Department for Education (2018), to redress the problem of specific training in schools, if children's mental health is to be placed on a similar footing to those of other pupils with SEND. Currently special educational needs coordinators (SENCos) take responsibility for coordinating and supporting an inclusive approach to children's mental health in schools. Allied to this, schools have recently created mental health champions (Gov UK, 2017) to promote this aspect of work within schools. Schools have also been advised to create mental health leads or dedicated leads to coordinate and support those most vulnerable and needy of pupils within our schools (Department of Health and Social Care and Department for Education, 2018). This drive to support mental health may also be seen by the employment of school-based counsellors or the training of teachers in youth mental health first aid (Mental Health First Aid England, 2018). Such initiatives have been supported by the government's pledge of funding which will drive forward and support the mental health of children and young people in our schools (Department for Education, 2018).

Such initiatives championing the mental health and well-being of children and young adults are surely much needed, though the scale of mental health and well-being issues facing our schools still seems unsure. As research suggests, there is a lack of reliable and up-to-date information (Health Select Committee, 2014) regarding the statistical significance of such issues. Whilst recent research has indicated an increase in the number of children and young people with mental health difficulties, accurate research figures are important to ensure professionals are not working in a 'fog'. That provision both in schools and in the community is both appropriate and timely. As stated by research, estimates indicate that one in ten children and young people experience clinically significant mental health difficulties (Green et al., 2005; Maughan et al., 2005), with such figures being seen as very similar to research in the USA (Waller et al., 2006). It is these children, young people and their families who will come into come into contact with schools, in the main, for support. Green et al. (2005) suggest that, of the families who had sought help, nearly three-quarters had first approached a teacher, in contrast with a quarter who had visited their family doctor. Greenberg (2010, p28) suggests:

> *By virtue of their central role in lives of children and families and their broad reach, schools are the primary setting in which many initial concerns arise and can be effectively remediated.*

Having access to supportive and understanding teachers can be very helpful for these children, young people and their parents given that the school setting will make up a significant proportion of the time in a child's life. It is very often at school where difficulties and problems are first noticed since teaching staff – the professionals who spend the longest contact time with children – are uniquely placed to foster mental health and well-being inclusively. However, as O'Reilly et al. (2018, p659) indicate:

> *training for teachers cannot tackle mental health promotion in isolation from the practical difficulties of supporing children who have a diagnosed condition.*

Mental health and well-being also depend on teaching and support staff having a fundamental knowledge and understanding of infant and child development and the management of transitional stages. However, while expecting schools to focus on mental health, Weare (2000, p6) suggests:

> *it is not simply to add yet another demand to teachers' already impossible workload; effective social and affective education is directly beneficial to academic attainment and can therefore help teachers be more effective.*

Government directives in England have increasingly emphasised the role of a public health approach, with schools being instrumental in preventive work around mental health problems and promoting well-being – for example, *Every Child Matters* (Department for Education and Skills, 2003); *National Healthy Schools* (Department of Health/Department for Education and Employment, 1999) and *Social and Emotional Aspects of Learning* (Department for Education and Skills, 2005, 2006; Department for Children, Schools and Families, 2007). Most recently this has included the *Government Response to the Consultation on Transforming Children and Young People's Mental Health Provision: a Green Paper and Next Steps* (Department of Health and Social Care and Department for Education, 2018). Such policies and frameworks offer up a vison for both universal and targeted mental health interventions and support for children and young adults.

It must be remembered, however, that such initiatives should be framed against what may be seen as ongoing historic rhetoric and concerns. For example, Targeted Mental Health in Schools (TaMHS) (Department for Children, Schools and Families, 2008) was rolled out from 2008 onwards and provided a much-needed framework through which local authorities could develop their own way of working, aiming to foster the role of schools in England in promoting children and young people's mental health. TaMHS was funded for 3 years between 2008 and 2011 at some targeted schools and areas. It was well received by school staff, including teachers, parents and pupils, with some schools having adopted and continued with aspects and principles of this project.

It could be concluded therefore that successive governments have held varying priorities which have resulted in a rather 'hotchpotch' approach to projects instead of an enduring longer-term, universal and consistent approach to what may be seen as a mental health crisis in our schools. Such a situation is even more worrying given the current government's proposal and direction for all schools in England to become academies, where there will be individual interpretations of inclusivity regarding mental health and ways to support pupils.

As a result of research and government strategy, the theme of 'inclusion' and a move towards an emphasis on prevention of mental health difficulties rather than a reactive approach is now thought to be the way forward, as with the *Government Response to the Consultation on Transforming Children and Young People's Mental Health Provision: A Green Paper and Next Steps* (Department of Health and Social Care and Department for Education, 2018). For children and young people there is a strong correlation between mental health issues in childhood and those within adulthood.

Research suggests that figures equate to 50 per cent of young adults with mental health difficulties having been diagnosed between the ages of 11 and 15 (Kim-Cohen et al., 2003). Over half of lifetime mental health problems (excluding dementia) begin to emerge by age 14 and three-quarters by the mid-20s. Up to 80 per cent of adults with depression and anxiety disorders first experience them before the age of 18 (Department of Health, 2011, 2015). Therefore, early identification and support for mental health and well-being within schools for all children and young people are of particular importance. It could be suggested that universal mental health provision within schools offers the ability to 'immunise' children and young people from later difficulties (Merrell and Gueldner, 2010). This 'immunisation' potential is closely linked to the potential protective factors from improving resilience, as discussed in Chapter 4.

Rutter (1991), in addition to his work on resilience, showed that school experiences are not just important for educational attainment, but also for psychological development. Greenberg (2010) suggests that a universal 'inclusion-based' approach also reduces the potential for stigmatising participants. With these thoughts in mind, a review of 599 primary schools and 137 secondary schools and their emotional health promotion strategies cited that, although two-thirds of schools' approaches focused on all pupils, these were still largely reactive rather than preventive interventions (Vostanis et al., 2012). This study suggests that we have some way to go before a totally inclusive approach to promoting mental health and well-being for children and young people in schools is realised.

The benefits of inclusivity to the child/young person, the school, staff and the wider community

The following case study aims to provide an insight into the benefits of inclusivity to the child/young person, the school and the wider community. Consider ideas for practice around inclusion and mental health with this example in mind.

──── CASE STUDY: JENNY ────

Jenny is 11 and has moved into a new county to join a Year 6 class in an urban primary school. Her attendance has been sporadic. Jenny has previously been presented to Child and Adolescent Mental Health Services (CAMHS) following an act of self-harm. Jenny's education experience has included several exclusions following events of unacceptable behaviour in class. She has been subject to numerous school moves, including three primary schools. Jenny is not able to tell the time on the clock and says she cannot read beyond a very basic level. She is unhappy about this and wishes things were different. Jenny's ethnic and cultural background is Gypsy/Traveller. Jenny and her family are settled Travellers and though they have moved to a new house they are again on the point of eviction. Jenny's sister, who is 17, has just had a baby and has returned to live in the family home. Her younger brother has a diagnosis of ADHD and is also violent at times. Jenny's older brother is away at college. Her parents are together; Mum has recently had a health scare but has just had the all clear.

(Continued)

(Continued)

Case study reflections

- What are the major factors that put Jenny at risk?
- What can the school do to support this situation?

Jenny is an example of a young person trying to deal with multiple layers of problems and has been left with an overwhelming sense of hopelessness. One way she has managed her incapacity to read is through behaving badly as that worked in a way to remove her from what was, for Jenny, an intolerable situation, especially as she grew older and it became clearer she was behind her peers. She is now even more isolated from any peers that she was friendly with. Unless Jenny's parents disclose their Traveller status on admission to their new school it may be some time before the school can access advisory support services which seek to improve the outcomes for Gypsy, Roma and Traveller children and families.

The school may wish to seek an urgent referral to their integrated behaviour outreach team or social inclusion officer in order to find the best outcomes for Jenny. This may alert the school to the previous CAMHS referral. Given her low levels of academic achievement, the school will need to do all it can, in consultation with the SENCo, to liaise with her prior settings as to what strategies may best support her needs. Jenny will need a lot of support given her complex needs and will require assigned and targeted support to help her cope in class. They will need to understand quickly what is driving her previous levels of poor behaviour so that the most appropriate interventions can be put in place.

Inclusive practice in schools

Having a positive inclusive school climate will in part be mainly dependent on the individual leadership from both the head teachers and governors. However, having said this, schools have a statutory responsibility to create a teaching and learning environment which is inclusive no matter what the child's needs may be, whether they are defined by physical, ethnic, gender or with regard to social, emotional and mental health needs.

All schools should make clear reference in their school policy how they intend to admit and support the equality, diversity and inclusion of those children with such needs in their school. This is in order to create a supportive, appropriate and purposeful teaching and learning environment. Such policies will have been informed by two key pieces of legislation. The Equality Act 2010 clearly sets out the legal obligations that schools have towards their children and young people. This includes not discriminating, harassing or victimising such groups as well as making reasonable adjustments to ensure that such individuals are not disadvantaged. The *SEND Code of Practice: 0 to 25 Years* (Department for Education, 2015 a) highlights how a range of needs can be assessed and supported. It helps schools to acknowledge in their inclusive policy and practice the importance of social, emotional and mental health difficulties within pupils. It allows schools to consider a whole school approach to supporting such needs by identifying the issues schools face when supporting such vulnerable individuals. These include:

becoming withdrawn or isolated, as well as displaying challenging, disruptive or disturbing behaviour
… anxiety or depression, self-harming, substance misuse, eating disorders or physical symptoms that
are medically unexplained. Other children and young people may have disorders such as attention
deficit disorder, attention deficit hyperactive disorder or attachment disorder.

(Department for Education, 2015 a, p98)

Strategies for inclusive practice in schools

For any inclusive school-based strategy to be successful it is important for educational professionals to understand the relationship between the child, family, school and the wider community. The
Extended Schools initiative, which commenced in 2001, was very much about embedding schools as
part of their wider community and using them as a resource for their communities as a longer-term
agenda. Principal messages were about making parents and families welcome, engaging health and
social care professionals in the school setting, including child and adolescent mental health professionals, and participation in community activities (DeBelle et al., 2007).

Children often receive a home visit from the class teacher prior to starting primary school. This is a
really helpful way of making home and family links and for school staff to see their pupils within a
context. It also eases the transition for starting school for both family and child and helps to build
a firm foundation for future relationship building. It is now common practice to have breakfast
clubs in schools as well as after-school clubs. These are a good example of promoting inclusivity
as they are open to all children. After-school clubs provide opportunities for children to engage in
extracurricular activities, often of a non-academic nature, such as sports, music and cookery. They
provide further opportunities for children, who may not find the classroom an easy place to excel
in, to do so in another area.

Positive family and friendship relationships scaffold a child's experience of life; this can also be
said of positive relationships in the school setting with peers and school staff. Before- and after-
school clubs often expose children to additional staff outside their classrooms with opportunities
for further positive relationships to develop. Other supportive strategies include developing friendships and social networks through having similar characteristics and shared common interests.

CASE STUDY: AMID

Amid is 7 and has just joined Year 3. He has struggled somewhat with his academic work in Key
Stage 1 but the school has not in the past been overly concerned about Amid. However, with
his move to Key Stage 2 he is becoming more aware of how he is not like his peers academically. This has meant he is now reluctant to work and has a sense that he is no good at anything.
To avoid work and to garner popularity with his class friends he is starting to disrupt the lessons
by calling out and disturbing others on the carpet. The school are becoming more concerned
that he is falling behind his classmates and allied with his disruptive nature the staff are concerned for his future.

(Continued)

(Continued)

Case study reflections

- What factors are influencing Amid's behaviour?
- Do you think his behaviour will continue to deteriorate?
- What can the school do to support Amid?

Usually, before a range of interventions and support are put in place for children like Amid, the school must assess his level of SEND and, linked to this, his emotional and mental health needs. In order to achieve this, an initial assessment will take place to ascertain how Amid's needs may be best supported given his move to Key Stage 2. This assessment has originated from concerns from his new teacher who has started to share her concerns regarding his progress, actions and behaviours with the SENCo and Amid's parents. This assessment will now take a more formal route which will include a full analysis of Amid's needs, the views of his parents being sought and teacher assessments and observations being made. Parents must be informed before any SEND intervention can be implemented for Amid. Early interventions can often prevent any emotional issues from escalating so it is important that swift action is taken. It is also important that, whatever the school does, it forms part of what may be seen as a graduated approach to support inclusion.

Such a graduated approach to promoting mental health and well-being in children and young people may faciliate a targeted and progressive approach to their delivery and support in schools. With universal provision for individuals being made available through approaches such as personal, social, health and economic education, targeted interventions, for example, through the use of nurture groups and also through more specialist interventions such as, for example, CAMHS.

A graduated response

Initially interventions may take the form of strategies linked to what is known as 'quality-first teaching'. Such strategies provide a safe, happy and welcoming school environment so that all children can flourish. For any aspects of inclusive practice to be effective all practitioners need to buy into the belief that all children are important and that they deserve the best educational opportunities and care. They must model inclusive values by being accepting and open to the range of needs given the many stresses that may be brought to the situation.

Strategies to support aspects of inclusion can include developing the culture of the classroom, adapting teaching styles and methods, adopting a range of access strategies and supplying additional class-based support or making referrals.

Developing the culture of the classroom

- Put in place agreed, acceptable and negotiated ground rules for any undesirable behaviour. Often it will be necessary for a consistency of approach to be maintained to promote progress with children with social, emotional and mental health difficulties. Despite the needs, everyone should be clear about the non-negotiables for unacceptable behaviour, such as harming others.

- Make children feel valued and raise their self-esteem through giving them class-based responsibilities, promoting success in the curriculum and through the use of social and emotional aspects of learning scheme circle time activities.

- Promote a 'can do' culture within the classroom and school, where all children's work is displayed and all forms of achievement are acknowledged. For children who have behavioural needs as a result of any of their issues, social success is valued just as highly as academic prowess.

- Give the child a 'voice' where children are listened to and no concerns will be dismissed.

- Foster a culture of accepting difference. Children with particular needs may not wish to work as a group and may prefer to work individually. They may have a short attention span or they may become angry and disruptive. Children may need to be given the space and time to calm down or a safe place to go until they are ready to be reintegrated into activities. The systems in the classroom and school need to be flexible enough to support such needs whilst minimising disruption to all other pupils.

Adapting teaching styles and methods

As part of a school's drive to include pupils whatever their need, it is important that children's work is structured to support them and to move them from the known to unknown items that are achievable. Sometimes learning objectives may have to be changed to take into account the need so that a child is able to succeed in order to build self-esteem as well as improve levels of motivation to continue with any work. Some work will need to be modified in light of potential triggers that can take a child into less desirable moods or emotions, for example asking a child to write about a birthday party or best friend when a child has experienced isolation from friends and family. For some children, strategies such as pre-teaching words or concepts before a lesson starts may lead to a greater involvement of children in the lessons, facilitating success as well as reducing aspects of negative self-esteem regarding a child's academic prowess as well as providing reassurance that the child can engage in the lesson. Teachers may also wish to find alternative ways to support children to record their ideas, such as taking photographs or using a teaching assistant as a scribe.

Adopting a range of access strategies

Many schools now adopt a range of inclusive access strategies in relation to children and young people's mental health and well-being in schools. These include:

- visual timetables to reassure pupils who are anxious or have short-term memory issues. Visual timetables give children the security of knowing what each day or lesson may hold for them;

- simple auditory meter displays, which a child can access to show when the noise in class may be too high, and can support pupils with limited social skills or children on the autism spectrum;

- the use of stress balls and fidgets to help pupils with autism or ADHD focus and seek a means to manage stress during their school day. These simple and effective toys allow pupils to engage their hands and fingers in movement rather than them distracting others in the class or when on the carpet;

- access to supportive resources such as number lines, word mats and working walls;

- emotion cards so that children who may find difficulty in verbalising their emotions can inform adults of their need to be left alone since they may be angry or sad.

Additional school-based support or referrals

Under the new *SEND Code of Practice*, schools are required to hold a record of the level of need/ register, indicating the level of need children may face with regard to their SEND. If a child is failing to make progress and there is a marked deterioration in any of his or her needs after using class-based support strategies, a more graduated, focused approach may be taken by the school. This will mean the children may be placed on the register needing 'SEN support' which will involve taking actions to remove any further barriers to learning and to put relevant special educational provision in place.

Working together, the teacher, SENCo and parents may create a 'provision map' for the child to map out the interventions that may be used over a particular timeframe. As part of developing this, a school may seek input from a specialist agency such as an educational psychologist, who will further assess the child's needs and suggest other agencies or a support package that may be carried out by a trained teaching assistant linked to the provision map. For example, this may lead to work being deemed necessary on developing a child's social and emotional skills. Targeted interventions may be used, such as 'socially speaking', involving the children in a board game which helps them focus on listening skills, social interactions and pupils' ability to develop and use receptive and expressive language. By interacting with a range of social scenarios – such as, if a child keeps interrupting when another child wishes to speak – children are given the opportunity to practise skills such as taking turns and how best to go about achieving the best outcomes.

Such activities can help children negotiate more challenging situations whilst also diminishing the chance of riskier behaviours escalating from situations. Carrying out group social skills interventions in school can also mean that schools can address concerns relative to the school setting (Kasari et al., 2016). Other agencies such as CAMHS or a child's general practitioner might also be accessed to help support a child's needs in school. Some schools may make use of a 'nurture group' as a means of providing a short-term, focused intervention which seeks to remove barriers to learning as a result of social, emotional and mental health difficulties (this was formerly referred to as behavioural, emotional and social difficulties).

Though the child or young person continues to remain a part of his or her own class, opportunities to join this group in school provide a safe, nurturing environment which seeks to foster positive relationships with both teachers and the child's peers. Finally, if parents are in agreement, a Common Assessment Framework may be initiated to back a coordinated effort to support a child's inclusion in school and possibly reduce the likelihood of an exclusion from school.

If, after all other avenues of support within school are exhausted and the child still exhibits severe causes of concern for the school and/or parents, they may need to seek through the local authority a needs assessment to review the education and health care of the child. If successful, this review may lead to securing statutory funding for the child's educational future through an Education, Health and Care plan.

KEY REFLECTIONS

- What strategies can a class teacher employ to support the range of a pupil's needs?
- How might parents support the school to help their child?
- What can a school do to promote the inclusion of pupils with concerns?

CHAPTER SUMMARY

- Inclusion is an evolving concept linked to the concept of special educational needs.
- Inclusive practice supports pupils with mental health and well-being needs alongside a range of physical and learning needs.
- Schools have statutory duties to secure the inclusion of pupils with mental health and well-being needs.
- Successful inclusion involves working with parents.
- The school should respond to supporting pupils using graduated means.
- 'Quality-first teaching' can form the basis for class-based inclusion.
- Schools may need to seek the help of outside agencies to promote inclusion.
- Funding can be sought to support a child's mental health and well-being needs if the school cannot support the child using their own school budget.

FURTHER READING

Atkinson, M. and Hornby, G. (2002) *Mental Health Handbook for Schools*. London: Routledge.

Glazzard, J., Stokoe, J., Hughes, A., Netherwood, A. and Neve, L. (2015) *Teaching and Supporting Children with Special Educational Needs and Disabilities in Primary Schools*, 2nd edn. London: SAGE/Learning Matters.

Goepel, J., Childerhouse, H. and Sharpe, S. (2015) *Inclusive Primary Teaching*, 2nd edn. Northwich: Critical Publishing.

REFERENCES

Avramidis, E., Bayliss, P. and Burden, R. (2002) Inclusion in action: an in-depth case study of an inclusive secondary school in the south-west of England. *International Journal of Inclusive Education*, 6(2): 143–163.

DeBelle, D., Buttigieg, M., Sherwin, S. and Lowe, K. (2007) The school as location for health promotion, in DeBelle, D. (ed.) *Public Health Practice and The School Age Population*. London: Edward Arnold.

Department for Children, Schools and Families (2007) *Social and Emotional Aspects of Learning (SEAL) Programme: Guidance for Secondary Schools*. Nottingham: DCSF.

Department for Children, Schools and Families (2008) *Targeted Mental Health in Schools Project.* Nottingham: DCSF.

Department for Education (2015 a) *Special Educational Needs and Disability Code of Practice: 0 to 25 Years.* Available at: www.gov.uk/government/uploads/system/uploads/attachment_data/file/398815/SEND_Code_of_Practice_January_2015.pdf (accessed 15 February 2016).

Department for Education (2015 b) *Mental Health and Behaviour in Schools.* Available at: www.gov.uk/government/uploads/system/uploads/attachment_data/file/416786/Mental_Health_and_Behaviour_-_Information_and_Tools_for_Schools_240515.pdf (accessed 15 February 2016).

Department for Education and Skills (2003) *Every Child Matters.* Nottingham: DfES.

Department for Education and Skills (2005) *Primary Social and Emotional Aspects of Learning (SEAL): Guidance for Schools.* Nottingham: DfES.

Department for Education and Skills (2006) *Excellence and Enjoyment: Social and Emotional Aspects of Learning (Key Stage 2 Small Group Activities).* Nottingham: DfES.

Department for Education and Skills/Department of Health (2006) *Extended Schools and Health Services: Working Together for Better Outcomes for Children and Families.* London: CSIP.

Department of Health (2004 a) *National Service Framework: Children, Young People and Maternity Services: The Mental Health and Psychological Wellbeing of Children and Young People.* Standard 9. Available at: www.gov.uk/government/uploads/system/uploads/attachment_data/file/199959/National_Service_Framework_for_Children_Young_People_and_Maternity_Services_-_The_Mental_Health__and_Psychological_Well-being_of_Children_and_Young_People.pdf (accessed 1 April 2016).

Department of Health (2004 b) *Choosing Health: Making Healthier Choices Easier.* Available at: https://www.yearofcare.co.uk/sites/default/files/images/DOH2.pdf (accessed 19 September 2019).

Department of Health (2011) *No Health Without Mental Health: A Cross Government Mental Health Outcomes Strategy for People of All Ages.* Available at: www.dh.gov.uk/en/Publicationsandstatistics/Publications/PublicationsPolicyAndGuidance/DH_123766 (accessed 1 April 2016)

Department of Health (2015) *Future in Mind: Promoting and Improving our Children and Young People's Mental Health and Wellbeing.* Available at: www.gov.uk/government/uploads/system/uploads/attachment_data/file/414024/Childrens_Mental_Health.pdf (accessed 15 February 2016).

Department of Health and Social Care and Department for Education (2018) *Government Response to the Consultation on Transforming Children and Young People's Mental Health Provision: A Green Paper and Next Steps.* Available at: https://www.gov.uk/government/consultations/transforming-children-and-young-peoples-mental-health-provision-a-green-paper (accessed 11 September 2018).

Department of Health/Department for Education and Employment (1999) *National Healthy Schools Programme.* Nottingham: DfEE.

Gee, J. (2018) *Mental Health Statistics in the UK.* Available at: https://www.childrenssociety.org.uk/news-and-blogs/our-blog/mental-health-statistics (accessed 18 December 2018).

Gov UK (2017) *Secondary School Staff Get Mental Health 'First Aid' Training.* Available at: https://www.gov.uk/government/news/secondary-school-staff-get-mental-health-first-aid-training (accessed 12 October 2018).

Green, H., McGinnity, A., Meltzer, H., Ford, T. and Goodman, R. (2005) *Mental Health of Children and Young People in Great Britain, 2004*. A survey carried out by the Office for National Statistics on behalf of the Department of Health and the Scottish Executive. Basingstoke: Palgrave Macmillan. Available at: www.hscic.gov.uk/catalogue/PUB06116/ment-heal-chil-youn-peop-gb-2004-rep2.pdf (accessed 15 February 2016).

Greenberg, M. (2010) School-based prevention: current status and future challenges. *Effective Education*, 2: 27–52.

Health Advisory Service (1995) *'Together We Stand': The Commissioning, Role and Management of Child and Adolescent Mental Health Services*. London: HMSO.

Health Select Committee (2014) *Children's and Adolescent's Mental Health Services and CAMHS*. Available at: www.publications.parliament.uk/pa/cm201415/cmselect/cmhealth/342/34202.htm (accessed 15 February 2016).

Kasari, C., Dean, M., Kretzmann, M., Shih, W., Orlich, F., Whitney, R., Landa, R., Lord, C. and King, B. (2016) Children with autism spectrum disorder and social skills groups at school: a randomized trial and comparing approach and peer composition. *Journal of Child Psychology and Psychiatry*, 57(2): 171–179.

Kim-Cohen, J., Caspi, A., Mot, T.E., Harrington, H., Milne, B.J. and Poulton, R. (2003) Prior juvenile diagnoses in adults with mental disorder: developmental follow-back of a prospective longitudinal cohort. *Archives of General Psychiatry*, 60: 709–771.

Maughan, B., Iervolino, A. and Collishaw, S. (2005) Time trends in child and adolescent mental disorders. *Current Opinion in Psychiatry*, 18: 381–385.

Mental Health First Aid England (2018) Available at: https://mhfaengland.org/ (accessed 12 December 2018).

Merrell, K. and Gueldner, B. (2010) *Social and Emotional Learning in the Classroom: Promoting Mental Health and Academic Success*. London: Guildford.

O'Reilly, M., Svirydzenka, N., Adams, S. and Dogra, N. (2018) Review of mental health promotion intervention in schools. *Social Psychiatric Epidemiology*, 53: 647–662.

Rutter, M. (1991) Pathways from childhood to adult life: the role of schooling. *Pastoral Care in Education*, 9(3): 3–10.

Save the Children (2002) *Schools for All*. Available at: www.eenet.org.uk/resources/docs/schools_for_all.pdf (accessed 15 February 2016).

UNESCO (2005) *Ensuring Access to Education for All*. Available at: http://unesdoc.unesco.org/images/0014/001402/140224e.pdf (accessed 24 February 2016).

Vostanis, P., Humphrey, N., Fitzgerald, N., Deighton, J. and Wolpert, M. (2012) How do schools promote emotional well-being among their pupils? Findings from a national scoping survey of mental health provision in English schools. *Child and Adolescent Mental Health*, 18(3): 151–157.

Waller, R.J., Bresson, D.J. and Waller, K.S. (2006) The educator's role in child and adolescent mental health, in Waller, R.J. (ed.) *Fostering Child and Adolescent Mental Health in the Classroom*. Thousand Oaks, CA: SAGE.

Weare, K. (2000) *Promoting Mental, Emotional and Social Health*. London: Routledge.

9

WHO'S LOOKING AFTER WHOM?

CHAPTER OBJECTIVES

By the end of this chapter you should be aware of:

- the current issues relating to the mental health and well-being of educational professionals;
- how leaders can seek to understand and support professionals within their setting with regard to their own mental health and well-being;
- how schools can support resilience amongst professional staff;
- what outside agencies are available to support schools;
- how leaders can help and support a return to work for their staff given a period of prolonged illness.

TEACHERS' STANDARDS

This chapter supports the development of the following Teachers' Standards:

TS8: Fulfil wider professional responsibilities

- Make a positive contribution to the wider life and ethos of the school.
- Develop effective professional relationships with colleagues, knowing how and when to draw on advice and specialist support.

Introduction

This chapter will focus on the current levels of mental health and well-being issues linked to the educational workforce and to those new to the profession. It will examine the risk factors associated with generating such health conditions as well as considering the impact it has on individuals' educational settings.

The current situation

The mental health and well-being of children and young people have become a major topic of concern in UK primary schools over successive years. Previous publications include, for example, the Department of Health's (2015) *Future in Mind: Promoting, Protecting and Improving Our Children and Young People's Mental Health and Wellbeing*. Other more recent guidance and policies from the government, education and health have included, for example, the government's Green Paper (Department of Health and Social Care and Department for Education, 2017) entitled *Transforming Children and Young People's Mental Health Provision*, as well as the Scottish Government's *Mental Health Strategy 2017–2027* (Scottish Government, 2017) and the Welsh Government's *Written Statement: Providing for the Emotional and Mental Health Needs of Young People in Schools* (Welsh Government, 2017).

This clear need for the identification and support of children and young people who encounter daily mental health issues in education is clearly outlined in statutory guidance through the *Special Educational Needs and Disability Code of Practice* (Department for Education, 2015). Through, for example, the introduction of Education, Health and Care plans there is a real desire to promote more integrated and comprehensive support for those most vulnerable of cases through access to education, health and social care.

Alongside the concern that has been raised for children's long-term well-being, there has been an emerging realisation of the influence that this has on the lives of the professionals working with them. Such influences can extend to all professionals whether new or longer-established members of staff. Though currently there is limited detailed research into what statistically the existing status for the mental health and well-being of staff employed within schools may look like 'at the chalk face', studies undertaken within the press and by teacher unions can provide some insight into the scale and scope of such an issue. Articles such as that by Stanley (2018), for example, suggest that a third of education professionals' jobs resulted in them feeling stressed most or all of the time when questioned about their recent week's experiences. This was in contrast to 18 per cent of the UK workforce overall.

Ongoing mental health and well-being concerns may present in a school's staff in the form of low-level anxiety, seasonal affective disorder and phobias. Many issues may have developed as a direct result of the impact of work-related pressures, including factors such as pupil behaviour, the pressures and demands being currently placed on educational professionals and the lack of funding to support them when dealing with the large range of needs of pupils presenting in schools currently. The research of Tyers et al. (2009) sought to identify six major components of stress in the workplace. These include workload demands, the level of individuals' ability to influence their working conditions, how change is managed, levels of support provided, relationships and an ability to understand their role.

The impact of these issues may be felt not only in terms of individuals' own personal health and staff absence, but also in relation to their ongoing effectiveness and commitment as educational practitioners. Work by Day et al. (2006) has clearly shown the influence that interactions around teachers' sense of well-being and work–life balance can have on their effectiveness, their sense of a teacher's commitment and the impact this can have on pupil progress.

Furthermore, statistics from the Chartered Institute of Personnel and Development (CIPD, 2015) provide evidence of the clear link between professional absence and health-related illness. The CIPD (2015) indicates that, of the five most common causes of long-term absence for non-manual workers, stress-related absence was the highest of all factors with public-sector workers. In this case, 79 per cent of absences reported were due to stress, compared to 58 per cent as a sector average. Statistics reported by Bloom (2016) indicate that 84 per cent of the 2,000 teachers sampled in a study by the Education Support Partnership had suffered from mental health problems over a period of the last 2 years. This report also suggested that the number of teachers who have had mental health problems has risen over the last 5 years. As concerning was the suggestion that such impact upon professionals' health was leading high levels of teachers to consider leaving the profession.

These rising figures are not surprising given that one in four adults will experience a mental health problem during their lifetime, to varying degrees. The Health and Safety Executive (2018, p3) has indicated that:

> in 2016/17 stress, depression or anxiety accounted for 40% of all work-related ill health cases and 49% of all working days lost due to ill health.

It is important to note that mental health disorders are one of the leading causes of ill health and disability worldwide, with two-thirds of people never seeking help due to stigma and potential discrimination (World Health Organization, 2001; MIND, 2013). Looking after those who look after and educate our children and young people has to be a priority.

Demands of workload

A range of workplace factors, such as the setting's health and safety practices, can obviously impact upon an individual's health and well-being (Patterson, 1997). This too can be said to be true for the working conditions in which teachers find themselves housed in terms of the positive role that schools can play as regards teachers' motivation, morale and job satisfaction (Howard, 2013). Undoubtedly, as Garner (2016) indicates through the work of the Education Support Partnership, teacher workload is a major factor of teaching professionals' mental health issues. For some of those new to the profession, such high levels of workload may come as an unwelcome surprise compared to those who have been in the profession for a longer period and who have had time to adapt and change to cope with such demands. These high levels of workload have led to many teachers feeling stressed, which has ultimately resulted in their feeling anxious and depressed. Given the constant level of public scrutiny through items such as the current inspection regime, it is not unexpected that surveys such as that conducted by the Association of Teachers and Lecturers in 2014 should draw links to damaged mental health and well-being resulting from the now constant inspections of schools and a culture of target setting (Ratcliffe, 2014). However, such claims are not without their critics, who suggest that the attribution of blaming others should be avoided by school leaders (Richardson, 2012). Most worrying, however, is the revelation that 68 per cent of teachers who stated that they had experienced mental health issues had not informed employers of their conditions (Ratcliffe, 2014), which tends to be in line with the above World Health Organization commentary around stigma.

Levels of support

Another major factor that has been attributed to the diminished level of teachers' professional mental health and well-being is the level of access available to them in the form of training to support pupils in their care. Concerns include supporting individuals with mental health issues linked to coping with parental separation, substance abuse and domestic violence. However, with regard to this aspect of teachers' professional lives, training such as youth mental health first aid (Mental Health First Aid England, 2018) is now available to them to prepare them for issues as they arise. Despite such training, research undertaken by the National Foundation for Educational Research for the Department for Education (2014) concluded that primary schools were less able to supply the provision needed to support pupils' mental health compared to secondary schools. Though teachers felt well equipped to identify pupil behaviour linked to an issue around pupils' mental health, most concerning was that 32 per cent of respondents felt they had not been appropriately trained to identify mental health problems among pupils. It is interesting given such findings that it is proposed that all secondary schools should be offered mental health training by 2020, alongside the development of mental health champions (Gov UK, 2017 a, b), whilst every primary school should receive training by 2022 (Department of Health and Social Care and Department for Education, 2018).

The National Association of Head Teachers (NAHT) published a survey in 2016 outlining the concerns of teachers, which suggests that over 10 per cent of pupils have a mental health problem before they are aged 11 (NAHT/Place2Be, 2016; Richardson, 2016). This is further evidenced in the British Child and Adolescent Mental Health Survey in 1999 and 2004, where it was identified that amongst 5–10-year-olds, 10 per cent of boys and 5 per cent of girls had mental health problems. For 11–16-year-olds the prevalence was 13 per cent for boys and 10 per cent for girls. The most common problems for this age group are attention deficit hyperactivity disorder, anxiety and depression and autistic spectrum conditions (Murphy and Fonagy, 2012). All of these will manifest with potential problems in classrooms, impacting on concentration and learning potential, together with the quality of the overall school day. Of the 1,455 English head teachers in the NAHT/Place2Be (2016) report sample, two-thirds of those in primary schools felt they were unable to deal with such issues. This was attributed to lack of resources despite the government claims of £1.4 billion funding being available for children's mental health.

For any teacher new to the profession, such reports will no doubt form the basis of professional concerns and anxiety. Such concerns may be fuelled by the level of training that their course may have provided for them in how to help and deal with issues around mental health and well-being in schools in general. Such worries may also be exacerbated with the reality of their now having to deal with the demands placed on them in terms of their new professional roles and responsibilities.

Given such a situation it is heartening for practitioners to note that there is currently a real desire from government to support professional practice, as signalled by the response to their Green Paper on transforming mental health provision for children and young people (Department of Health and Social Care and Department for Education, 2018). Such proposals include the desire to provide further courses to train additional teaching professionals in mental health first aid as well as supporting the development and training of a Designated Senior Lead in Mental Health in education settings. Such leads, trained professional and mental health champions, will be seen as a means to promote, support and deliver better mental health through a whole school approach. Let us hope that these proposed changes may go a long way to providing better support for the many new and more experienced professionals who may often find themselves potentially at risk or underskilled when dealing with this aspect of their work in schools.

It must be remembered that the necessity to support the mental health and well-being of children and young adults effectively also extends to the need to support employees in their places of work. This may be seen in terms of a statutory duty of care placed upon employers regarding their employees under the Equality Act 2010 (UK.Gov, 2013). This Act clearly states that individuals may be deemed to have a disability if they have a physical or mental impairment that can have a substantial, adverse, long-term effect on their normal daily working lives. It is also the duty of the employer to make 'reasonable adjustments' so that individuals can do, and progress in, their job. Therefore, feel reassured that as a teacher you will not be alone if you are faced with any issues around dealing with your own mental health and well-being. Not only are there statutory duties placed on employers to support you, but given the caring nature of the profession, no doubt if you have any concerns your colleagues will do their best to support your future needs.

KEY REFLECTIONS

- What influences can mental health and well-being have on educational professionals?
- What are the main contributing factors to teachers' mental health issues?
- Are there currently any new proposals to support the future training of teaching professionals when dealing with mental health and well-being issues?

The role of leaders

As any educational professional should realise, the mental health and well-being of any employee must start from the very top of any school organisation. This will involve the head teachers, senior leaders and governors creating a culture in your school where the duty of care for safeguarding individuals is seen as of paramount importance. It is their responsibility that staff are deployed effectively and in the best interest of the setting, giving due regard to individuals having a reasonable work–life balance. The leadership team should make certain that you and all employees feel that you should not suffer in silence, that there is someone who can be approached given any concerns, no matter how small, and that no stigma will be attached to any individuals admitting to work-related symptoms linked to mental health and well-being. As Weare (2015, p7) suggests:

It is helpful if the school climate and ethos routinely acknowledges the reality of staff stress and finds ways to make it safe for staff and leaders (as well as pupils) to acknowledge their human distress, weakness and difficulty and seek support and help for their mental health needs in non-stigmatising ways.

If you do not seek help this will inevitably lead to deterioration in your health, so obtaining help and advice at the earliest of times is vital. Though many factors can lead to teachers suffering mental health issues, many of which are associated with stress in the workplace, it is important to realise that all individuals deal with stress differently. It is also important for an individual to remember that 'stress' is 'normal' according to one's own acceptable levels of stress – without it we would not get up in the morning. However, some people are able to continue to work without realising the signs that they are becoming too stressed. It can be reassuring to you to note that your senior staff who lead you in your settings are not themselves exempt from stress. However, what is important is that a school should have some mechanism in place to help and support any individual who has any concerns and worries.

It is therefore important for you to realise that the common signs of stress can make people act in a particular way, as shown below.

Signs of stress	Behaviours	Physical symptoms
Feeling anxious	Picking at the body, avoidance behaviours, becoming overly attached to a safety object/person	Panic attacks, chest pains, shortness of breath, sweaty palms, racing heart, sleep disturbance/fatigue, diarrhoea
Feeling depressed	Tearful, crying, not wanting to get up or go to work, lack of concentration at and during work	Physically feeling tired, waking early, headaches, loss or change of appetite
Feeling isolated/lonely	Feelings that no one likes you or that they do not wish to talk to you. Feelings that everyone is against you. Not wanting to talk to others, finding somewhere out of others' way	Feeling depressed, sad, lethargic
Feeling a sense of dread/ unhappy	Feeling down about things, not seeing the positives in life and not happy to laugh or make light of things	Morbid feelings, tearful or crying
Feeling overloaded with work	Confusion, poor memory	Unable to sleep, waking early, mood swings, withdrawn, increased smoking or drinking 'to cope'
Feeling uninterested	Loss of drive for life and the job	Lethargy, lack of willingness to engage with the world and work
Feeling irritable	Not willing to listen to others, or restless	Snappy, being short-tempered with people, impatient

To help leaders in schools identify the levels of stress that their staff are suffering, stress audits could be carried out. This may go some way to addressing the school's legal obligation to individuals, as with other employers, to make an appropriate and suitable assessment of the risks to the health and safety of their employees. This type of audit may help leaders understand the types and levels of stress that exist in their particular workplace and may help them see where individuals' issues are coming from. To take an audit you may be required to fill in a questionnaire and the results are then used to seek improvements in the areas of concern identified. In addition the school leaders may monitor staff sickness and absence through a monitoring policy so as to start to identify if any staff absences need a supporting investigation.

KEY REFLECTIONS

- How are you currently feeling about work?
- What signs might you need to look for to gauge your mental health and well-being?
- Who in school might you feel comfortable talking to regarding any issues you may have?

Managing work-related stress

The following case study aims to provide an insight into the sort of pressures a teacher can face and how it can impact upon their mental health and well-being. Read the case study and consider ideas for practice strategies to support this person.

CASE STUDY: SUNIL

Being responsible for the SATs, I feel personally responsible for each of the children and their results. I have started to feel sick and anxious when I think about it, and I am now shouting at my close friends and they are getting worried about me. They worry about the way I will react and this is also making me feel anxious. Given the parents I have it has all got very competitive. Also, with the result trends from last year, I know that we need some good results in writing to show an upward progress with regard to children. I am trying not to put pressure on the children but I find that I spend my evenings marking practice papers and analysing them to see how I can target work for each child to improve. I am finding I am waking up in the night thinking about things and when I think about it I am getting anxious. I am trying not to let it all get me down.

Case study reflections

- What are the triggers for Sunil's feelings towards his work?
- Who should he be sharing his feelings with?

Sunil is clearly being affected by the pressures placed on him at work. It is starting to affect his own health and the health of others around him. If he does not seek help this feeling will only grow and so will his isolation and levels of discontentment with his lot in life. The first step he must take is to realise he needs help before things get even worse for him. He must start by realising he is not alone and must talk to someone. This realisation is not a judgement on Sunil as a professional, or a sign of weakness, but a much-needed heightened awareness that, due to the pressure of work, he is struggling to cope. It may be worth considering that there are probably other staff in a similar position. He might not feel that he can talk to the staff or his head teacher at school since he may not wish to signal his own fallibility; if this is the case he should see his doctor. Hopefully the head teacher may have become aware of Sunil's fragile nature and if this is the case the head teacher might try and speak to him to signpost him to places for help.

Supporting well-being and fostering resilience

It is important that any school setting provides an environment that nurtures and promotes a sense of control over professional work and workload as well as the means by which resilience can be nurtured amongst colleagues and groups of employees. As Weare (2015, p7) suggests:

Schools need to ensure staff experience connection, through celebrating and sharing everyday successes and achievements, and are encouraged to know when to let go, to make more realistic demands on themselves, and have the kind of work/life balance that can help them recover and recuperate from the full-on nature of everyday school life.

Weare's (2015) suggestions around celebrating skills and achievements work for adults and professionals in relation to the work setting in the same way as they do for children and young people, as discussed in Chapter 4. By improving resilience factors, risk factors have the potential to be minimised. Surely one of the most important means of promoting resilience amongst current and future teaching professionals must be found in the active support by government to support the education and training of such frontline professionals, as signalled by the government's response to the Green Paper (Department of Health and Social Care and Department for Education, 2018). Such outlined measures may enable teachers to feel more confident and competent, and therefore less stressed and anxious in such situations.

Due to every school's demographic and situational context you will find that each setting will have its own particular strategies to support staff in their particular context. Some strategies that schools and leaders might consider suggesting include:

- encouraging a climate where staff are encouraged to be able to share worries and concerns. This could be done at an individual level through an individual's own self-identified network within schools or meetings where concerns about the impact of new initiatives are shared;

- allowing staff to attend training outside their schools so they can meet with other colleagues to share experiences and to build up a different support network who they can also turn to when things get tough. This continuing professional development could be related to a curriculum responsibility, that of mental health first aid, or a related academic qualification through that of a Master's degree. Some courses could also be identified to support issues around workload or classroom management. Further support can be found in courses run by relevant unions, and again such attendance can be a means of building up a support network for individuals;

- encouraging staff to do what can be done now and not later. Try and avoid 'busy work' which has no real purpose beyond making you feel better because you are doing things;

- trying to organise times when staff are clearly valued and can be together. Perhaps on a Friday, organise cake or sandwiches to be made available in the staff room and make certain you say to all the staff this is a time for them and you want them to come no matter what. Show them it is important by giving clear signals that they are more important than that last task;

- trying to dedicate a space in the school for a quiet area where staff can just go and not hear about work. Perhaps it can be a place where, if the school is committed to the staff's well-being, an activity such as meditation could take place;

- considering supporting opportunities for 'supervision' for all staff. 'Clinical' supervision is a mandatory, not a luxury, feature and an aspect of work for clinicians in practice, but is less practised in education settings. It can, however, provide a supportive, reflective and restorative framework (Andrews, 2016). Teaching staff similarly deal with difficult situations with pupils which are stressful and impact on the self and person. It is vital therefore to create a thinking space with a respected colleague, to provide supervision or debriefing so that individuals can offload the emotional result of working with children and young people (O'Reilly et al., 2018; Robert-Holmes et al., 2018);

- consider how each organisation can mitigate the negative impact such work has on their own mental health;

- formalised peer mentoring or 'buddy' systems. Teaching staff are very good at formalising these supporting strategies for their pupils, with good evidence of their effectiveness. Why not consider implementing similar systems across staff teams? This fits with the Teachers' Standards (2011, p13): *develop effective professional relationships with colleagues.*

As Gardner (1993) suggests in his theory around multiple intelligences, there are many facets within individuals that will impact upon a person's professional and personal life. Goleman (1996) also suggests that emotional intelligence can influence individuals' ability to be self-aware with regard to knowing how they are feeling, whether they can handle such feelings and also control their level of motivation. Given this, it is important that you take notice of how you are feeling in your daily life, since such positive or negative feelings will have a profound influence on your ability to do the job and your mental health and well-being. Such scrutiny of your feelings may also, in turn, provide a cue to signify that something must be done to mediate against any reductions in positive emotions towards the job and an individual's life in general.

For any staff, maintaining a work–life balance will often provide the key to greater resilience against stress. It is important that you find times when you are free from thinking about the job in hand in order to spend time with family and friends or to take part in a sport or hobby. No doubt some of the greatest barriers to all of this are excuses such as 'being tired' or it being 'too expensive', but remember there is always a way around this. If you feel tired, build up your commitment or find a time when you feel that doing this activity is most likely to happen. If things are too expensive try and find something for free, such as a walk in the countryside.

Though everybody's work patterns will be different, try and set yourself a clear timetable of slots of time when you will not be on task or tempted to dip into work. This may be, for example, that you work up until 6 p.m. on a Friday and then start looking at work again at an agreed time on Sunday – though this is easier said than done, given that sometimes things will get in the way, and sometimes you will be your own worst enemy. Nobody is indispensable and surely it is better you do your job well rather than on half a tank of energy or mental ability.

The practice of mindfulness offers the opportunity to foster inner resilience. It is being aware of and focused on what we are doing in the here and now, monitoring experiences in a non-judgemental way (Kabat-Zin, 1994 as cited in Jennings, 2015). Mindfulness has been proven to enhance emotional self-regulation, increasing a sense of well-being and self-efficacy. Early research demonstrates that, when used by teachers, it can increase their ability to manage classroom behaviour and improve relationships with others (Meiklejohn et al., 2012). Nurturing a teacher's resilience using mindfulness-based training can also create a relational foundation in the classroom, in so much as it offers pupils, by default, mindful skills that nurture their own inner resilience. It is important to be aware that mindfulness is a skill that has to be practised regularly and over a period of time to realise its benefit fully. Mindfulness activities and training courses are widely available through a variety of means, such as self-help books, online training courses and those requiring attendance. Mindfulness practice is recommended by the National Institute for Health and Care Excellence for recurring symptoms of depression (National Institute for Health and Care Excellence, 2016). It is also used in a variety of ways within the NHS to relieve symptoms of sleep problems, headaches and depression and for stress reduction (King's College Hospital NHS Foundation Trust & Guys and St Thomas' NHS Foundation Trust, 2013). More information regarding mindfulness practice and its benefits can be found at **https://mindfulnessinschools.org**.

Outside agency support for schools

Despite some leaders' and schools' best efforts in supporting you and their staff with issues around mental health and well-being, these concerns may not always be resolved at school level. In this case or with an extended period of absence due to illness, the school may need to access specialist agency support to support you, such as occupational health, to help with an individual's issues.

Normally most schools will have paid into some form of a school level agreement to buy in such an agency if required. Such services, as a matter of course, should be clearly signposted in schools to any individuals, alongside any other organisations such as unions that can help and advise you given any such issues. This specialist support could come through an approved medical practitioner or even a member of staff's own doctor. The benefits of such support may be centred on the objective specialist overview that such practitioners can provide to meet the needs of each individual.

If the employer starts to be concerned about your mental health and well-being, they should seek your agreement, so that they can make a referral to such agencies as soon as possible. They will need an individual's written consent before any other medical practitioner is allowed to access confidential medical records when being involved in such a case. You should be given a chance to understand the process that they are embarking on as well as why you think this is important for you. Often, given such conditions, any suggestions to access support may cause an individual to feel irritated, agitated or even victimised. However, if this is the case and you have any concerns, you should remind yourself that they are suggesting this for your well-being; such a referral should be encouraged and seen as a positive move to support you. It should be seen as a means of offering specialist support by a professional who understands the cause and impact of such issues upon both your personal and professional life. It will provide a specialist who can understand your condition as well as suggesting or signposting treatments that may support your recovery. If you are off on sick leave, then such agencies can also suggest ways of offering you a phased return to work. It is important to note, however, that the work of these services is advisory. Normally a report will be sent to the human resources department linked to the local authority. The report will include a return-to-work date, advice for the employer to support your recovery and return to work and any reasonable adjustments that could be made to support your condition when at work. Since the report does not produce statutory guidance it is the decision of the employer whether to act on or take up this advice.

Other agencies that can provide you with support could include the person's union and those shown below.

Organisational overview	Website link
The Health and Safety Executive provides a range of useful links and guidance linked to matters surrounding health and safety	www.hse.gov.uk/stress/mymental.htm
The FitforWork website provides access to a range of occupational health professionals who can offer advice and support around work-based issues	http://fitforwork.org/employee
Anxiety UK provides information and support for those with anxiety disorders	www.anxietyuk.org.uk/
The Samaritans provides free confidential advice and support	www.samaritans.org/
Mind is a mental health charity	www.mind.org.uk/
The Mental Health Foundation provides guidance and research around issues relating to mental health	www.mentalhealth. org.uk/
Time to Change challenges mental health stigma and discrimination	www.time-to-change.org.uk/about-us

Reasonable adjustments

Your setting should realise and comply with the Equality Act 2010 with regard to making reasonable adjustments to help individuals who have developed a long-term mental health issue which has been longer than 12 months, or who have an existing mental health issue. It is important to realise that you do not need to have any one particular mental health condition to be protected under the Equality Act. What is important however is that it should be seen as a disability; your general practitioner may be able to help you evidence such a claim. Some conditions recognised by the Act include depression, bipolar affective disorder and schizophrenia. Whatever your condition, it is important that your setting publishes information to demonstrate how they are complying with the Public Sector Equality Duty.

Reasonable adjustments will mean that your setting will have to make certain that any disabled workers are not disadvantaged compared to non-disabled workers as a result of the setting's policy, procedures or practice.

Such adjustments can involve:

- adjustments to the physical working environment;

- a reallocation of some duties to other individuals;

- changes to the individual's working practices or hours;

- support from trained individuals, mentor support or counselling.

It is important that you, as the employee, are consulted with regard to how you feel you can be best supported upon your return to work. Such measures must be seen by the employee as being supportive rather than punitive.

It is important, however, that when assessing if reasonable adjustments can be made you realise that the employer will need to bear in mind the extent to which such adjustments are practical. This may include the financial costs or the extent to which such adjustments may cause internal disruption.

Following some conditions, a phased return to work may be considered as an option to support your return to work. This could include you taking part in a job share arrangement with an internal colleague or having someone who has been employed to help support you in your daily duties. This option may include making adjustments in the form of flexible working hours, such as mornings only to start with. Extra class-based support may be introduced or a suggestion made that additional duties can be avoided, such as clubs or supervision at break times.

Given the ongoing stresses related to your mental health condition in such situations, it might be appropriate that the school suggests that you also find some form of advocacy to support or help you during this difficult time. This could be someone you get on with at work, a friend or family member. If this is not an option, information can be sought regarding the help and support you may get from organisations such as Mind or Mind Infoline. Given what may be for you a time of ongoing fragile mental health, an advocate may help you by being there to listen, in confidence. This may help you to see things more objectively and therefore you may feel in a better position to explore options with the person, or the advocate may signpost you to legal support. Such support may help you to make the right informed decision, and, if needed, the advocate may accompany you to meetings as a means of additional support.

CASE STUDY: TARA

Tara has been struggling with her work for over 12 months; this has manifested itself with week-long bouts of sickness absence. Despite seeing her general practitioner and getting medication, the situation has not improved. She has opened up to her manager regarding her issues and the manager has now persuaded Tara to go back and see her doctor to discuss her ongoing worries around her work-related depression and feelings of anxiety with regard to her ability to cope with her job on a day-to-day basis. She has now been issued with a fit note by her doctor and she has handed this into her setting. Tara has been signed off sick for a month.

Case study reflections

- What can the setting do to support her?
- What can be done to help her return to work?

Given Tara's long-term mental health issues and the lack of improvement despite her ongoing medication, it seems likely that Tara will be able to get protection under the Equality Act. This means her condition will be recognised as a disability and some adjustments will need to be made to support her at work. It is important that an agreed line of communication between the setting and Tara is set up so that she is not left feeling socially isolated. Tara should not be made to feel that she is being a nuisance or that it is all her fault. It is vital that the setting lets Tara know that there is no stigma attached to her illness and that her friends and colleagues are always availaible to listen and support her.

The school could seek her agreement to attend a referral to occupational health to understand and assess the barriers that are now stopping Tara from working. As soon as Tara is considered fit for some form of return to work, she will need to arrange a return-to-work meeting so that an agreed strategy can be put in place to support her return. Tara may feel that she needs the support of an advocate to help her through this process. The result of the return-to-work meeting may be a phased return or some support plan being put in place. It is important that this is mutually agreeable given the setting's limitations.

Ill-health retirement

Unfortunately, even following the best efforts of everyone involved, sometimes a solution cannot be found to make a return to work possible. If this is the case, for you or any individual, it may be that ill-health retirement is the only option. This will signal that you are now permanently incapable of carrying out your normal duties due to ill health. This should not be seen as defeat but a means by which you can still have a good quality of life freed from the burdens that may have led to your health issues. Sometimes the occupational health service can suggest that individuals might consider ill-health retirement. Remember that you or any individual can decide to apply for such an option as long as you have your doctor's or even a consultant's support. In such situations, it is anticipated that the setting manager will support the application to comply with the relevant statutory duties. An application will need to be made to either the Teachers' Pension Scheme or Local Government

Pension Scheme in order to set this process in motion by the employer or individual as required by the relevant scheme.

KEY REFLECTIONS

- What are some of the key risk factors that can trigger issues around mental health and well-being?
- What strategies can schools and leaders put in place to support their staff?
- What outside agency support is available to a school and its staff with regard to issues around mental health and well-being?
- How can a school and leaders support a return to work for those individuals who may have suffered longer-term illness?

CHAPTER SUMMARY

- Mental health and well-being issues can be triggered by a range of factors found in a professional's working life.
- Mental health and well-being issues can influence individuals' physical well-being.
- Schools have statutory duties to secure and include their staff with mental health and well-being needs.
- Providing clear strategies to support individuals, a climate of openness and no stigma is vital to reducing the isolation felt by staff with mental health and well-being issues.
- Provision of strategies should come from a 'top-down' approach that becomes embedded in the school system.
- Outside agencies can support schools and leaders who have issues around staff's mental health and well-being.
- Schools should find ways to support a return to work if there is long-term illness.

FURTHER READING

Healthy Schools. *Guidance for Schools on Developing Emotional Health and Wellbeing.* Available at: www.healthyschools.london.gov.uk/sites/default/files/EHWB.pdf (accessed 24 August 2016).

Public Health Agency. *A Guide to Mental Health.* Available at: www.publichealth.hscni.net/sites/default/files/Mind_Your_Head_Booklet_LR_08_15_0.pdf (accessed 16 August 2016).

Workplace. Available at: http://mind.org.uk/workplace (accessed 25 August 2016).

━━ REFERENCES ━━

Andrews, L. (2016) Family nurse partnership: why supervision matters. *Nursing Times*, 25 January. Available at: www.nursingtimes.net/roles/nurse-educators/family-nurse-partnership-why-supervision-matters/7001826.article (accessed 9 June 2016).

Bloom, A. (2016) *8 in 10 Teachers Have Had Mental-health Problems and Workload to Blame*. Available at: www.tes.com/news/school-news/breaking-news/eight-10-teachers-have-had-mental-health-problems-and-workload-blame (accessed 7 April 2016).

Chartered Institute of Personnel and Development (2015) *Absence Management Annual Survey Report 2015*. Available at: www.cipd.co.uk/binaries/absence-management_2015.pdf (accessed 23 April 2016).

Day, C., Stobart, G., Sammons, P., Kington, A., Gu, Q., Smees, R. and Mujtaba, T. (2006) *Variations in Teachers' Work, Lives and Effectiveness*. London: Department for Education and Skills.

Department for Education (2014) *NFER Teacher Voice Omnibus: Questions for the Department for Education: March to May 2014 and May to June 2014*. Available at: www.gov.uk/government/uploads/system/uploads/attachment_data/file/363735/RB391_-_NFER_Teacher_Voice_Omnibus.pdf (accessed 29 April 2016).

Department for Education (2015) *Special Educational Needs and Disability Code of Practice: 0 to 25 Years*. Available at: https://assets.publishing.service.gov.uk/government/uploads/system/uploads/attachment_data/file/398815/SEND_Code_of_Practice_January_2015.pdf (accessed 12 September 2018).

Department of Health (2015) *Future in Mind: Promoting, Protecting and Improving Our Children and Young People's Mental Health and Wellbeing*. Available at: www.gov.uk/government/uploads/system/uploads/attachment_data/file/414024/Childrens_Mental_Health.pdf (accessed 15 February 2016).

Department of Health and Social Care and Department for Education (2017) *Transforming Children and Young People's Mental Health Provision: A Green Paper*. Available at: https://www.gov.uk/government/consultations/transforming-children-and-young-peoples-mental-health-provision-a-green-paper (accessed 11 September 2018).

Department of Health and Social Care and Department for Education (2018) *Government Response to the Consultation on Transforming Children and Young People's Mental Health Provision: A Green Paper and Next Steps*. Available at: https://www.gov.uk/government/consultations/transforming-children-and-young-peoples-mental-health-provision-a-green-paper (accessed 11 September 2018).

Equality Act 2010. Available at: www.legislation.gov.uk/ukpga/2010/15/contents (accessed 23 July 2016).

Gardner, H. (1993) *Multiple Intelligences: The Theory in Practice*. New York: Basic Books.

Garner, R. (2016) Inside the "Samaritans for teachers" hotline that shows just how stressful the classroom can be. *The Independent*. Available at: www.independent.co.uk/news/education/education-news/education-support-partnership-samaritans-for-teachers-hotline-that-shows-just-how-stressful-the-a6798136.html (accessed 8 April 2016).

Goleman, D. (1996) *Emotional Intelligence: Why It Can Matter More Than IQ*. London: Bloomsbury.

Gov UK (2017 a) *Prime Minister Unveils Plans to Transform Mental Health Support*. Available at: https://www.gov.uk/government/news/prime-minister-unveils-plans-to-transform-mental-health-support (accessed 12 October 2018).

Gov UK (2017 b) *Secondary School Staff Get Mental Health 'First Aid' Training*. Available at: https://www.gov.uk/government/news/secondary-school-staff-get-mental-health-first-aid-training (accessed 12 October 2018).

Health and Safety Executive (2018) *Work Related Stress, Depression or Anxiety Statistics in Great Britain 2017*. Available at: http://www.hse.gov.uk/statistics/causdis/stress/stress.pdf (accessed 14 September 2018).

Howard, C. (2013) *The Influence of New School Buildings Upon the Motivation, Morale and Job Satisfaction of Their Teaching Staff*. PhD thesis, University of Birmingham. Available at: www.eprints.worc.ac.uk/cgi/search/archive/advanced?exp=0%7C1%7C-date%2Fcreators_name%2Ftitle%7Carchive%7C-%7Ccreators_name%3Acreators_name%3AALL%3AEQ%3Acolin+howard%7C-%7Ceprint_status%3Aeprint_status%3AANY%3AEQ%3Aarchive%7Cmetadata_visibility%3Ametadata_visibility%3AANY%3AEQ%3Ashow&_action_search=1&order=-date%2Fcreators_name%2Ftitle&screen=Search&cache=2298764&search_offset=20 (accessed 12 October 2018).

Jennings, P. (2015) *Mindfulness for Teachers*. New York: W. W. Norton.

King's College Hospital NHS Foundation Trust & Guys and St Thomas' NHS Foundation Trust (2013) *Mindfulness-based Stress Reduction (MBSR)*. Available at: www.guysandstthomas.nhs.uk/resources/patient-information/elderly-care/mindfulness-based-stress-reduction.pdf (accessed 28 July 2016).

Meiklejohn, J., Philips, C., Freedman, M., Griffin, M., Biegel, G., Roach, A., Frank, J., Burke, C., Pinger, L., Soloway, G., Isberg, R., Sibinga, E., Grossman, L. and Saltzman, A. (2012) Integrating mindfulness training into K–12 education: fostering the resilience of teachers and students. *Mindfulness*. DOI: 10.1007/s12671-012-0094-5

Mental Health First Aid (2018) Available at: mhfaengland.org (accessed 18 September 2019).

MIND (2013) *Mental Health Facts and Statistics*. Available at: www.mind.org.uk/information-support/types-of-mental-health-problems/statistics-and-facts-about-mental-health/how-common-are-mental-health-problems (accessed 29 July 2016).

Murphy, M. and Fonagy, P. (2012) Mental health problems in children and young people, in Annual Report of the Chief Medical Officer (2012) *Our Children Deserve Better: Prevention Pays*. Available at: www.gov.uk/government/uploads/system/uploads/attachment_data/file/252660/33571_2901304_CMO_Chapter_10.pdf (accessed 29 July 2016).

NAHT/Place2Be (2016) *Children's Mental Health Matters: Provision of Primary School Counselling*. Available at: http://website.place2be.org.uk/media/10046/Childrens_Mental_Health_Week_2016_report.pdf (accessed 9 February 2017).

National Institute for Health and Care Excellence (2016) *Depression in Adults: Recognition and Management*. Available at: www.nice.org.uk/guidance/cg90?unlid=4306996020163922547 (accessed 28 July 2016).

O'Reilly, M., Adam, S., Whiteman, N., Hughes, J., Reilly, P. and Dogra, N. (2018) *Whose Responsibility is Adolescent's Mental Health in the UK? Perspectives of Key Stakeholders*. School Mental Health, pp1–12.

Available at: https://link.springer.com/content/pdf/10.1007%2Fs12310-018-9263-6.pdf (accessed 10 October 2018).

Patterson, J.M. (1997). Vpp companies' best practices. *Occupational Health & Safety*, 66: 60–61.

Ratcliffe, R. (2014) Ofsted inspections and targets harming teachers' mental health, finds survey. *The Guardian*, 14 April. Available at: www.theguardian.com/education/2014/apr/14/ofsted-inspections-targets-harming-teachers-mental-health (accessed 15 April 2016).

Richardson, H. (2012) Ofsted chief Sir Michael Wilshaw: teachers not stressed. *BBC News*. Available at: www.bbc.co.uk/news/education-18025202 (accessed 11 April 2016).

Richardson, H. (2016) Heads warn over pupils' untreated mental health issues. *BBC News*. Available at: www.bbc.co.uk/news/education-35502394 (accessed 24 April 2016).

Robert-Holmes, G., Mayer, S., Jones, P. and Fung Lee, S. (2018) *An Evaluation of Phase One of the Youth Mental Health First Aid (MHFA) in Schools Programme: "The training has given us a vocabulary to use."* Available at: https://mhfastorage.blob.core.windows.net/mhfastoragecontainer/5603 f429f9cae811814fe0071b668081/Youth-MHFA-in-Schools-programme-UCL-evaluation-report. pdf?sv=2015-07-08&sr=b&sig=ymj3QDGofbxrqdRoqSnwmqGUet3Ed0So3j2IaSmYwI4%3D &se=2018-10-12T11%3A28%3A59Z&sp=r (accessed 13 October 2018).

Scottish Government (2017) *Mental Health Strategy 2017–2027*. Available at: https://beta.gov.scot/ publications/mental-health-strategy-2017-2027/ (accessed 11 October 2018).

Stanley, J. (2018) *Teachers are at Breaking Point. It's Time to Push Wellbeing up the Agenda*. Available at: https://www.theguardian.com/teacher-network/2018/apr/10/teachers-are-at-breaking-point-its-time-to-push-wellbeing-up-the-agenda (accessed 14 September 2018).

Tyers, C., Broughton, A., Denvir, A., Wilson, S. and O'Ragan, S. (2009) *Organisational Responses to the HSE Management Standards for Work-related Stress: Progress of the Sector Implementation Plan Phase 1*. Research Report RR693. London: Health and Safety Executive.

UK.Gov (2013) *Equality Act 2010: Guidance*. Available at: www.gov.uk/guidance/equality-act-2010-guidance (accessed 12 February 2016).

Weare, K. (2015) *What Works in Promoting Social and Emotional Well-being and Responding to Mental Health Problems in School?* London: National Children's Bureau.

Welsh Government (2017) *Written Statement: Providing for the Emotional and Mental Health Needs of Young People in Schools*. Available at: https://gov.wales/about/cabinet/cabinetstatements/2017/ mentalhealthneeds/?lang=en (accessed 10 October 2018).

World Health Organization (2001) *Mental Disorders Affect One in Four People*. Available at: www.who. int/whr/2001/media_centre/press_release/en (accessed 29 July 2016).

INDEX